Doing Business
with the New Japan

Doing Business with the New Japan

Succeeding in America's Richest International Market

Second Edition

James Day Hodgson, Yoshihiro Sano, and John L. Graham

ROWMAN & LITTLEFIELD PUBLISHERS, INC.
Lanham • Boulder • New York • Toronto • Plymouth, UK

ROWMAN & LITTLEFIELD PUBLISHERS, INC.

Published in the United States of America
by Rowman & Littlefield Publishers, Inc.
A wholly owned subsidiary of The Rowman & Littlefield Publishing Group, Inc.
4501 Forbes Boulevard, Suite 200, Lanham, Maryland 20706
www.rowmanlittlefield.com

Estover Road, Plymouth PL6 7PY, United Kingdom

British Library Cataloguing in Publication Information Available

Library of Congress Cataloging-in-Publication Data

Hodgson, James D., 1915–
  Doing business with the new Japan : succeeding in America's richest
international market / James Day Hodgson, Yoshihiro Sano, and John L.
Graham.— 2nd ed.
      p. cm.
  Includes bibliographical references and index.
  ISBN-13: 978-0-7425-5533-4 (pbk. : alk. paper)
  ISBN-10: 0-7425-5533-X (pbk. : alk. paper)
  1. Negotiation in business—United States. 2. Negotiation in business—Japan.
3. United States—Commerce—Japan. 4. Japan—Commerce—United States.
5. Intercultural communication—United States. 6. Intercultural communication—
Japan. I. Sano, Yoshihiro. II. Graham, John L. III. Title.
  HD58.6.H63 2008
  658.4'052—dc22

                                                                    2007028438

Printed in the United States of America

♾™ The paper used in this publication meets the minimum requirements of
American National Standard for Information Sciences—Permanence of Paper
for Printed Library Materials, ANSI/NISO Z39.48-1992.

Contents

Illustrations

TABLES

FIGURES

BOXES

Acknowledgments

Several people influenced our research on Japan, which provides the foundation of this work: Richard P. Bagozzi, George A. Devos, John J. Gumperz, Richard H. Holton, John Gerretsen, Edward T. Hall, and Roy A. Herberger Jr.

We wish to thank three people for their help in producing the book. Lindsey Lambert helped us prepare the first draft of the manuscript. Jehanne Schweitzer has done a wonderful job as production editor. Susan McEachern as editorial director at Rowman & Littlefield has provided both her encouragement and patience. Thanks to all!

Introduction

No region of the world at any time in history has seen the transformation of multiple national economics proceed more rapidly than in Northeast Asia during the last few decades. There we witness the Greater China, Japan, Russia, and the two Koreas interweave and, at times, clash. American business has watched with awe as China's economy surged ahead, coming on with the impetus of a thousand-pound gorilla. Meanwhile, an upstart dictator in pint-sized North Korea has triggered worldwide apprehension with his bluster and nuclear arms threats. These developments head a parade of uneasy cross-currents that now swirl around this dynamic region. This book intends to examine these cross-currents and other fundamental features of interest to today's business world. It will lay out a picture of the historical and cultural influences that underpin the stage on which today's and tomorrow's international business will be played. Japan will provide our centerpiece. We will then go on to cast a sharp eye on the way face-to-face negotiations are now conducted between business practitioners of the contrasting cultures. Included will be specific prescriptions for managing the often central and seminal activities of trans-Pacific commercial negotiations.

Japan is a fascinating land with ancient cultural roots and the most modern capabilities. First, some observations about the Japanese people. Though they live longer than almost any of the world's peoples, they do not consider their demographic picture encouraging. It is not hard to understand why. The country's birth rate has been slipping, now sinking below a level needed to sustain the present numbers. A whopping 28 percent of their population of 120 million are now sixty years of age or older. With their insular traditions, the Japanese probably cannot count on infusions of immigrants to meet any labor shortages in the years ahead. Japan, however, can proudly boast about the quality of its workforce, an exceptionally well trained and highly motivated national asset. The country can lay claim to top-flight primary and secondary school systems. A higher percentage of its high school graduates go on to college than in any society other than the United States. Importantly, in today's technologically sophisticated industrial world, they outscore us in students who graduate with science and math degrees. Finally, underpinned by ancient Confucian principles, the Japanese work ethic is a match for the world's best. Thus, when all this is added up, it becomes clear that today the Japanese can face the industrial world confident of a highly competitive work capability.

Now let us shift our attention to Japan's economy. Here we will recall how in the latter half of last century, the world became startled by the country's speedy recovery from wartime devastation. "How did they do it?" we asked.

Perhaps the best overall explanation lies in a brilliantly conceived and beautifully executed national strategy. Raw materials, of which Japan had almost none, would each day be brought in from elsewhere in the resource-rich Pacific basin. Once in hand, these materials would be converted by newly built modern plants into superior quality products for sale to an eagerly awaiting world. At home, the value added by this process became widely shared. Everyone benefited. By the mid-1980s worker wage and benefit levels had risen to match those of the American counterparts.

The 1990s brought the thunder of Japan's bursting asset price bubble. However, despite the precipitous crashes in their stock market (down some 64 percent) and real estate prices (down more than 67 percent), GDP in Japan has remained relatively stable. They managed the crash remarkably well, actually. Indeed, as we will detail in chapter 13, Japanese per capita income continued to climb through the macroeconomic tribulations of the 1990s. And toward the end of the decade, America's information technology revolution and the associated consumer feasting helped the Japanese stay afloat in their export-driven lifeboat.

Here we will shift gears to briefly examine the country's political picture. Despite the unease that can be expected to accompany a sluggish economy, Japan's political scene, to outsiders at least, reflects remarkable stability. The same political party that held power when the nation fell into stagnation years ago remains solidly in power today. Prime ministers come and go, a few modest economic reforms are made, inflation is kept under control, and just enough gain is achieved to satisfy a remarkably passive electorate. On the Japanese political front, stability reigns today.

No doubt one compelling reason for this stability lies in the impressive gains the country has made in its foreign relations. The country deftly weathered the end of the Cold War, avoided being overwhelmed by the emerging Chinese powerhouse, finessed the recurrent trade spats with the United States, and has reacted responsibly to each new source of international tension. Unsurprisingly, the Japanese are terrified by North Korea's next-door nuclear threats. But even here they have worked patiently in concert with other regional powers to deal with this bizarre circumstance. So today the world sees the nation reflecting new confidence, assuming greater responsibility, and asserting greater influence in world affairs than at any time since World War II.

Behind these impressive achievements, of course, lies Japan's secure bond with the United States. Thus it has become almost a cliché for leaders of both countries to now regularly assure us that "relations between our two countries have never been better." And in so saying, they are exactly right.

In sum, the current climate for pursuit of continued trans-Pacific commercial relationships must be seen as bright with promise.

A WELCOMING JAPAN

Any business contemplating a venture in another country always has a vital question: Will we be welcome?

Despite today's galloping economic globalization, a fully open market to foreign capital is rare. The welcome facing a new business from abroad can vary widely, anywhere from "come right in" to "forget it." A not uncommon greeting goes something like this: "We, of course, welcome your investment in this country, but . . ."

Examination of these "buts" may provide a useful key to the nature of your welcome. Almost always, a variety of permits or licenses will await application, both at national and local levels. In some countries those requirements may simply serve as devices for delay or denial. Normally, however, they are little more than a reflection of local regulatory practices.

What sort of welcome can a new business venture expect in Japan now? In earlier years, during Japan's postwar industrial rebuilding, restrictions could prove difficult. So-called "infant" industries were often protected from outside competition through, and well beyond, infancy. Years of delay were not uncommon. But even then a few American corporations (one thinks of Hewlett-Packard and IBM) persisted and sweated it out. Today they thrive. We also find more recent amazing success stories like that of McDonald's Golden Arches setting records on Tokyo's Ginza.

Today, entry into the Japanese market by ventures from abroad happily reflects quite a different story. Sure, certain permits and procedures are still needed, but as a member of the World Trade Organization (WTO), Japan at minimum must comply with international standards.

What is perhaps the most heartening indicator of Japan's present welcoming posture goes beyond mere procedural approval. Today the Japanese boldly advertise their new appetite for American investment capital. We find U.S. business publications plastered with Japanese invitations that read something like "Y'all come on over." Good reasons are offered for doing so. Rewards, they boast, outweigh any possible risk. Expert outside observers seem to agree. The chairman of the European Trade Commission in Tokyo speaks glowingly of Japan's "lucrative market." Senior American trade officials concur.

The Japanese have also come up with another attraction they contend is going for them in their pursuit of outside investment. They point to their status as the single most solidly established international business nation in East Asia. Their location, they suggest, provides a favorable site from which investors can tap into neighboring economies. This region, they note, is now home to a newly well-heeled middle class of consumers. Figures suggest they are right. As recently as 1980 the region's share of worldwide GDP stood at 17 percent. Today that figure has climbed to nearly 30 percent. Indeed, Japan now remains the largest foreign market for American products and services on the planet, nearly double that of both China and Germany.

We also find a Japanese government trade agency, JETRO, dangling another interesting carrot. JETRO now suggests that Japanese lifestyles are converging with those prevailing in the Western world. A well-established foreign business venture in Japan can use its base there as a springboard from which to pursue investment opportunities elsewhere in the region.

Adding up all these favorable factors, we believe something exists here that historians call a positive "confluence-of-forces." Among the forces prevailing in today's Japan we find:

- Significant opportunity for outside capital investment,
- An attitude that welcomes that capital,
- An economy seemingly on the brink of an upward economic cycle,
- A country surrounded by several other flourishing economies,
- A country unthreatened by political instability, and
- A country whose relationship with the United States is strong and enduring.

This strikes us as an impressive array of favorable circumstances. They must also be coupled with several positive regional developments of recent years. We will briefly enumerate them here before dealing with them in a more detailed way in the chapters that follow.

1. As we move into the twenty-first century, China's astounding forward economic charge has startled the world. This now thriving neighbor offers Japan both an appetizing new market for its superior industrial products and an area of expanding investment opportunity. The presence of a nearby ambitious competitor is, of course, part of the package.

2. No nation has had greater reason to be heartened by the end of the Cold War than Japan. Gone is a lurking security threat. Ahead lies Russia's promising market.
3. For forty years Japan has endured what it considers to be harassment on trade issues by its friend the United States. Japan now senses some relief as the United States shifts its attention to more demanding troubles elsewhere in the world. Besides, China's bilateral deficit of $202 billion in 2007 diminishes Japan's deficit in our eyes.
4. Meanwhile, Japan has gained impressive—very impressive—new respect in world affairs. Strong new leadership has undertaken welcome outreach and has shown a broadened sense of national responsibility.

A troublesome regional development has been North Korea's nuclear saber-rattling rhetoric. Japan has thus far shown admirable restraint in reacting to this matter, working with other regional powers to keep the lid on.

Finally, Japan now continues to be a fun, innovative, and interesting place. Perhaps Amy Chozick puts it best in a recent *Wall Street Journal* article:

> Next up from the land that introduced the world to Godzilla, Hello Kitty and "Iron Chef": Jesus-themed restaurants, T-shirts that release vitamin C to the skin, and hot-tub karaoke.
>
> Japan has long been a world trendsetter, launching icons like the Sony Walkman and Honda Civic and sparking crazes for Tamagotchi and the wide-eyed characters of *anime* films. But lately, thanks to an economic transformation a decade in the making, Japan has shifted its trend-making machine into high gear. As its economy grows again, quirky creativity has become one of its biggest growth industries.[1]

To sum up, the foregoing examination of contemporary Japan stimulates us to suggest that the enterprising American business world now has abundant reason to give that country most serious attention. The purpose of our book is to help prepare American managers and public officials for negotiations with Japan Now. In Part I of the book we provide four chapters focused on the topic of Japanese and American cultural differences. In Part II (chapters 5 to 9) we get down to the business of face-to-face negotiations. Part III (chapters 10 to 13) covers a variety of topics important for trans-Pacific negotiators including the two best case studies we can find on Japanese/American negotiations. We conclude the book with speculation about the maturing marriage of the two economies and the implications for managers and public officials on both sides of the Pacific.

NOTE

1. Amy Chozick, "Land of the Rising Karaoke Hot Tub," *Wall Street Journal*, March 9, 2007, page W1.

I

CULTURAL DIFFERENCES

1

The *Aisatsu*

The initial meeting was scheduled weeks in advance for a Thursday afternoon in the Japanese firm's corporate offices in Tokyo. The primary purpose was the introduction of a high-level American executive to the president of a Japanese firm in a typical Japanese *aisatsu* (a formal greeting). The principal American negotiator was a relatively young (early forties), recently promoted sales vice president of an American capital equipment manufacturer. The two firms were in the final stages of establishing an important agreement for distribution of the American products in Japan. Protocol dictated a visit by a high-level representative of the American firm. A visit by the vice president was convenient because at that time he was scheduled to tour some of his new areas of responsibility, including Japan.

I [John Graham] had spent the early part of the week with the American firm's Tokyo representative observing a variety of Japanese-American business meetings. Much of that activity involved preparations for the Thursday meeting, working with lower level executives of the Japanese firm to coordinate final details.

As Thursday approached things began to go wrong. Final approval of the distribution agreement from the U.S. corporate headquarters and legal counsel was expected before the meeting. However, the Tokyo representative received news that, if the approval came at all, it would be delayed until after the vice president's arrival and scheduled meetings. This presented the ticklish problem of holding the scheduled meetings but avoiding making commitments—acting positive but not saying yes.

The American vice president was due to arrive in Tokyo on Wednesday evening before the Thursday *aisatsu*. He was to be briefed regarding the commercial aspects of the deal by the company's Far East district sales manager accompanying him on the flight. The flight from Singapore was delayed twelve hours and the two executives arrived at their Tokyo hotel at 9:00 a.m. Thursday. The Tokyo representative and I met them for a quick breakfast at the hotel.

The Tokyo representative briefed his superiors on the recent developments. The three Americans decided on a strategy of "dancing" with the Japanese—avoiding discussion of business for as long as possible and avoiding making any firm commitments.

This was the vice president's first visit to Japan. His previous international experiences were extensive and included business negotiations in Europe, the Middle East, and Africa. He appropriately asked the Tokyo representative about protocol and other cultural considerations. He was told generally not to worry and to just act naturally. He was also told that substantive business discussions were not appropriate at the *aisatsu*. Following the briefing, the two senior executives retreated to their rooms to shower and take a rest before the 2:00 p.m. meeting.

The three representatives of the American firm and I arrived at the Japanese corporate offices at 2:00 p.m. We were greeted by a female employee in the uniform of the company. She escorted us to a nearby formal meeting room. The room was furnished in expensive but conservative easy chairs with several coffee tables. The sixteen chairs were arranged in a square. We were not asked to sit, and shortly after our arrival three Japanese executives entered the room. These executives, whom I had met earlier in the week, were assigned specific management responsibilities related to the distribution of the American products. Introductions were made and business cards exchanged, but in a relatively more formal manner than I had previously observed in other interactions with the same managers. The American vice president was treated with obvious respect. The seven of us chatted in English about travel from Singapore and other nontask-related matters.

Behavioral scientists tell us that Americans are relatively uncomfortable with obvious status distinctions. As the conversation progressed, it became apparent that all four Americans (including myself) were unconsciously imitating the respectful and formal behaviors of the three Japanese, thus equalizing the initial status distinctions. About the time this interpersonal equalization had been completed, three more Japanese executives entered the room. These three were members of the president's executive staff, much older than the first three (late fifties) and treated with utmost respect by the first three Japanese. Because the Americans had successfully established an ambiance of status equality with the first three Japanese, there now existed a large status gap between the Americans and the three Japanese executive staff members. This again was an uncomfortable situation for the Americans, who began to try to establish status equality with the three new Japanese executives. However, before this nonverbal status manipulation could be completed, the Japanese company president entered the room. The six Japanese already in the room acted most formally and respectfully, and thus, the status position of the Americans took another dip from which it never fully recovered.

Once again business cards were exchanged and formal introductions made. One of the first three Japanese acted as an interpreter for the Japanese president, even though the president spoke and understood English. The president asked us to be seated. We seated ourselves *in exact order of rank.* The interpreter sat on a stool between the two senior executives. The general attitude between the parties was friendly but polite. Tea and a Japanese orange drink were served.

The Japanese president controlled the interaction completely, asking questions of all the Americans through the interpreter. The attention of all participants was given to each speaker in turn. After this initial round of questions for all the Americans, the Japanese president focused on developing a conversation with the American vice president. During this interaction an interesting pattern in nonverbal behaviors developed. The Japanese president would ask a question in Japanese. The interpreter then translated the question for the American vice president. While the interpreter spoke, the American's attention (gaze direction) was given to the interpreter. However, the Japanese president's gaze direction was at the American. Thus, the Japanese president could carefully and unobtrusively observe the Americans facial expressions and nonverbal responses. Alternatively, when the American spoke the Japanese president had twice the response time. Because he understood English, he could formulate his responses during the translation process.

This interesting conversational interaction continued on nontask-related matters for several minutes; the Japanese viewing business discussions at an *aisatsu* as inappropriate and the Americans specifically avoiding business discussion for strategic reasons. The weight of the conversation was clearly directed toward the senior American executive by the Japanese president. The seating arrangement also served to focus everyone's attention on the American vice president, who often filled the gaps in the conversation. When the topic turned to golf, a favorite sport of the American, his mood noticeably improved. He mentioned the several golf courses in the local area of the American headquarters and an upcoming professional golf tournament.

Then, to everyone's disbelief, the American vice president invited the Japanese president to the golf tournament when the president traveled to the United States *to sign the distribution agreement!* The American continued to talk about business and the distribution agreement and predicted a long and prosperous relationship between the two firms. The Japanese president courteously responded to the American's statements. He also ended the meeting shortly thereafter by excusing himself and suggesting moving to another conference room for a presentation by his executive staff.

It seemed incomprehensible that the American vice president would make such statements and commitments given his briefing prior to the *aisatsu*. A brief recap of the antecedent conditions helps to explain this major error. Four characteristics of the vice president seem to be relevant. He was younger than his Japanese counterpart by approximately twenty years. He was inexperienced in the Far East, particularly in Japan. He was physically fatigued after a long flight and little sleep. And finally, he was unprepared, having been told to "act naturally" in his morning briefing. The process of the meeting also appears to have worked against the American. In particular, the hierarchical introductions and vertical status relations put him in an unfamiliar and uncomfortable status position. The Japanese president's use of the interpreter further disadvantaged him. Also, the vice president obviously felt the weight of both the conversational responsibility of answering questions and filling gaps and of being the distinct physical focus of attention.

Thus, contrary to the Americans' agreed game plan, a verbal commitment was made at the *aisatsu*. The district sales manager later explained to me the potential consequences of this faux pas. The most obvious was a loss of face by the Americans because business is never to be discussed at an *aisatsu*. Worse yet, if headquarters failed to agree with the vice president's commitments, business with the Japanese firm would be finished. Even if headquarters did agree, the Tokyo sales representative lost an important degree of control over management of the relationship. Because the Tokyo sales representative and the vice president presented somewhat different positions to the Japanese group, the Japanese would tend to bypass the representative on important issues and contact the vice president directly. The district sales manager did mention one possible benefit of the error: The vice president would work harder to conclude the agreement once he returned to headquarters in the United States.

This description of an *aisatsu is* excerpted from John Graham's field notes taken during our long-term study of international negotiation styles. We have found that situations such as the one described occur all too frequently when Americans call on Japanese clients. We feel the major problem has to do with the "natural" behavior of American negotiators. This is a book primarily about an American style of business negotiation. The fact that such a style exists is not apparent until negotiation behaviors of Americans are compared to those of business executives in other countries. Thus, a second purpose of this book will be to compare the American negotiation style to that of perhaps our most important international trading partner, Japan.

As any American businessperson who has traveled to Japan will quickly point out, the Japanese have a style of bargaining distinctly their own. Discussion of these two very different styles of negotiation leads to the central theme of the book: American businesspeople, by *nature,* will have great difficulties bargaining with Japanese businesspeople. When Americans travel to Japan to negotiate with prospective clients or partners, the natural bargaining behavior that achieves good results at home can cause major problems. Business negotiations in Japan will have to be handled differently, and we intend the book to be a useful guide toward this end.

But, before we get down to details it's worthwhile to consider the long view and the view from the top regarding American and Japanese negotiations. It was some time before we began our systematic studies of international bargaining styles that Ambassador James Hodgson began his own relationship with Japan. He well describes the big-picture essentials of working with Japanese in the next chapter.

2

A View from the Ambassador's Chair

Years ago when I [Jim Hodgson] arrived in Tokyo to take up my duties, I found Japan's economic promise had already been discovered by American business. From my ambassadorial window I could look out on the huge IBM building down the street. A major 3M building was just across the Shuto Expressway, and in suburbia a Hewlett-Packard subsidiary was spewing out electronic products by the carload. Yes, I found that American business had already arrived in force, something that made me feel right at home.

I had spent thirty years in the hard-charging U.S. corporate world so I had more than mere diplomatic interest in American business ties with Tokyo. Happily my ambassadorial perch gave me a unique perspective from which to examine those ties. Obviously a diplomat doesn't get into the nitty-gritty of business operations. Nonetheless, when on the scene, one soon develops some strong impressions.

I have found that a recounting of salient stories can oftentimes prove more instructive than narrow analyses. So I thought I would open this chapter by picturing a series of experiences—experiences that served to form much of my outlook on what I continue to consider to be the world's most fascinating two-country business relationship.

While these early experiences won't provide a road map through Japan's business/cultural jungle, they may offer at least something of a "feel" of where the high ground may lie. Further, recounting these experiences serves to demonstrate the resiliency of both Japanese and American business cultures.

BRUISED INNOCENCE

As I recall, it usually happened on a Thursday, often in the early afternoon. My secretary would buzz my office saying, "An American businessman now in Tokyo, a Mr. Smith, is calling. He wants to see you. Says it is important. What shall I tell him?"

"I'll be free after four o'clock. I'll see him then."

Later that day an energetic but obviously distressed American executive would be ushered into my office. Almost before being seated he would burst out with an anguished tale of woe that would go something like this: "Ambassador, I am in trouble. As your secretary probably told you, I am the International VP of the Smith-Jones Company. Last week our company president called me in and told me to get myself over here and sew up a joint venture we have been working on with a local Japanese company. Since a lot of groundwork had already been laid, it seemed to me the remaining negotiations shouldn't take more than a week. My boss agreed, then he went on to tell me not to come back empty-handed. Anyway, I wired our prospective partners here, saying I would like to arrive on what was last Sunday. That was fine with them. In fact they even met me at the airport, where they asked how long I could stay here. I told them I had promised our president I would be back in a week. That was all right with them. I spent Monday at their headquarters here getting acquainted with their top brass. Tuesday we took the bullet train to Nagoya and toured their plant there. For Wednesday they insisted we all relax together with a game of golf, telling me that no American should be allowed to return home without being treated to a bit of Japanese golfing hospitality. Each night there was a company dinner or geisha party."

At about this point it seemed to me the fellow was getting pretty well wound up, so I broke in to ask him just what the problem was.

"My problem is simply this," he continued, "not until this morning did we get down to doing any actual negotiating. Then they came up with a whole new list of demands that I knew we could never properly cover in a day and a half. So now I'm faced with either caving in and accepting their position on a lot of key items or blowing the whole deal and outraging my boss."

Then he began pouring out questions.

"Do you have any suggestions for me? Where did I go wrong? Have you seen this sort of thing happen before?"

I couldn't help but feel sorry for the poor guy. Wounded innocence is always a pitiable sight. Had I seen it happen before? Yes. Yes indeed. With variations I had seen it happen a dozen times. To me, his critical question was, "Where did I go wrong?" Since he had asked, I proceeded to tell him—tell him with what I hope was more diplomatic tact than I set forth here. I said:

1. You should never—never—set inflexible time limits for yourself when dealing with the Japanese, especially not when establishing an initial working relationship. Japan is not a one-stop shopping service.
2. Arriving here you told them you only had a week to do the job. When you did that you gave your Japanese friends exactly what they needed to know to develop the timing of their own negotiating strategy. One thing you will soon find out here is that the Japanese are grand masters at making time work for them tactically.
3. You let them set the agenda and then you waited too long to learn their complete list of demands. Spending time getting to know their management, to tour their plant, and to play a round of golf is a normal way the Japanese use to get to know those with whom they intend to do business. Doing that was okay. Yet in allowing it to compact your negotiating time, you also let it serve their tactical interest.

I am sure my distraught friend didn't need me to tell him these things. His experience had already done that for him. Nor could I give him much consolation with respect to what he should do about his problem. When you find yourself between the rock of an inflexible time limit and the hard place of boss's orders, there's not much room to maneuver.

But I did tell him one thing. I said I had watched several others get caught in a similar predicament. When they did, they would reluctantly bite the bullet, sign up for the best deal they could get in the time allotted and then fly home, probably to brag about how well they had done.

Readers will recognize that despite the best of intentions my visitor had done just about everything wrong. In business matters the Japanese are not amateurs. Their respect for Americans does not translate into a willingness to set aside their own business interests. One is reminded of the old W. C. Fields admonition, "Never give a sucker an even break." As with most business people, if you give the Japanese a chance to drive a hard bargain, they will often drive it unashamedly.

THE DEVELOPMENT OF TRUST

It seems to me that over their long history, the Japanese have produced few illustrious philosophers in the Western sense of the term. Great leaders—yes; brilliant artists—yes; but Olympian philosophers—not many.

One of late last century, however, is Yukichi Fukuzawa, an astute educator who founded Keio University (a school I am fond of calling Japan's Stanford). Fukuzawa placed *trust* at the top of a man's virtues. I found the Japanese have an unusually strong reason for valuing trust. That crowded society is bound together by an intricate web of relationships that simply cannot abide weak links of trust. An outsider soon notices that between persons in Japan trust is neither casually given nor capriciously compromised.

At times American businessmen find it curious that their Japanese counterparts often insist on developing strong personal relationships before undertaking business ties. I believe this practice is simply a matter of habit with them. Unless a feeling of trust exists between business parties, the Japanese are apt to feel uncomfortable. With the Japanese, relationships are not merely negotiated, they are built.

Long before I became an ambassador, I had my eyes opened to the importance the Japanese place on trust among people who do business together. That year I was with other U.S. Cabinet officials visiting Tokyo. I had the good fortune to visit with one of Japan's elder business statesmen, a Motosume Kobayashi, president of the huge Fuji Film Company. I questioned him about his various ties with American executives. He said he found them all capable but a few reflected attitudes that were hard for a Japanese to understand. So I asked him point blank, "Is there a single American business leader you have particularly come to appreciate?"

"Certainly, it would be Sol Linowitz," he quickly replied. Since Mr. Linowitz had built his Xerox Company into a commanding position, I was not wholly surprised at the respect he had gained from my new friend. Yet I sensed the Fuji president's answer reflected more than mere respect. So I asked, "What was there about Mr. Linowitz that impressed you?"

"I found we could do business together simply on the basis of trust," he said. "We did almost everything by mutual agreement. We never had to bring in a bunch of lawyers. That's the way I have always liked to do business, one person trusting another."

Today I believe most Japanese business executives, perhaps reluctantly, have learned to be more accepting of the American way of business—a way that features formal contracts complete with endless boilerplate. But personal trust among business associates still ranks high in the Japanese lexicon. Very high.

More than anything, these experiences of mine exemplify the need for all players in our fast globalizing economy to think anew about many aspects of their business. When products and services flow across political borders, are traded in volatile currencies, and run up against unusual practices, new safeguards must be coupled with new flexibilities. "Be prepared" then becomes more than a scout's motto.

NEVER BE SURPRISED

I suppose most American companies who venture abroad are prepared to find regulatory and legal differences in their targeted country. They will certainly find them in Japan. While there I noticed that though an American might feel prepared for such differences, actual exposure to them, Japanese-style, could become frustrating to the point of madness. Seemingly inexplicable business practices and mystical cultural no-nos often pile up to puzzle him. When that happens, an otherwise composed American may react a bit like old G. K. Chesterton. In a burst of frustration, that early Britisher once exploded, "I have seen the truth and I can tell you, it doesn't make sense."

Don't expect all things to make sense in Japan, at least not Western-style sense.

TACTICS AND TRUST

One should be cautious in recommending specific tactical approaches for dealing with the Japanese. I have seen instances of what I considered to be a properly tailored approach fail, and then go on to watch some ham-handed approach succeed. So I resist suggesting hard and fast rules on this subject. Yet, this of course does not mean one shouldn't try to improve the odds.

When considering opening a new relationship with almost any Japanese enterprise, ways must often be found to test the other's sincerity. I recall one circumstance that involved this matter.

After returning from Tokyo, I was called by the owner of a highly successful office design company. He had been asked to submit a proposal for furnishing a new Tokyo office building. He was concerned because of the way he had previously been burned. It seems he had then been asked by another Japanese company to come to Tokyo and submit a proposal for furnishing a new skyscraper. Since he was eager to expand his activities into the international arena, he had poured big money into preparing an elaborate proposal. Then he took it to Tokyo and presented it to a group of seemingly enthusiastic executives. But then—nothing. He never heard a word from them again. Later he learned the job had gone to a Tokyo company that had used many of the concepts embodied in my friend's proposal.

Once burned, twice shy. My friend didn't want to make the same mistake twice. So together we discussed ways of testing the sincerity of his latest request from Tokyo. What we came up with was this:

1. My friend would go to Tokyo but without a specific proposal in hand. There he would discuss his company's capabilities and suggest a few concepts that might be appropriate for their project.
2. While there he would offer to prepare a complete detailed proposal should the client be willing to pay half the cost of preparing it.

3. Should the client agree, he and the client would then further agree to a "ball park" figure that the client would be willing to spend on the overall project.

What happened? The Japanese firm at first said "they could not do business that way." Since I had counseled patience, however, my friend waited them out. Eventually they came around. Ultimately he got the full contract and later on did several other projects for that same client. Our sincerity test had worked.

One thing needs to be made clear about this circumstance. Going into this game, my friend held some strong cards. His firm was known to be top in its field. He could make demands of a client that a less prestigious firm could not. Here it was simply a case of him capitalizing on his strengths, not a bad idea in any business situation.

Another thing about this "sincerity test" factor needs remarking. Most Japanese themselves are experts at similar testing. An American hoping to do business with them had better be prepared to respond. But once a relationship of trust has been established, sincerity tests become perfunctory.

Long after leaving my Tokyo post, I continued to find myself involved in various U.S.-Japan business matters, especially where either a Japanese or an American company was seeking to develop an initial across-the-sea tie. Knowing I had spent a few years in that island nation, many American executives would seek me out in the belief that my experience would provide answers to their questions. A lot of their problems simply had no one "right" answer. I have come to believe that the best most advisors can do is to help narrow the range of suitable courses of action and thereby improve odds of success.

NOT A "DREAM WORLD"

So far in this chapter I have written only of circumstances where Americans were doing business in Japan. A reverse situation now comes to mind, one involving the need for a different kind of sincerity test. In the early eighties an American-based official of a Japanese bank came to me asking that he be introduced to the president of a prestigious American trust company for the purpose of developing a "mutually beneficial" bond. He told me his bank in Tokyo had never been in trust work and needed to learn the business from an experienced American firm. I asked if he had a specific proposal to make. He responded that he had only an "impossible dream" of getting his bank into the trust business.

Dealing in dreams is not my specialty so I was more than normally skeptical. Further, I knew the Japanese usually prefer to deal on a peer-to-peer basis. Yet here was a second-level bank officer seeking to meet with a top-level American CEO. I was concerned that I might have an overly ambitious junior executive on my hands. Not only sincerity but legitimacy needed testing. So I told him I couldn't oblige him unless he did two things.

First, he should obtain from his bank's Tokyo-based president a letter authorizing him to proceed on his bank's behalf. The letter should be addressed to the American CEO and should express a willingness by his president to come to the United States to finalize terms should initial discussions prove promising. Chances for success are always enhanced if the two top executives personally participate. Second, when meeting with the American trust people, he should forget his "dream." Instead, he should present a finite list of inter-company activities that would be involved, together with an account of what financial benefits might ensue for the American company. (As mentioned earlier, the Japanese are often loath to talk financial terms in initial meetings. But knowing this particular American CEO as I did, I knew this step was necessary.)

At first my suggestions met with what I can only describe as great reluctance. But after lengthy convincing, the young banker finally assented. The project went forward, negotiations succeeded, and a long-term relationship was eventually established. I find dreams are more easily fulfilled when their fulfillment is carefully planned.

LONG-TERM STRATEGIES

Thus far I've mainly pictured instances involving the opening of a new business association, or of solving a specific relationship problem. Among the more sizable American companies, however, a major policy decision may be made to seek a specific initial international objective, which will then be coupled with a long-term strategy for achieving that objective. I was witness to several such circumstances when I served in Tokyo. Here I will cite a couple of examples, one of failure and one of success.

A major American chemical company had examined the potential need for its products in Japan's thriving industrial future. They saw the country as a promising market for one of their major products, one that would have to be produced in Japan. So the company chose an unusually capable executive to go and live in Tokyo, there to steer the company's project through what it knew would be a lengthy effort to gain government permits, lay the necessary public relations groundwork, choose a suitable plant site, and so on. He was given instructions to avoid "ugly American" methods, that is not to use bullying and bulldozing techniques.

When I met him in Tokyo, the man had already been on the scene for three years pursuing various permits, schmoozing with authorities, and gaining a highly favorable impression for himself and his company. And he continued this diligence for several years thereafter. Finally he had solved all the permit problems and had selected a suitable site. Nothing further stood in the way. Nothing, that is, but a new problem. During the intervening years a Japanese chemical company had also noticed the same promising market right in their own backyard. By the time the patient Americans were ready to build, they found the Japanese had already beaten them to it. The need for the American plant had disappeared. The American executive sadly folded his tent and slunk back to the States with a decade of effort and countless dollars sacrificed in futility. I suppose the lesson here is, never expect your competition to remain asleep if there is a promising market around, especially in Japan.

In another case I did, however, see a strategy of endless patience pay off, this time for an American agricultural group. Japanese agricultural interests have political power far out of proportion to their numbers. They can thwart almost any intrusion of their cherished home market monopoly. Only strong American political pressure can neutralize their local clout. This American agricultural group soon realized that operating alone without U.S. government pressure on the Japanese was getting them nowhere. But eventually, with American government help, a breakthrough occurred. Here I suppose the moral is, never try to use power you don't have. Instead, team up with another source that has the needed power.

A third example of seeking entry into the Japanese market presents still another picture. The makers of Ritz Crackers saw no reason why their tasty morsels should not sell well in Japan's middle-class society. Observing Japan's inefficient multitiered distribution system, the company decided to distribute directly to the retailer. But their product was met with a big yawn. After conducting some tests, the company modified its product formula to meet Japanese taste preferences. Yet no matter what they tried, they still couldn't get Japanese retailers to show an interest in stocking their crackers.

After several months on the scene, the company's local executive sat next to a Japanese trading company executive on a social occasion. He described the futility of his efforts.

"Why don't you make a joint venture with us," said the trading company man. "We can get your product into 90 percent of Japan's retail markets in thirty days."

The company knew a good thing when they heard it. They quickly revised their distribution decision and accepted the joint venture offer. Ritz Crackers soon adorned just about every market shelf in the country. Moral: if one strategy doesn't work, try another.

CROSS-CULTURAL COMPETENCE

Now let's shift gears and drive off down a wholly new road. Behind us we leave a parade of anecdotes and ambassadorial experiences that I hope may have provided at least some business insights. Ahead of us lies a formidable thicket of Japanese behavior. From where I sat, it seemed to me various American business people took polar opposite approaches in hacking through the thicket. One group seemed so intimidated by the complex knowledge involved and the cultural gaffes they might commit during their early relationship with Japanese counterparts, they became overly cautious. At times, this excess of caution actually made them look ridiculous.

On the other hand, there were those who chose simply to ignore local cultural niceties, either out of indifference, or from having concluded that the Japanese would excuse them as just "stupid Americans." Neither course is recommended.

In the last forty years, as more and more Japanese business people have ventured out into world markets, they have come to realize the singularity of their own culture. This experience has made them more tolerant of those Americans whose behavior at times reflects a lack of cross-cultural sensitivity.

As usual, I believe a middle ground will be the most suitable here. One should not be intimidated by cultural differences, neither should one be indifferent to them. Conspicuous indifference or outright neglect is naturally resented by the Japanese. On the other hand, excessive concern for local proprieties can be carried so far at times as to defeat possible progress. With that said, let's examine some aspects of the cultural thicket of which Americans should be aware in seeking to smooth the path of a business relationship with the Japanese.

Matters of Form

First of all, we must understand that the mish-mash of behavior, of life styles, of differing practices and habits that we Americans extol as pluralism holds absolutely no attraction for the men and women of Japan. In those people-packed islands there exists an explicitly preferred way of doing and saying just about everything. Their now accepted patterns of speech and behavior have been nurtured and refined through the centuries. In Japan, orderliness is "in"; shortcuts are "out." Following tradition is "in," casualness is "out." One of the reasons Japanese society functions so smoothly, perhaps more so than any other society, is that its citizens know the "rules," and what's more, they play by them. Technological creativity may be appreciated, but creativity in manners and mores is not. American buoyancy and brashness is rarely appreciated.

Customs and Practices

The Japanese appreciate those Americans who become acquainted in advance with their more standard business customs. One, of course, is the exchanging of business cards on being introduced. And remember—not only should your business card be printed in Japanese on one side, but any written material you wish to employ should be offered in the Japanese language. Not to do so not only reflects insensitivity, but may also be interpreted as reflecting a shallowness of interest.

I do not believe it necessary to elaborate on this subject here. Rather, I would suggest anyone seriously considering a Japanese venture should arrange for a few sessions with a knowledgeable bicultural business consultant. They are available most places. Your presentation can then be better tailored to your express needs.

Business Communication

I won't try to get into the nuts and bolts of this subject, much of which is covered elsewhere in this book. I will, however, point to a few fruits of my experience.

First, as I see it, in business correspondence Americans should realize no news is bad news. If a request goes unanswered, the answer is "no." This is just another Japanese avoidance of the hated word "no." And remember, if an answer to any of your proposed actions turns out to be, "That will be difficult," you've just been given a conclusive "no." When a language is short on definitiveness, as is the Japanese language, and when people are reluctant to appear disagreeable, as are the Japanese people, patience and lots of penetrating talk must occur before certainty can exist on any subject.

A distinction must also be noted with respect to when to talk and when not to talk business with the Japanese. With many Japanese there are business occasions and there are social occasions. Some of them consider it bad form to talk business on social occasions. Golf outings and seven-course dinners are more opportunities to relax and become acquainted than to discuss business. If business is to be discussed on such occasions, let the Japanese be first to bring it up, especially if they are the host.

An illuminating personal experience is worth noting here. A business friend who owned a sizable California insurance company asked me to provide some guidance in negotiating a joint venture with a Tokyo insurance company. All was going well in Los Angeles discussions. An agreement seemed within reach. A senior official of the Japanese company told me he was prepared to return home with an American proposal that had his endorsement. On the evening before his flight back to Tokyo, a festive dinner was scheduled. The American CEO, however, was called away at the last minute. His marketing vice president substituted in hosting the dinner. I counseled the vice president to keep the evening purely social—no mention should be made of business unless the Japanese official spoke first.

The dinner was delicious, the wine superb, and camaraderie began to flower. But then it happened, just as described in the previous chapter. Perhaps emboldened by the vintage wine, the vice president could not resist. He broke into a long dissertation on how wonderful the new business relationship would be, how he would personally take charge, and how much money both companies would make. On he went. After dinner we dropped our noncommittal Japanese dinner partner at his hotel. The vice president, still euphoric, then turned to me and exclaimed, "What a great evening; what a wonderful fellow, we'll make great business partners." Then he asked, "What do you think?"

Disgusted, I let him have it. "I think you blew it," I said. I guess I was right. Next morning the Japanese took a plane back to Tokyo. We never heard from him or his company again.

General Knowledge of Japan

I believe most Americans who venture into the Japanese business world will feel more comfortable and be more favorably received if they provide themselves with some general knowledge of the country and its people before they pursue a business objective there with them. As a start I suggest simply reading an encyclopedia's entry on the country. At minimum this should be coupled with a more intensive examination of available materials devoted to the specific Japanese sector, company, or institution that will be involved. For rigorous preparation, reference to some of the books and studies set forth in the final pages of this book is suggested. Nothing, of course, is more important than a study of this book itself.

3

The American Negotiation Style

Picture if you will the closing scenes of John Wayne's Academy Award–winning performance in *True Grit*. Sheriff Rooster Cogburn sitting astride his chestnut mare, a Colt .45 in one hand, a Winchester in the other, whiskey on his breath, reins in his teeth, stampeding across the Arkansas prairie straight into the sights and range of villains' guns. A face-to-face shootout with four bad guys, and sure enough, the John Wayne character comes through again.

Great entertainment, yes! We know it's all fantasy. We know that in real life Sheriff Rooster Cogburn would have ended up face down in the blood and dust, alongside his dead horse. But it's more fun to see the fantasy nonetheless.

Such scenes from movies (think Clint Eastwood in *Unforgiven*, Daniel Day-Lewis in *The Last of the Mohicans*, or even Uma Thurman in *Kill Bill*), TV, and books influence our everyday behavior in subtle, but powerful ways. We tend to model our behavior after such John Wayne figures. And when everyone else plays the same game, the bluff and bravado often work. But such behavior becomes a problem when we sit face-to-face across a negotiation table with business executives who haven't grown up on a steady diet of American action heroes. Our minds play out the familiar scenes. But instead of six-guns, flintlocks, or samurai swords, our weapons are words, questions, threats and promises, laughter, and confrontation. We anticipate victory, despite the odds—four against one is no problem. But we are often disappointed to find it's not the movies. It's a real-life business negotiation. At stake are the profits of our companies, not to mention our own compensation and reputation. And like a real-life sheriff, we lose.

This scenario repeats itself with increasing frequency as American enterprise turns more global. The cowboy bargaining style, which has served us well in conference rooms across the country, does us great disservice in conference rooms across the sea.

Probably no single statement better summarizes the American negotiation style than "Shoot first, ask questions later," a phrase straight out of an old Saturday afternoon Western. But the roots of the American negotiation style run much deeper than movies and television reruns. To understand the American approach to bargaining, we must consider more basic aspects of our cultural background—in particular, the seeds of Western thought, our immigrant heritage, our frontier history, the fundamental competitiveness of our social and business systems, and finally, much of the training in our present-day business and law schools.

THE ROOTS OF AMERICAN CULTURE

Culture starts with geography.[1] Our ancestors adapted social systems and thinking processes to the problems and opportunities their environments presented. The cradle of ancient Western civilization is Greece 500 BC. Look at a map and you'll see thousands of islands. That's the prominent geographical feature of Greece. Islands allow for individualism. Indeed, the word "isolation" has its roots in the Italian word *isola*, or island. If you get mad at your neighbor you can always move to another island, particularly when the seas are Aegean calm. You don't need his or her help to cast your net. In fact, you can't fit many folks into your boat anyway. And, of course, boats did get bigger and trade brought a flood of new ideas from all over the Mediterranean. Personal freedom, individuality, objective thought, and even democracy all come to us from this ancient island realm.

Now fast forward two millennia. Throughout its history, America has been a nation influenced by its immigrants. Certainly the continuous mixing of ideas and perspectives brought from across the seas has enriched all our experiences. Every newcomer has had to work hard to succeed; thus the powerful work ethic of America. Another quality of our immigrant forefathers was a fierce individualism and independence—characteristics necessary for survival in the wide open spaces. But this latter quality does us disservice at the negotiation table. Negotiation is by definition a situation of *inter*dependence—a situation that Americans have never handled well.

We inherit more of this island/individualistic mentality from our frontier history. "Move out West where there's elbow room," ran the conventional wisdom of the first 150 years of our nation's existence. Americans as a group haven't had much practice negotiating because they have always been able to go elsewhere if conflicts arose.

The long distances between people allowed a social system to develop with not only fewer negotiations but also shorter ones. A day-long horseback ride to the general store or stockyard didn't favor long, drawn-out negotiations. It was important to settle things quickly and leave no loose ends to the bargain. "Tell me yes, or tell me no—but give me a straight answer." Candor, laying your cards on the table, was highly valued and expected in the Old West. And it still is today in our boardrooms and classrooms.

We must also recognize the uniqueness of the fundamental driving forces behind our social and business systems. Adam Smith in his *Wealth of Nations*, published in 1776, well justified their emphasis in perhaps the most important sentence ever written in English: "By pursuing his own interest he frequently[2] promotes that of the society more effectually than when he really intends to promote it." In a stroke of his pen Smith solved the age-old conundrum of group versus individual interests. And, through his co-author, one Benjamin Franklin, he inseminated the philosophy and structure of the most dynamic social system ever devised by Man.

Thus, in no country in the world are individualism and competitiveness more highly valued. Indeed, see the empirical evidence for this assertion reported in table 3.1. Compare the ninety-one for the U.S. to the forty-six for

Table 3.1. Hofstede's Individualism/Collectivism Index

Country	Score	Country	Score
USA	91	**Japan**	46
Australia	90	Argentina	46
Great Britain	89	Iran	41
Canada	80	Brazil	38
Netherlands	80	Turkey	37
New Zealand	79	Greece	35
Italy	76	Philippines	32
Belgium	75	Mexico	30
Denmark	74	Portugal	27
Sweden	71	Hong Kong	25
France	71	Chile	23
Ireland	70	Singapore	20
Norway	69	Thailand	20
Switzerland	68	Taiwan	17
Germany	67	Peru	16
South Africa	65	Pakistan	14
Finland	63	Colombia	13
Austria	55	Venezuela	12
Israel	54		
Spain	51		
India	48		

the much more collectivistic Japanese culture. We're at the top of the list, the end of the scale. Americans place higher values on individualism than folks from any other country. These numbers are based on the research of a Dutch international management scholar, Geert Hofstede. In 1970 he surveyed IBM employees around the world about their work-related values. From those data he developed four dimensions of cultural differences, the most salient of which is his "Individualism/Collectivism Scale."

The Individualism/Collectivism Index (IDV) refers to the preference for behavior that promotes one's self-interest. Cultures that score high in IDV reflect an "I" mentality and tend to reward and accept individual initiative, whereas those low in individualism reflect a "we" mentality and generally subjugate the individual to the group. This does not mean that individuals fail to identify with groups when a culture scores high on IDV, but rather that personal initiative and independence are accepted and endorsed. Individualism pertains to societies in which the ties between individuals are loose; everyone is expected to look after himself or herself and his or her immediate family. Collectivism, as its opposite, pertains to societies in which people from birth onward are integrated into strong, cohesive groups, which throughout people's lifetimes continue to protect them in exchange for unquestioning loyalty.

Of course our educational system also reflects Adam Smith's profundity. And, what goes on in the classrooms in our business and law schools in turn has a strong influence on our negotiation style. Throughout the American educational system we are taught to compete, both academically and on the sporting field. Adversarial relationships and winning are essential themes of the American socialization process. But nowhere in the American educational system is competition and winning more important than in case discussions in our law and business school classrooms. They who make the best arguments, marshal the best evidence, or demolish the opponents' arguments win both the respect of classmates and high marks. Such skills will be important at the negotiation table, but the most important negotiation skills aren't taught or, at best, are shamefully underemphasized in both business and legal training.[3] We don't teach our students how to ask questions, how to get information, how to listen, or how to use questioning as a powerful persuasive strategy. In fact, few of us realize that in most places in the world, the one who asks the questions controls the process of negotiation and thereby accomplishes more in bargaining situations.

A combination of attitudes, expectations, and habitual behaviors constitutes the John Wayne negotiation style. Each characteristic is discussed separately below, but it should be understood that each factor is connected to the others to form the complex foundation for a series of negotiation strategies and tactics typically American. We hope it is obvious that what we are talking about is the typical or dominant behavior of American negotiators.

Obviously not every American executive is impatient, a poor listener, or argumentative. Nor does every American manager encounter difficulties during international negotiations. But many do, particularly when compared with businesspeople from other countries.

I CAN GO IT ALONE

Most American executives feel they should be able to handle any negotiation situation by themselves. "Four Japanese versus one American is no problem. I don't need any help. I can think and talk fast enough to get what I want, what the company needs." So goes the John Wayne rationalization. And there's an economic justification "Why take more people than I need?" Another more subtle reason might be, "Why not take full credit for success? Why split the commission?" Often, then, the American side is outnumbered when it shows up for business discussions.

Being outnumbered or, worse yet, being alone is a severe disadvantage in a negotiation situation. Several things are going on at once—talking, listening, preparing arguments and explanations, formulating questions, and seeking approval. Numbers help in obvious ways with most of the above. Indeed, on a Japanese negotiation team one member is often assigned the task of carefully listening with no speaking responsibilities at all. Consider for a moment how carefully you might listen to a speaker if you didn't have to think up a response to his or her next question. But perhaps the most important reason for having greater, or at least equal, numbers on your side is the powerful, subtle influence of nodding heads and positive facial expressions. Negotiation is very much a social activity, and the approval and agreement of others (friend and foe) can have critical effects on negotiation outcomes. Numbers can also be a subtle indicator of the seriousness and commitment of both parties to a negotiation.

JUST CALL ME MARY

Americans more than any other cultural group value informality and equality in human relations. The emphasis on first names is only the tip of the iceberg. We go out of our way to make our clients feel comfortable by playing down status distinctions such as titles and by eliminating unnecessary formalities such as lengthy introductions. But all too often we succeed in making only ourselves feel comfortable, while our international clients are often uneasy or even annoyed.

While Japanese society is changing, interpersonal relationships are traditionally vertical; that is, in almost all two-person relationships a difference in status exists. The basis for this status distinction may be any of several factors: age, sex, place of education, position in a firm, which firm, or even industry of employment. For example, the president of the number one firm in an industry holds a higher status position than the president of the number two firm in the same industry. The Japanese are very much aware of such distinctions and of their positions in the hierarchy. And for good reason, knowledge of their status positions dictates how they will act during interpersonal interactions. Thus, it is easy to understand the importance of exchanging business cards in Japan; such a ritual clearly establishes the status relationships and lets each person know which role to play. The roles of the higher status position and lower status position are very different, even to the extent that different words are used to express the same idea depending on which person makes the statement. For example, a buyer would say *otaku* (your company), while a seller would say *on sha* (your great company). Status relations dictate not only what can be said, but how it is said.

Such rules for conducting business discussions are difficult for Americans to understand. We can perhaps get by with our informal, egalitarian style when we're dealing with foreigners in the United States. However, we only make things difficult for ourselves and our companies by asking executives in Tokyo, Paris, or London to "just call me Mary (or John)."

PARDON MY FRENCH

Americans aren't adept at speaking foreign languages. Often we aren't even apologetic about it. We rightly argue that English is the international language, particularly with regard to technology and science. Wherever we go we expect to find someone who speaks English. Often we do; but when we don't, we are left to the mercy of third-party translators.

Even when our clients, partners, or suppliers do speak English we are at a disadvantage at the negotiation table. First, the use of interpreters gives the other side some subtle but very real advantages. As exemplified in chapter 1, foreign executives will sometimes use interpreters even when they have a good understanding of English. This permits them to observe our nonverbal responses. Alternatively, when we speak, the executives have longer to respond. Because they understand English, they can formulate their responses during the translation process.

Having to bargain in English puts a second, very powerful negotiation tool in the hands of our opponents. On the face of it, bargaining in our first language should be an advantage, but even the most powerful argument fizzles when the other side responds, "Sorry, I'm not sure I understand. Can you repeat that please?" Bargainers listening in a second language have more freedom to use the tactic of selective understanding. It also works when they speak. Previous commitments are more easily dissolved with the excuse, "That isn't exactly what I meant. "

A third disadvantage concerns our assumptions about those who speak English well. When facing a group of foreign executives it is natural to assume that the one who speaks English best is also the most intelligent and influential in the group. This is seldom the case in foreign business negotiations. Yet, we often direct our persuasive appeals and attention toward the one who speaks the best English, thus accomplishing little.

CHECK WITH THE HOME OFFICE

It is not always easy to identify the key decision maker in international business negotiations. Indeed, American bargainers become very upset when, halfway through a negotiation, the other side says, "I'll have to check with the home office," thus making it known that the decision makers aren't even at the negotiation table. In such a situation, Americans feel they've wasted time or even been misled.

Having limited authority at the negotiation table is a common circumstance overseas and can be a useful bargaining tactic. In reality the foreign executive is saying, "In order to get me to compromise you have to convince not only me, but also my boss who is 5,000 miles away." Thus, your arguments must be most persuasive. Additionally, such a bargaining tactic helps to maintain harmony at the negotiation table by letting the home office take the blame for saying no.

But such tactics go against the grain of the American bargaining style. Americans pride themselves in having full authority to make a deal. After all, John Wayne never had to check with the home office!

GET TO THE POINT

As mentioned earlier, Americans don't like to beat around the bush, but prefer to get to the heart of the matter as quickly as possible. Unfortunately, what is considered the heart of the matter in a business negotiation varies across cultures. In every country we have studied we have found business negotiations to proceed in the following four stages:

1. Nontask sounding
2. Task-related exchange of information
3. Persuasion
4. Concessions and agreement

The first stage includes all those activities that help establish a rapport. It does not include information related to the business of the meeting. The information exchanged in the second stage of business negotiations regards the parties' needs and preferences. The third stage involves their attempts to change each other's mind through the use of various persuasive tactics. The final stage is the consummation of an agreement, which is often the summation of a series of concessions or smaller agreements.

From the American point of view, the heart of the matter is the third stage—persuasion. We have a tendency to go through the first two stages quickly. We do talk about golf or the weather or family, but relative to other cultures, we spend little time doing so. We state our needs and preferences, and we're quick about that, too. We tend to be more interested in logical arguments than in the people with whom we're negotiating.

In many other countries the heart of the matter is not so much information and persuasion as the people involved. In Japan, much time is spent getting to know one another. Since the Japanese would prefer not to depend on a legal system to iron out conflicts, a strong relationship of trust must be established before business can begin. Americans new to the Japanese way are particularly susceptible to what we call the "wristwatch syndrome." In the United States, looking at your watch usually gets things moving along. In Japan, impatience signals apprehension and thus necessitates even longer periods of nontask sounding.

LAY YOUR CARDS ON THE TABLE

Americans expect honest information at the negotiation table. When we don't get it, negotiations often end abruptly. We also understand that, like dollars, information must be traded. "You tell me what you want, and I'll tell you what we want." And there is an uncommon urgency to this request for reciprocity. Compared to the negotiation styles of managers in the twenty other cultures we have studied, Americans expect information in return almost instantly. We begin to feel very uncomfortable if something is not given in return that day. Reciprocity is important in all cultures, but because relationships tend to last longer elsewhere, foreign negotiators are willing to wait until later to see their partner's cards.

Another problem with our American approach is that negotiators in other countries may have different attitudes and values about "honest information." In Japan it can be very difficult to get a straight answer for two reasons. First, the Japanese team may not have decided what it wants out of the deal. Second, if the answer is no, the Japanese side may not be willing to say so. Because it is the Japanese style to avoid conflict and embarrassment, they may sidestep, beat around the bush, or even remain silent. We misread and often feel misled by such subtle negative responses. Japanese executives—particularly those educated since World War II, with international experience—say they are learning to value directness. But here too the tradition is a long one and is a powerful influence on behavior at the negotiation table.

DON'T JUST SIT THERE, SPEAK UP

Americans are uncomfortable with silence during negotiations. This may seem a minor point, but we have often witnessed Americans getting themselves into trouble—particularly in Japan—by filling silent periods.

The American style of conversation consists of few long silent periods—that is, ten seconds or greater. Alternatively, the Japanese style includes occasional long periods of silence, particularly in response to an impasse. We have found that American negotiators react to Japanese silence in one of two ways. Either they make some kind of a concession or they fill the gap in the conversation with a persuasive appeal. The latter tactic has two counterproductive results: (1) the American does most of the talking, and (2) he or she learns little about the Japanese point of view.

DON'T TAKE NO FOR AN ANSWER

Persistence is highly valued by Americans. We are taught from the earliest age to never give up. In sports, classrooms, or boardrooms, we are taught to be aggressive and to win. Subsequently, we view a negotiation as something to be won. We expect a negotiation to have a definite conclusion, a signed contract. Moreover, we are dissatisfied and distressed if we don't get the bigger piece of the pie. But even worse than losing a negotiation is not concluding a negotiation. We can take a loss, consoling ourselves that we'll do better next time, but not the ambiguity of no outcome.

This competitive, adversarial, "persistence pays" view of negotiation is not necessarily shared by our foreign clients and vendors. Negotiations are viewed in many countries as a means of establishing long-term commercial relations, which have no definite conclusions. Negotiations are considered a cooperative effort where interdependence is manifest and each side tries to add to the pie.

ONE THING AT A TIME

Americans tend to attack a complex negotiation task sequentially. That is, they separate the issues and settle them one at a time. For example, we have heard American bargainers say, "Let's settle the quantity first and then discuss price." Thus, in an American negotiation, the final agreement is a sum of the several concessions made on individual issues, and progress can be measured easily. "We're halfway done when we're through half the issues." However, in other countries, particularly Eastern cultures, concessions tend to be made only at the end of a negotiation. All issues are discussed using a holistic approach, and nothing is settled until the end.

Because negotiators on the other side "never seem to commit themselves to anything," American executives invariably feel that little progress is being made during cross-cultural negotiations. Agreements are often unexpected and often follow unnecessary concessions by American bargainers.

A DEAL IS A DEAL

When an American makes an agreement, he or she is expected to honor the agreement no matter what the circumstances. But agreements are viewed differently in other parts of the world. W. H. Newman put it well:

> In some parts of the world it is impolite to openly refuse to do something that has been requested by another person. What a Westerner takes as a commitment may be little more than friendly conversation. In some societies, it is understood that today's commitment may be superseded by a conflicting request received tomorrow, especially if that request comes from a highly influential person. In still other situations, agreements merely signify intention and have little relation to capacity to perform; as long as the person tries to perform he feels no pangs of conscience, and he makes no special effort, if he is unable to fulfill the agreement. Obviously, such circumstances make business dealings much more uncertain, especially for new undertakings.[4]

I AM WHAT I AM

Most Americans take pride in determination, not changing one's mind even given difficult circumstances. John Wayne's character and behavior was constant and predictable. He treated everyone and every situation with an action-oriented, forthright style. John Wayne could never be accused of being a chameleon—changing colors with changing environments.

Many American bargainers take the same attitudes with them to the negotiation table. Competition, persistence, and determination no matter what. But during international business negotiations, inflexibility can be a fatal flaw. There simply isn't a strategy or tactic that always works. Different countries and different personalities require different approaches.

FINAL COMMENTS

Most Americans are not aware of a native negotiation style. We tend to perceive bargaining behavior in terms of personality as the Texas "good ole boy" approach, or the Wall Street "city slicker" approach, or the California "laid-back" style. But when viewed through the eyes of our foreign clients and partners, we Americans have an approach to bargaining all our own. And this distinct flavor we bring to the bargaining table, this John Wayne style, is the source of many problems overseas. We must learn to adjust our behavior and gain an appreciation for subtler forms of negotiation.

NOTES

1. There are two hugely important books on this topic well worth the read on your next flight to and from Japan: Jared Diamond's *Guns, Germs, and Steel—the Fates of Human Societies* (New York: Norton, 1999) won a Pulitzer Prize. Richard E. Nisbett's *The Geography of Thought—How Asians and Westerners Think Differently . . . and Why* (New York: Free Press, 2003) is essential reading for anyone doing business in Asia. Use your jet-lag recovery days to read your reports, etc.

2. We think this is the most often forgotten word in his sentence. He says "frequently," not "always" or even "most of the time." Through his use of the term "frequently" Smith granted that competitive behavior can have negative consequences for society and organizations, and cooperative behavior can be a good thing. This subtlety in his lesson is most often missed (ignored?) by our colleagues in the finance departments of our business schools and on Wall Street. Gordon Gecko actually should have said, "Greed is *frequently* good."

3. We note that this situation is improving, as negotiation courses are now popular electives at many business schools around the world (e.g., The Merage School at UC Irvine and Wharton). Some B-schools have taken the bold step of requiring a negotiation course as part of the curriculum (e.g., George Washington and Harvard, the latter beginning in 1993!).

4. "Cultural Assumptions Underlying U.S. Management Concepts," in *Management in an International Context*, ed. James L. Massie, Jan Luytjes, and N. William Hazen (New York: Harper & Row, 1972), 75.

4

The Japanese Negotiation Style

Japanese business culture has been rapidly changing during the last two decades as both firms and their managers have become more integrated with the world economy. World Trade Organization membership and foreign ownership and leadership of major Japanese corporations such as Nissan and Sony have had important impacts in recent years. (Please see box 4.1 for details regarding foreign executives leading Japanese organizations.) Also, massive foreign capital investments in Japan during the 1990s economic slowdown have affected everyday views of businesspeople at all levels of commerce. Attitudes and behaviors are becoming more "Westernized" particularly for younger executives. For example, the once taboo practice of job hopping is today much more acceptable among the newly minted, multilingual businesspeople of the more cosmopolitan business centers in Japan. Working for a foreign company does not carry the stigma it did just ten years ago.

Despite such noticeable changes, the Japanese negotiation style remains perhaps the most distinctive in the world.[1] Moreover, contrary to what one might expect, the Japanese style is far different from negotiation styles in Taiwan and Korea, Japan's closest neighbors. Compared to the aggressive haggling more typical of Korean and Chinese businesspeople, the subtle, low-key bargaining of Japanese executives appears foreign indeed.

The historical and cultural roots of the Japanese negotiation style run far deeper than those of the American style. Their history is much longer and relatively free of influence from the outside. Another characteristic that sets the Japanese style apart from all others is the suitability of the Japanese style for international use. An important aspect of the Japanese style of business negotiations includes adapting bargaining behaviors to

BOX 4.1. FOREIGN EXECUTIVES
AT THE HELM OF JAPANESE COMPANIES

Sony—Howard Stringer

Howard Stringer is annoyed. Since becoming Sony Corp.'s first foreign chief executive almost two years ago, he has been slammed by Japanese financial analysts and Sony employees for being disconnected from the company's daily operations, especially during two big crises. Investors in the U.S., meanwhile, have put him under constant pressure to fix Sony's problems more quickly. And he was hearing conflicting advice from both sides.

"Look, in America, I was told to cut costs," Mr. Stringer says. "In Japan, I was told not to cut costs. Two different worlds. In this country, you can't lay people off very easily. In America, you can."

In a series of interviews at the end of a tumultuous year for Sony, Mr. Stringer says he balanced those competing demands to squeeze 4% growth out of Sony's electronics business and beat earnings estimates for four successive quarters. Sony's stock price has risen 44% since he took over in June 2005. He bristles at criticism, mostly from Japanese, that he lives in a hotel when in Tokyo and spends too much time in New York and London to run the company effectively.

Says [Welsh born] Mr. Stringer, sitting in a conference room in Sony's Tokyo headquarters: "If I'm not running the company, who the hell is?"

Fixing this iconic Japanese company is one of the biggest challenges in business. Mr. Stringer's dilemma is that he is caught between different management styles and cultures. He says he recognizes the risk of falling behind amid breakneck changes in electronics. But he says there's an equal risk in moving too aggressively.

"I don't want to change Sony's culture to the point where it's unrecognizable from the founder's vision," he says. "That's the balancing act I'm doing."

Source: Yukari Iwatani Kane and Phred Dvorak. "Howard Stringer, Japanese CEO," *Wall Street Journal*, March 3–4, 2007, A1, A6.

Nissan Motors—Carlos Ghosn
Considered the most successful Western manager in Japan

In 1999, France's Renault bought a controlling stake in the troubled Japanese carmaker and put Ghosn in charge. He slashed headcount, suppliers, and debt, pledging to return Nissan to profit in 2001. He beat his target.

Vodafone Japan—Darryl Green
Quit in 2004

Vodafone Japan replaced Green, hired in 2001, after sales declines and complaints that the unit wasn't paying attention to local customs. It hired a British manager, then a Japanese executive, then another American, before selling the unit to Japan's Softbank in 2006.

Mitsubishi Motors—Rolf Eckrodt
Resigned in 2004

Controlling shareholder DaimlerChrysler dispatched German Rolf Eckrodt to turn around the struggling Japanese automaker. Eckrodt became CEO in 2002. After a restructuring plan failed to stem losses, DaimlerChrysler sold in 2005.

Chiba Lotte Marines—Bobby Valentine
The most successful American to manage a Japanese major league team

Bobby Valentine was a major league player in the United States and manager for the Texas Rangers and New York Mets. He's managed the Marines twice. He was fired after one year of his two-year contract by the Marines general manager in 1995, but was re-signed in 2003. In 2005, he led the Marines to win the Pacific League pennant after thirty-one years, in a close playoff with the Fukuoka SoftBank Hawks. His Marines then went on to beat the Hanshin Tigers in the Japanese Series. He then challenged the winner of the U.S. World Series to a seven-game series, but it was never played. Valentine is also infamous in the States for a 1999 incident where he was discovered to have sneaked back into the team dugout after being ejected by wearing a disguise consisting of a change of clothes, sunglasses, and a "mustache" painted on with eye black.

Most recently Mr. Valentine has engineered a path-breaking agreement with the Boston Red Sox to share player evaluations and statistical analyses. In addition to exchanging scouting reports, coaches, training staff, and front-office personnel will be traded as well, all toward developing baseball in China and other Asian nations.

Sources: Associated Press, "Boston Red Sox Form Alliance with Japan's Marines," July 4, 2007; Wikipedia contributors, "Bobby Valentine," Wikipedia, The Free Encyclopedia, http://en.wikipedia.org/wiki/Bobby_ Valentinewikipedia (accessed March 14, 2007).

those of the host country or firm. This idea will be developed later in the book. For now, let's consider the historical and cultural foundations of the Japanese negotiation style.

THE ROOTS OF THE JAPANESE STYLE OF BUSINESS NEGOTIATION

The natural environment of Japan has had a pervasive influence on the character of social systems, personal relationships, and, yes, *even* the process of business negotiations. Three environmental factors are salient: (1) the insular and mountainous geography, (2) the dense population, and (3) the importance of rice as the basic food crop.

Throughout its history Japan has been an isolated country. Until the fifteenth century the surrounding seas formed a substantial barrier, preventing invasions and limiting influence from the Asian continent. Even with the dramatic changes throughout the rest of the world brought about by Western European maritime power in the sixteenth century, the political policies of the Tokugawa Shogunate kept foreigners out of the country. Indeed, Japan was the country least influenced by Western European culture through the mid-nineteenth century. And not only did the maritime barriers keep foreigners out, but they also kept Japanese from leaving. Thus social systems and personal relationships developed in a concentrated environment where geography dictated that cooperation was essential. Ethnicity, cultural values, and behavioral norms are therefore uniquely consistent and homogeneous.

The mountains in Japan have always made travel within the country difficult, adding further to the isolation of social groups. Because of the mountains, only about 10 percent of the land can be cultivated. Japan is the most densely populated of all countries in the world with respect to people per square mile of arable land. This crowding has fostered a tightly organized society that highly values obedience and cooperation. Crowding does not permit the aggressive independence and equality so characteristic in the United States.

The final environmental factor influencing values and behaviors in Japan is the historical importance of rice cultivation. Until a hundred years ago, five-sixths of the population of Japan was employed in rice cultivation. Rice production requires community effort and cooperation. Irrigation, planting, and harvesting are most efficiently accomplished with the participation of groups of families. Thus, the small group has evolved as the salient social unit in Japan. Individual needs and desires are deemphasized in favor of one's social unit. In the historical agrarian society, the family and village were key. Now in Japan, one's family and one's work group are central. Loyalty and consensus decision making are key elements that bind such groups together.

Because of this unique combination of environmental influences, a social system has evolved in Japan that avoids conflict and promotes harmony. And as in America, classroom behavior is influenced by and tends to reinforce these cultural values and behavioral norms.

Lively case discussions are not part of the educational experience in Japan. Rather, professors present lectures with no questions or feedback from students. Listening skills and obedience, rather than debating skills and independent thinking, are rewarded in the Japanese educational system. It should be understood that the Japanese negotiation style characterized in the paragraphs to follow is deeply influenced by and reflects these salient environmental factors and the values and social structures associated with them.

Tate Shakai (Living and Working in a Vertical Society)

Although many argue that Japan is becoming more egalitarian as it connects with the rest of the planet, still one of the most important differences between the Japanese negotiation style and others, particularly the American, concerns status relationships. At the interpersonal level the bases for the status distinction might be age, sex, education, or occupation. The power position in business relationships has more to do with size and prestige of the company, industry structure (e.g., number of competitors), and very often, which company is the buyer. There are cases when sellers are more powerful—large manufacturers versus small retailers—but most often Japanese buyers expect and receive deference from Japanese sellers. Indeed, in Japan the buyer is said to be "kinger." Note the following excerpt from a pamphlet provided by the Manufactured Imports Promotion Organization of Japan:

> In Japan, as in other countries, the "buyer is king," only here he or she is "kinger." Here, the seller, beyond meeting pricing, delivery, special specifications, and other usual conditions, must do as much as possible to meet a buyer's wishes. . . . Many companies doing business in Japan make it a practice to deliver more than called for under the terms of their contracts.

The key point here is that the roles of the buyer and seller are very different in Japan. Status relations dictate what is said and what bargaining strategies may be used during Japanese business negotiations. The norms of behavior for the seller are very different from those for the buyer.

In America the way in which status distinctions affect how we behave is almost the opposite of that in Japan. In Japan people at all levels feel somewhat uncomfortable if status distinctions do not exist or are not understood. But in our egalitarian American society we often go out of our way to establish an interpersonal equality. There is little distinction between roles and relatively few rules for adjusting behavior.

Americans expect to, and do, affect business outcomes at the negotiation table. For Japanese, negotiation is more of a ritual, with actions predetermined and prespecified by status relations.

Amae (Indulgent Dependency)

Hierarchical personal and business relationships are difficult for Americans to understand. "Doesn't the lower status seller get taken advantage of?

That's what would happen in the United States." However, understanding an additional aspect of Japanese hierarchical relationships is essential for full appreciation of the Japanese business system. It is true that Japanese buyers have the freedom to choose the deal they want. They will get little argument from the Japanese sellers. But along with this freedom goes an implicit responsibility to consider the needs of the sellers. Japanese sellers can trust the buyers not to take advantage of them. This theme of *amae is* woven into every aspect of Japanese society. Consider, for example, the relationship between management and labor. Management has much more control over labor in Japan than in the United States. But with that control comes a large measure of responsibility for the welfare of the labor force, exceeding that in America.

In Japan, buyers take care of sellers. Buyers consider the needs of sellers before making demands that sellers defer to. In America, conversely, we all take care of ourselves. If buyers make unreasonable demands, they will most likely hear an argument.

Nagai Tsukiai (Long-Term Relationships)

Another aspect of business relationships in Japan that influences negotiation behavior regards the importance and expectation of long-term relationships. The fact that Japanese managers are more predisposed than American managers to take a long view of business affairs has been given much attention. The importance of establishing long-term relations is grounded in the cultural heritage of being isolated and having no other place to go. Personal and group relationships are for life and therefore entered into slowly, carefully, and in a socially prescribed way. The same is true for business relationships.

Perhaps no society values reliability and trust in relationships more than the Japanese. These are ingredients on which they have built their sturdy culture. The intricate web of interdependence between persons and institutions in that society both creates and depends on a foundation of trust. So in Japan trust must not be merely sought, it must be won. But once won, a legacy of trust between the parties can become their most valuable joint asset, an asset worth preserving.

This aspect of Japanese values has two important implications for business negotiations with Japanese clients or partners. First, the Japanese side will want to spend more time getting to know prospective American associates. They will be more willing to invest time and money in negotiation preliminaries and rituals. The second and perhaps the more important implication regards the structure and presentation of the business deal itself. Japanese bargainers will be looking for long-term commitments. Short-run profits are important, but secondary to a long-run business association benefiting both sides.

Shinyo (Gut Feeling)

In the previous chapter we mentioned four stages of the negotiation process nontask sounding, task-related information exchange, persuasion, and concessions and agreement. We also pointed out that, from the American point of view, the persuasion stage is the heart of the matter. It is different in Japan. Compared to Americans, Japanese spend a considerable amount of time in nontask sounding activities. The Japanese view the time and money spent in the initial stages of bargaining as an important investment.

The typical Japanese negotiation involves a series of nontask interactions and even ceremonial gift giving. The *aisatsu* described in chapter 1 is prescribed behavior in Japan. To the American critic this may seem a waste of time. However, the Japanese place great importance on establishing a harmonious relationship. This helps them avoid expensive litigation if things go wrong, which seems more and more common in the United States.

Naniwabushi (A Seller's Approach)

In Japan, information exchange during the second stage of negotiations is generally unidirectional. Sellers describe in great detail what they need, and buyers consider this information and make a decision. Sellers don't object to or question the decision because they can trust the buyers to take care of them. Thus, the information flows principally from sellers to buyers.

Robert March, author of two excellent books on Japan, explains that the seller's agenda is often ordered like a Japanese narrative chant going back to the fifteenth century. A *naniwabushi* (both the chant and the negotiation approach) consists of three phases: The opening, which is called *kikkake*, gives the general background of the story and tells what the people involved are thinking or feeling. Following this is the *seme*, an account of critical events. Finally there is the *urei*, which expresses pathos and sorrow at what has happened or what is being requested. The request comes last, after long explanation of the reasons why it is being made.

Alternatively, the American style of information exchange we have observed starts with the request (without the sorrow), and the explanation is provided only if necessary. American persuasive appeals are couched in terms of "you should . . ." rather than the Japanese, "my company needs . . ." To the American mind the *naniwabushi* seems melodramatic and a waste of time. However, this is the kind of behavior higher status buyers expect from lower status sellers. It is the kind of behavior that makes Japanese negotiators feel comfortable.

We have seen many examples of this approach to business negotiations. One case stands out. Safeway Stores, Inc. and Allied Import Company (AIC was a consortium of four of Japan's major retailers JUSCO, UNY, Izumiya, and Chujitsuya) were discussing an agreement for the distribution of Safeway products in Japan. The Japanese presentation followed the *naniwabushi* approach. All aspects of the partnership had been agreed upon except for the exclusivity provisions. That is, the AIC representatives wanted to be the sole distributor of Safeway products in Japan. The presidents of the four Japanese companies had flown into San Francisco International Airport in preparation for signing ceremonies scheduled for that day. Yet no agreement had been reached regarding the exclusivity provision. Finally, at the last minute, the head Japanese negotiator resorted to *urei* and "cried on the shoulder" of an executive vice president of Safeway, using an emotion-drenched personal appeal. Thus, the time pressure and the *urei* broke the impasse; the deal was consummated that day with the Japanese receiving the exclusive rights of distribution.

Banana No Tataki Uri (The Banana Sale Approach)

In the days of street vendors in Japan, banana salesmen were notorious for asking outrageous prices and quickly lowering the prices when faced with buyers' objections. The term *banana no tataki uri* is now used in Japan to describe a similar approach often taken by Japanese businesspeople. But instead of bananas, factories, distribution chains, even banks are sometimes bargained for using the "banana sale" approach. Japanese executives are more likely to use such a tactic during international negotiations because they don't know what to expect from foreign buyers and they feel that it's safer to leave much room to maneuver. While less prevalent than even ten years ago, you may still run into the banana sale approach if not a more simple cultural difference in the aggressiveness of price padding by some Japanese.

Wa (Maintaining Harmony)

Western negotiators universally complain about the difficulties of getting feedback from Japanese negotiators. There are three explanations for this complaint. First, the Japanese value interpersonal harmony, or *wa*, over frankness. Second, the Japanese perhaps have not come to a consensus regarding the offer or counteroffer. Third, Westerners tend to miss the subtle but clear signals given by the Japanese.

Wa, like *amae*, is one of the central values of the Japanese culture. Negative responses to negotiation proposals are principally nonexistent, and when they are given, they are given very subtly. We've all heard the classic story about the Japanese response of, "We'll think it over," to an American's request. A simple response like this usually means no in American terms, for if the Japanese really wanted to think it over he would explain the details of the decision-making process and the reason for the delay. A Japanese negotiator would be loath, however, to use the word "no." Indeed, one Japanese scholar, Keiko Ueda, has described sixteen ways to avoid saying no in Japan (see box 4.2). Moreover, we have found that Japanese negotiators tend to use the word "no" less than two times per half-hour in bargaining simulations, while Americans use "no" five times per half-hour, Koreans seven times, and Brazilian executives forty-two times. And we must add a couple of other options to Ueda-san's table: (17) changing the topic, and (18) letting lower level negotiators say "no" in informal settings.

Regarding the ambiguous responses, Japanese negotiators follow the cultural double standard of *tatemae* and *honne*. (Please see items 13 and 14 in box 4.2.) *Tatemae* can be translated as "truthful" (or "official stance") and

BOX 4.2. SIXTEEN WAYS THE JAPANESE AVOID SAYING NO

1. Vague "no"
2. Vague and ambiguous "yes" or "no"
3. Silence
4. Counter questions
5. Tangential responses
6. Exiting (leaving)
7. Lying (equivocation or making an excuse—sickness, previous obligation, etc.)
8. Criticizing the question itself
9. Refusing the question
10. Conditional "no"
11. "Yes, but . . ."
12. Delaying answers (e.g., "We will write you a letter.")
13. Internally "yes," externally "no"
14. Internally "no," externally "yes"
15. Apology
16. The equivalent of the English "no"—primarily used in filling out forms, not in conversation

Source: Keiko Ueda, "Sixteen Ways to Avoid Saying No in Japan," in *International Encounters with Japan*, ed. J. C. Condon and M. Saito (Tokyo: Simul Press, 1974), 185–192.

honne as "true mind" (or "real intentions"). It is important for Japanese to be polite and to communicate the *tatemae* while reserving the possibly offending, but also informative, *honne*. Additionally, this difference in the Japanese value system manifests itself in statements by Japanese negotiators in retrospective interviews. The Japanese often describe Americans as honest and frank, but to the point of discomfort for the Japanese. Finally, eye contact is much less frequent during Japanese negotiations (13 percent of the time in negotiations between Japanese, 33 percent for both Americans and Koreans, and 52 percent in negotiations between Brazilian executives). Thus, in Japan, leakage of potentially offending feelings is limited and the *honne* is kept intact. To the American point of view this distinction between *tatemae* and *honne* seems hypocritical. However, the discrepancy is borne by the Japanese in good conscience and in the interest of the all-important *wa*.

Teresa Watanabe well described the problem in the *Los Angeles Times*:

> The Japanese reluctance to give a clear, definitive no has confused countless other foreigners and snarled international interactions, from casual chats to trade talks.
>
> The ambiguity of the Japanese no is so famous that President Clinton, at a dinner last year in Vancouver, Canada, with Russian President Boris N. Yeltsin, scribbled this advice to him: "When the Japanese say yes, they mean no."
>
> But times are changing. Five years after flamboyant legislator Shintaro Ishihara urged his nation to stand up to Washington in his controversial book, *The Japan That Can Say No*, Prime Minister Morihiro Hosokawa did just that by resoundingly rejecting U.S. demands for measurable trade targets in his recent summit meeting with Clinton in Washington.
>
> There was no hemming or hawing in the language Japanese negotiators used to reject the proposed targets. They said, *"Totei doi dekimasen,"* or "There is no way I can agree with that," according to translator Mariko Nagai, who has worked on dozens of U.S.-Japan trade negotiations.
>
> "I was a bit scared about interpreting it, because the language was so clear," Nagai said. She said she has seen a trend toward sharper language among Japanese negotiators in recent years.
>
> Hosokawa's definitive no to Clinton, widely applauded here as a sign of Japan's coming of age, symbolizes a shift away from the soft, indirect expressions that Japanese have long used to maintain harmony and save face with one another. As contact with foreigners increases and the tradition that frowns on direct expression weakens, more Japanese are learning to speak more clearly and daring to disagree—in daily life as well as in the international arena.

Ringi Kessai (Decision Making by Consensus)

Because of the importance of *wa* it is very difficult to get a "no" from a Japanese client. But because of group decision making by consensus, it may also be difficult to get a "yes." Often, the Japanese side simply hasn't made up its mind.

In the voluminous comparative management literature, much has been made of the bottom-up approach to decision making typical in Japanese organizations. It has the disadvantage of slowing down the decision making, but the advantage of quick and orchestrated implementation. Moreover, this approach to decision making has proved very successful in coordinating group efforts in modern companies as well as in the traditional rice-growing agricultural communities. However, it has also been a substantial stumbling block and source of frustration for executives of American companies dealing with Japanese firms.

In business schools in the United States we teach the importance of identifying the key decision makers in an organization. In marketing terms, we look for the key buying influences. Generally, these key executives are located higher up in the organization. Once the key decision makers have been identified, special persuasive efforts are directed toward them. We try to determine the special interests (commercial and personal) of these key individuals, and communications are tailored accordingly.

Such an approach isn't as likely to work in Japan. The decision-making power isn't quite so centralized in key or high positions. Rather, the decision-making power is spread throughout the organization, and all executives involved in or influenced by the deal are important. All of them will have to be convinced that your proposal is the best before anything happens. The key buying influence in Japan is the executive who says "no." Thus, the typical business negotiation in Japan will include talking to more people and will require repetition of the same information and persuasive appeals—much to the frustration of impatient Americans.

For American bargainers, perhaps the greatest source of frustration associated with the consensus style of decision making has to do with the difficulty of getting feedback. American bargainers asking, "What do you think of our proposal, or our counteroffer?" often receive no answer. The Japanese are not being cagey, or coy, or dishonest; more often than not, a consensus has not been reached and Japanese negotiators (even senior people) are simply unwilling and unable to speak for the group.

Ishin-Denshin (Communication without Words)

The third reason foreigners complain about little feedback from Japanese negotiators has to do with the importance of nonverbal communication and subtlety in Japanese history, society, and business talk. Japan's ethnic homogeneity, isolation, and tradition of lifetime personal relationships with daily contact all permit the use of very subtle forms of communications. Subtlety is not only possible in such a fixed social system but is also required from the standpoint of *wa*.

America's tradition as a melting pot and the general transience of our personal relations make explicit communication necessary. Words are considered to be the most important vehicle of communication. In Japan much more is communicated nonverbally—through tone of voice, eye contact, silence, body movements, and the like. It's difficult for Americans to appreciate this difference in communication style and the importance of nonverbal channels in Japan. Takeo Doi, at the University of Tokyo, explains that in Japan the most important information, the content of the communication, is transmitted via nonverbal channels. The verbal communication provides a context for the central information. The opposite is true in the United States, where communications researchers think of nonverbal signals as providing a context for the words spoken, the content of communication.

From the American point of view this Japanese mode of communication is incomprehensible. We know that nonverbal communication is very important, but how can a delivery date or a purchase price be communicated nonverbally? The explanation goes back to the concept of *shinyo* (gut feeling). To the Japanese, the key information in a negotiation concerns the qualities of the long-term, personal relationships that exist in the context of the business deal. The long discussion of minute details so prevalent in Japanese negotiations provides a context for development of comfortable personal relationships and a positive *shinyo*. And this *shinyo is* what makes the business deal go or not. Information about *shinyo is* communicated nonverbally and subtly. Delivery dates and purchase prices, which must be communicated verbally, are important; but these details are not the critical information in a Japanese business deal. So, Americans bargaining with Japanese are not only looking for the less important information but are also focusing on the wrong channel of communication. Thus, we have another explanation for the difficulty Americans have in getting feedback from Japanese clients and partners.

Kazuma Uyeno further explains the importance of nonverbal communication in his definition of *hara-gei*. Anatomically, *hara* is the abdomen or stomach. Used in figures of speech, the word can mean the heart or the mind of a man (but not of a woman.) *Hara* appears in a large number of expressions. The author, who devoted a whole book to *hara-gei* (stomach art), would probably say that it is presumptuous to try to explain in just a few lines this Japanese problem-solving technique. *Hara-gei* may be explained as a technique for solving a problem through negotiation between two individuals without the use of direct words. You don't reveal to the other party what is in your *hara* but you unmistakably and effectively communicate your purpose, desire, demand, intention, advice, or whatever through *hara-gei*.

To do this, you bring into play psychology, intuition, and your knowledge of the other party's personality, background, ambitions, personal connections, et cetera, and also what the other party knows about you. Only people with plenty of experience and cool nerves can make it succeed, but a lot of communication between Japanese in high positions is through *hara-gei*.

Nemawashi (Preparing the Roots)

"Care to prepare the roots and the tree grows tall and strong" is an old Japanese saying. Its traditional wisdom holds critical importance for Americans bargaining with Japanese executives. The idea is that, in Japan, what goes on at the negotiation table is really a ritual approval of what has already been decided before through numerous individual conversations in restaurants, bath houses, and offices. In Japan the negotiation table is not a place for changing minds. Persuasive appeals are not appropriate or effectual. If an impasse is reached, typical Japanese responses are silence, a change of subject, a request to consult the home office, or any of the several options for avoiding saying no. All members of the group must be consulted before new concessions or commitments are made.

As mentioned in the last chapter, the John Wayne approach to business negotiations is almost the opposite. Americans *do* expect minds to change at the negotiation table. Why else have the meeting? When an impasse arises we use our best arguments and persuasive appeals to change the other side's point of view. Although the *nemawashi* approach is often used in the United States—we sometimes call it lobbying—and it may often be the smart strategy, it is not the norm.

Shokai-Sha (Introducer), Chukai-Sha (Mediator)

In his book, *The Japanese Way of Doing Business,* Boye De Mente mentions the importance of friendly and neutral third parties in establishing relationships and settling disputes between Japanese firms. This is not a new idea in the West, but in Japan the functions of *shokai-sha* and *chukai-sha* are institutionalized.

Generally, business relationships in Japan are established only through the proper connections and associated introductions. "Cold calls" are simply not made. Indeed, Bruce Money at the Brigham Young University provides the most recent and strongest arguments for the importance of *shokai-sha* services.[2] Instead, a third party (often a bank or trading company executive) familiar with both parties arranges and attends the initial meeting. This third party is called *shokai-sha* in Japan. At later stages in the negotiation, if things go wrong, another outside party or *chukai-sha* may be asked to mediate the conflicts. However, the *shokai-sha* will usually act in both capacities. Only in rare instances will the *shokai-sha* feel it necessary to call in another person to act as *chukai-sha*.

In a recent joint venture negotiation, an executive vice president of a major Japanese trading company called on executives in an American firm's Product Planning Department prior to the negotiations. He had worked previously with American executives and was partially responsible for the American company's recent investment in another Japanese firm. He also participated in the initial discussion between the two firms. Because of his connections with both companies, this particular executive was the ideal *shokai-sha*.

THE SPECIAL PROBLEM FOR AMERICAN SELLERS

A special point of conflict exists when American sellers call on Japanese buyers. Given the horizontal relationship between American negotiators and the vertical relationship between Japanese negotiators, what happens in cross-cultural negotiations? It is our belief that a Japanese seller and an American buyer will get along fine, while the American seller and Japanese buyer will have great problems. Moreover, we believe this consideration to be a key factor in our trade difficulties with Japan. Our observations in the field and in the management laboratory (summarized in table 4.1) provide strong evidence for such a proposition.

When Japanese sellers come to America to market their products, they naturally assume the lower status position, act accordingly (showing great deference for the American buyer), and a sale is made. Initially, Japanese sellers are taken advantage of. After all, they expect American buyers to respect their needs. But in any case, a relationship is established between firms. The door is open and the Japanese sellers have the opportunity to learn the American way, to adjust their behavior, and to establish a more viable long-term relationship.

Such a conception of the Japanese experience in America is supported by both field interviews and experiences and by our laboratory observations. Universally, Japanese executives in the United States report that their companies "took a beating" when entering the American market. But they also report adjusting their business and negotiation practices to fit the American system. Moreover, in our management laboratory, the Japanese were more likely to adjust their behavior. In cross-cultural interactions, Japanese executives dramatically increased eye contact, increased the number of smiles, and decreased the number of aggressive persuasive tactics. The Americans were found to make a few comparable adjustments. Also, there were fewer silent periods in cross-cultural negotiations. But this is apparently not due

Table 4.1. Key Points of Conflict between American and Japanese Business Negotiation Styles

Category	American	Japanese
Basic Cultural Values	Individual competition	Individual cooperation
	Individual decision making and action	Group decision making and action
	Horizontal business relations	Vertical business relations
	Independence	*Amae*
Negotiation Process:		
1. Nontask Sounding	Short	Long, expensive
	Informal	Formal
2. Task-Related Exchange of Information	"Fair" first offers	"Banana sale" first offers include room to maneuver
	Full authority	Limited authority
	"Cards on the table"	*Tatemae* and *honne*
	Immediate reciprocity	Long-term reciprocity
	Explicit communication	Implicit communication
3. Persuasion	Aggressive persuasive tactics (threats, promises, arguments, and logic)	*Nemawashi* and *chukai-sha*
	"You need this"	*Naniwabushi*
4. Concessions and Agreements	Sequential	Holistic
	Goal = "good deal"	Goal = long-term relationship

to Japanese adjustments as much as to Americans filling potential silent periods with new arguments.

There is an important implication underlying this apparent adjustment made by the Japanese but not by the American negotiators.

Anthropologists tell us that power relations usually determine who adapts their behavior in a cross-cultural setting. Japanese executives in an American business setting are likely to be the ones to modify their behavior. Moreover, in American negotiations status relations are less defined and less important. Japanese sellers can apparently fit into such a situation without offending American buyers.

However, if American sellers take their normative set of bargaining behaviors to Japan, negotiations are apt to end abruptly. American sellers expect to be treated as equals and act accordingly. Japanese buyers are likely to view this rather brash behavior in lower status sellers as inappropriate and disrespectful. Japanese buyers are made to feel uncomfortable and thus, without explanation, politely shut the door to trade. American sellers do not make the first sale, and hence do not learn the Japanese system.

FINAL COMMENTS

Edward T. Hall is the seminal thinker when it comes to international business negotiations. With Mildred Reed Hall, he has written one of the best books on the topic, *Hidden Differences: Doing Business with the Japanese.* The three basic premises of the book are important.

First, cultural differences are crucial. The Halls state: "Despite popular beliefs to the contrary, the single greatest barrier to business success is the one erected by culture." Second, most cultural differences are hidden, affecting our behavior and attitudes below our level of awareness—thus the title of their book. And third, it would be difficult to find two cultures that are more different than the Japanese and the American, and therefore the two cultures are more susceptible to business disharmony. (The Halls' long experience in studying many cultures around the world qualifies them to make this last statement, and we couldn't agree more.)

Indeed, given these several and substantial points of conflict in negotiation styles it seems truly remarkable that American and Japanese businesspeople ever agree on anything. It is our belief that two things have made business deals between the two largest economic powers possible. The first is the powerful reality of commercial interdependence. American and Japanese companies can, and do, achieve substantial economic benefits from cooperation. Second, businesspeople on both sides of the Pacific have learned to manage these differences in negotiation styles. The Japanese have been better at making adjustments. It is the goal of this book to help Americans improve. Thus, in the next few chapters we present a comprehensive list of instructions for Americans bargaining with Japanese executives. Included are prescriptions regarding selection of representatives, negotiation preliminaries, management of the negotiation process itself, and finally, follow-up procedures.

NOTE

1. Please see the research appendix at the end of the book for more details regarding Japan's unique negotiations style.

2. R. B. Money, M. C. Gilly, and J. L. Graham, "National Culture and Referral Behavior in the Purchase of Industrial Services in the United States and Japan," *Journal of Marketing*, 62(4), October 1998, 76–87.

II

THE BUSINESS OF FACE-TO-FACE NEGOTIATION

5

Life Navigating a Cultural Thicket

Like humus on the forest floor, a culture requires centuries to accumulate.

—Primo Levi

I [Jim Hodgson] had a problem. My first ambassadorial speech in Tokyo was coming up. And to a mixed Japanese and American audience. In the United States one is well advised to begin remarks with a bit of trenchant humor. Not so in Japan. If not humor, then what. Almost unfailingly, an apology. Perhaps something such as:

"I'm afraid many present today may know more about this subject than I do," or "I'm sorry that you must spend your precious time this morning, listening to what little I have to say."

In Japan, propriety of form demands such a ritualized opening. But when facing a mixed audience as I was that day, what was one to do? Would it be humor or apology?

While still in America preparing for my diplomatic role, I learned of a young scholar who had come up with a unique solution to this dilemma. He began his remarks by apologizing for not telling a joke.

Now halfway around the world, I concluded I could safely indulge in a bit of pirating. So I led off with the same observation. It seemed to go over rather well. That is, it did until I had finished and was preparing to leave the hall. Then a smiling young fellow came up and introduced himself. Horrors! He turned out to be the author of my pirated statement. By co-incidence, he just happened to be in Tokyo at the time. Thus did I learn the hazards of cribbing in today's shrinking world. No place, however distant, is safe.

The same speech produced another minor personal trauma. As I approached the lectern and looked out I was stunned to see about half the Japanese out there seemingly asleep. There they sat, eyes firmly closed, as if to suggest, "It will be less painful this way."

Later that day I ran into Dr. Chie Nakane, a brilliant Japanese anthropologist. Just the person to explain my somnolent audience, I thought. "Oh Ambassador, I'm afraid you are mistaken," Dr. Nakane advised. "Those men weren't asleep, they were merely in repose." While I reflected on whether the response contained a distinction or a difference, Dr. Nakane continued, "You see Ambassador, in Japan neither the audience nor the speaker expect much of each other." Talk about great truths revealed. Here was ancient oriental wisdom handed me on a platter by a consummate authority.

For one who wants a better grasp of Japan's unusual culture, I discovered their proverbs may be a good place to start. Their lexicon is shot through with hundreds of them. Even before leaving Washington for Tokyo the role of proverbs in that society was brought forcibly home to me. And by a surprising source.

COUNSEL FROM KISSINGER

After Senate confirmation, my sole remaining departure agenda item was a briefing by Secretary Kissinger. The briefing went well. But as I rose to leave Kissinger held up a hand. "One more thing, Ambassador," he interjected. "When you get to Tokyo and ask questions of the Japanese, do not expect answers. All you will hear is proverbs." Then it was goodbye.

With Henry's curious admonition tucked away in a corner of my brain, off I flew to my new diplomatic post. Days went by, then weeks, even months, yet nary a Japanese proverb met my ears. Could his excellency have been misinformed, I wondered. But then it happened.

One gray November morning, along with Japan's 120 million citizens, I awoke to some startling news. Their prime minister had been unceremoniously sacked. How come, I thought. Curious, I made a date with the vice minister of foreign affairs. Next day at lunch, the two of us sat down to steaming bowls of rice curry.

"Please explain something, Togo-san," I began. "What happened? Why was Prime Minister Tanaka ousted?" After turning in his chair to gaze briefly at distant Mount Fuji, my companion swung back with a sigh and said, "Well you see Ambassador, here in Japan we have an old proverb." At this point deep inside me a bell sounded. I sensed Kissinger was about to be vindicated. "We say," continued the vice minister, "a nail that sticks out must get hammered down."

"Ah so," I responded with the only phrase that means exactly the same thing in Japanese as it does in English. The vice minister then went on to explain that in their ancient land, the Japanese frown on overt displays of personal power. The prime minister had become a bit too fond of throwing his weight around, so he had to go. Thus enlightened, I returned to my office to await, along with the 120 million Japanese, word of a successor.

Now it should be understood that in the Japanese version of democracy, the elected Diet, not the citizenry, selects the nation's chief executive. Diet members cluster into factions and when opportunity knocks, faction leaders proceed to maneuver for the prime minister's office. Normally the process is about as secretive as anything can be in a society that has raised public gossip to high art.

Yet the ensuing weeks saw leaders of the two strongest factions openly butting heads in a battle for the prize. In a most un-Japanese way, Messrs. Ohira and Fukuda publicly exchanged expressions of mutual distaste. How would it all end, we wondered.

Then one frosty December morning I came down to breakfast and opened my *Japan Times* to a screaming headline. "Miki is Japan's New Prime Minister." Miki? Who was this Miki? What had happened to Ohira and Fukuda? Time for another visit with the vice minister, I decided.

So once again the two of us faced rice curry and again, I asked, "Explain please." Barely restraining a smile, Togo-san leaned across the table, "Ambassador," he began, "to help understand why neither Ohira or Fukada could be chosen is to cite an old proverb." (What is this, a rerun, I thought.) "We say," he continued, "when two men fight, both must be punished."

Apparently Ohira and Fukada had offended Japanese custom. So Japan's political insiders decreed that both needed a lesson in manners. They learned their lesson well. Each went on to serve the nation as prime minister in later years. Meanwhile, a much enlightened American ambassador had gained enhanced respect for a prescient American secretary of state. "Proverbs," the secretary had said and proverbs it was.

FORM VERSUS SUBSTANCE

Like anyone who finds himself in an unfamiliar culture, when in Tokyo I tried to follow the old "when in Rome . . ." adage. Tokyo proved to be a unique Rome. I soon found that matters of *form* are almost deified in Japan. Doing and saying things the correct way and showing fastidious respect for proprieties prevail there.

Nothing could be more formalized than Japan's approach to pace—the speed with which things are done and decisions are made. When pressing for a quick decision, the impatient American can go bananas in Japan. Though they are not dawdlers, the Japanese do pursue decisions with agonizing deliberation. The worst tactical mistake an outsider can make in Japan is to set his own timetable for some venture and then attempt to force it on his hosts. Try it and you will wind up buffeted about and, in the end, outwitted.

For the Japanese, such deliberating serves a purpose. It buys them time to get everyone affected into the act. That, of course, is what Japan's famed consensus method is all about. To the outsider, Japanese meetings may seem interminable, delays unconscionable, and reasons obscure. But then one day it all comes resoundingly together and voilà, you've got a deal.

When the deal is made, the Japanese explode into action. They shift into high gear and are a joy to behold. They meet schedules, they meet cost projections and faithfully fulfill commitments. They expect you to do the same. And you had better be prepared.

Eventually I sought to synthesize something my early experience there taught me. I called it "Hodgson's Law for Dealing with the Japanese." It goes about like this: "If you will accommodate the Japanese in matters of form and pace, they will try hard to accommodate you on substance."

As trade-offs go, that's not a bad deal for Americans. Few people are more substance-minded than we.

In the Cold War days of September 1976, an unusual incident gave me an opportunity to watch my law in action. That month saw the unthinkable. A defecting Soviet Air Force pilot swooped down from the Siberian sky and came to ground on a northern Japanese airfield. With his late model MIG aircraft in Japanese hands, American intelligence officers drooled. They flooded embassy channels with messages imploring me to gain them immediate access. They pounded on Japanese embassy doors. Observing punctilious respect for propriety of form in such matters, the Japanese seemed slow to respond. Washington became impatient. Pressure mounted. Delay was interpreted as noncooperation. It decidedly was not. In fact, anything but. Given time to do it their way and at their pace, the Japanese responded in a highly satisfactory way. A major intelligence coup was achieved. And a law confirmed.

My law served only as a useful start in understanding the Japanese perspective, however. Each week that passed seemed to bring new insights. For instance, after only two months in Tokyo a tragic incident drove home to me Japan's incredible respect for history.

A SENSE OF HISTORY

Americans are often baffled by the attention to history older societies reflect. Only a bit more than two centuries into our nationhood, we are inclined to dismiss history as something that happened to other people elsewhere. Not so the Japanese.

Late last century an activist from among the 600,000 largely quiescent Koreans who live in Japan returned to Seoul intending to assassinate Korea's prime minister. He whipped out a pistol at a public gathering and fired twice. The prime minister escaped, but his wife was shot dead. Under ordinary circumstances even such a heinous crime as this would hardly foment an international crisis. But there is nothing ordinary about the relationship between the Japanese and Koreans. Their intense distaste for each other smolders barely below the surface. The assassin's bullets broke through that surface and triggered an eruption. Accusations were hurled and threats exchanged. Soon a 24-carat hullabaloo was raging.

"What will the United States do if Korea invades Japan?" Japanese officials implored.

"You can't be serious," was American reaction.

"But we are deadly serious," they snapped, "the Koreans tried to invade our islands once before you know."

"When?"

"In the thirteenth century," came the unblinking reply.

Respect, even reverence, for the past, for its events and accumulated tradition, spreads all across Japan's cultural landscape. It serves to influence their political and personal judgments.

I became particularly aware of that reverence when spending America's bicentennial year in Japan, as I witnessed a subtle Japanese reaction to that event. While our fledgling nation was whooping it up over birthday number 200, the Japanese watched with wry bemusement. With a more than 2,000-year history (some say 6,000), they could not help but see American exuberance as something of an adolescent indulgence.

QUESTIONS OF TRUST

Not surprisingly, I found the world of diplomacy has much in common with the world of personal relationships. The most perplexing questions often involve trust. In every society trustworthiness ranks as an uncontested virtue. Yet virtues are never absolute. I'm afraid we all must learn to deal with the untrustworthy as well as the reliable. As we do, some curious ethical behavior patterns can emerge. Many men of dubious trust, I have discovered, are more naive than malicious. And strangely, some men of otherwise reliable character often turn out to have a few blind spots of credibility. And so it goes; one simply must learn to distinguish.

I recall spending a long evening listening to a duel of wits on the respective merits of loyalty versus veracity between a visiting Elliot Richardson, then the U.S. secretary of commerce, and a Japanese cabinet official. Group loyalty, or fealty to the samurai master, is such an entrenched tradition in Japan, it often overrides personal veracity. In short, it is considered superior in principle. The concept is not wholly foreign to Westerners, but it is largely disdained. In every society, trust has its own pattern and limits. A diplomat's survival depends on understanding those limits.

SECRETS AND SHEARS

I have long been fascinated with patterns of "underground" communication. Discreet semi-clandestine networks are often created to share inside information among trusted peers. These networks cover, link, and often dominate the Japanese social, political, and business landscape. Many are openly acknowledged. Trusted ties between old schoolmates, for instance, run deep and last a lifetime. Schoolmates there are often not just "contacts," as in our parlance. They more nearly resemble blood brothers.

Other networks, equally pervasive, run deep and strong, but lie well below the surface. I found the subterranean conduits a Japanese executive may use to get a message to another without direct contact to be particularly interesting. He may do it through his geisha. Few outsiders, including me, will ever fully understand the geisha phenomenon.[1] But I was told their role in quiet communication linkage is extensive. Wives will even employ their husband's geisha to plant a seed of gossip in some interested ear. "She is a repository of a million secrets," so one geisha was described to me.

Gradually I became so intrigued with the delicate role of trust in Japan I put my thoughts about the subject into a traditional Japanese verse form, the standard haiku 5-7-5 syllable structure. It came out like this:

> When trust flows too deep
> And the channel grows shallow
> The craft will founder.

As this verse elliptically suggests, limits often exist on the level of trust that can wisely be extended. Miscalculating those limits can at some point shatter a relationship. The level of trust extended should carefully reflect the degree of dependability of the relationship. This, I believe is as true between men as between nations.

PERCEPTION VERSUS FACT

Public perception, the way things look rather than the way things are, is as important in Japan as in our own country. Misreading character traits, extrapolating a general impression from a specific event, or dwelling on an irrelevance, especially by the media, serves to twist public perception toward specious conclusions in both countries.

I recall one particularly amusing illustration. In the mid-seventies my friend, pipe-puffing James Schlesinger, served as America's secretary of defense. He was respected in the United States as a man of strong but moderate views. Not so in Japan. There, for unknown reasons, he had been labeled a "cold warrior." During my ambassadorial tenure, the secretary scheduled a visit to Tokyo on his way to China. The Japanese press screamed that America was sending its defense secretary across the Pacific to intimidate them. "Why does America's cold warrior come to Japan?" ranted a lead editorial. Obviously expecting less than a cordial welcome, the secretary arrived for a three-day visit. Within twenty-four hours I watched his public image do a flip-flop.

Though I was unaware of it at the time, Jim Schlesinger had a passion-driven hobby. He had been bitten by the bird-watching bug. Learning in advance that Japan's forests were home to some unusual feathered types, he arranged to spend the early morning of his first Japanese day in a local woods. Dawn found him, binoculars at the ready, peering through verdant Nipponese underbrush. Some clever Japanese photojournalists had learned of the secretary's plans and were on hand to take candid shots of his venture. By the evening of that day, local TV and newspapers were splashed with pictures of America's supposed cold warrior benignly stalking finch and thrush. By the next morning the editorial pages were awash with revisionist commentary, the general theme of which was that no man who watched birds could be a threat to anyone or anything. Thus an official who arrived under a cold warrior cloud left in triumph as a sensitive nature lover. Of such silly pontification is public opinion formed and deformed. The question is, should one react with bemusement or despair? I think both are warranted. Yet public perception cannot be ignored. It has a reality of its own. What people think often outweighs what they would think if better informed. Those who deal with public issues must understand the vital importance of public perception.

CULTURAL CONTRAST

For the outsider, it is often said that the process of becoming deeply acquainted with the unique Japanese culture turns out to be a bit like peeling back layers of a Bermuda onion. No matter how often one removes a layer another lurks beneath, even more exotic than the one just removed. I found this peeling process appealing. To dig into the innards of that society became as tantalizing to me as turning a scientist loose in a well-stocked laboratory.

To start with, almost from the hour Pan American Airlines deposited Maria and me at Haneda Airport, I was struck by the curious number of Japanese practices that were exactly the reverse—a mirror image—of those prevailing in our Western world. Pick up one of their hundreds of magazines, for instance; you will discover it reads from back to front. They drive, of course, on the left side of the road.

Toilet paper comes off the roller bottom rather than the top. What we call a first name turns out to be, in Japan, a last name. One can wander down the trail of a typical Japanese sentence until the very end before the verb emerges. Pity a poor interpreter. On and on go the contrasts. On the other side of the world things are other-worldly.

Fundamental features of their culture such as values and priorities also reflect many a startling disparity. One finds, for example, that gaining the approval of one's group ranks well above satisfying one's own personal desires. The American credo of looking out for number one would offend a Japanese. Then too, a Westerner will be surprised to observe that, in extreme anxiety to avoid social confrontation, the individual Japanese citizen will often forgo his just rights.

Behavioral patterns also amazed me. The go-getting assertiveness on which we Americans practically pin a halo is scorned there—a definite Japanese no-no, much too disharmonious it seems for their cultural taste. When dining at her table, if you wish to please your hostess, you will be expected to—can you believe it—slurp your soba (Japanese noodles). For the unsuspecting foreigner ordinary social intercourse erupts with many a surprise. When conversing in Japan, for instance, you will be well advised not to look your listener steadily in the eye, Western style, unless of course, you wish to be tagged as an arrogant upstart.

While the Western world places pluralism firmly on the top rung of its ladder of values, the Asian world does not. The French exclaim, *"Vive la différence."* The English cherish quirky eccentricity. We Americans revel in an exuberant mish-mash of lifestyles and flaunt our polyglot ethnic cauldron, extolling the diversity of both as national virtues. But in Japan one "correct" way to do or say almost everything is slavishly practiced. In the swarm of Tokyo's streets and shops, expressions and behavior—even dress—fall into an almost unvarying pattern. And to be uncorrupted either by external ideas or racially diluted bloodlines ranks high in that land.

Does this mean, as one hears at times, that "all Japanese are alike?" Of course not. Within these rigidities, individual citizens of that fascinating land have found myriad ways to make themselves distinctive. The discipline of doing so within a narrow compass actually seems to stimulate such creativity.

So it was that after repeatedly peeling back successive layers of East-West cultural distinctions, a gnawing itch arose within me. I kept puzzling over what might underlie and explain these differences. Knowing that with disparate values Japanese and Western peoples have both been able to build superior societies, I concluded that the proper form for my question was not, "Which society is better?" but rather, "Why the difference?"

Driven by curiosity and fortified by my academic grounding in three "ologies"—soci, psych, and anthrop—I set about to track down a personal answer. First I sampled the wares of a few Japanese anthropologists, particularly the writings of the brilliant Chie Nakane. Dr. Nakane explained something that often puzzles observers of the Japanese scene, the paradox of a nation where long-enduring tradition lives comfortably with the latest in Western fads and fashions. How, for instance, can a nation locked into veneration of a 2,000-year-old emperor lineage go overboard for everything from Big Macs to rock and roll?

"It is in the Japanese nature to accept superficial change with little resistance, but to do so without the slightest effect on the persistence of their basic nature," writes Dr. Nakane.[2] Later she further explained to me that the top 10 percent of Japanese culture, being superficial, is subject to constant change—all the while being underpinned by a rock-like 90 percent.

Next I sought to trace the history of Japan's unchanging 90 percent. External influences, both national and religious, seem to have played an early role in its evolution. Chinese and Korean values plus Buddhist and Confucian teachings had all reached Japan and been absorbed into her culture before the eleventh century. So the Japanese cultural base was clearly Oriental in origin. But why did Oriental patterns differ so markedly from those of the Western world?

As I came to see it, differences between Japan and the West can be traced to the very roots of our respective heritages. Back somewhere before the era of recorded time, human thinking must have come to a fork in the road. Down one fork traveled savants of the Orient, sowing seeds that flowered into Confucian, Buddhist, and other Oriental value systems.

Down the other fork traveled the sires of Western philosophy and religion. In the West the foremost value underpinning civilized society emerged as that venerable Judeo-Christian goal: justice—justice for the individual.

But then look at Japan. Nurtured by Oriental teachings, justice, especially individual justice, is less than a top-priority goal. So if not justice, then what? Something in many ways quite different: harmony—harmony within the group. To simplify, our contrasting value systems pit justice against harmony. And the individual versus the group.

And how does each society seek to attain its treasured value? We Americans use an adversary system to create a roster of rights. The Bill of Rights, human rights, civil rights, voting rights, rights of privacy—all devised to ensure justice for the individual. When a contingent of Americans feels put upon, just about their first reaction is to demand a set of legislated rights.

The Japanese seek to achieve their treasured harmony, not by demanding rights, but by creating smooth interlocking relationships. No wonder Japan doesn't need an army of lawyers as does the West. Almost no one sues anyone. To do so would create a disharmonious disturbance—and cause a loss of face. This pursuit of harmony gave birth to Japan's renowned consensus system, probably the most effective bonding technique yet devised by man. The contrast pits Western emphasis on rights against Japanese emphasis on relations. When we trace down through all the steps of cultural contrast and examine the end product, that is, the goal of human beings in each society, the bottom line is this: In America, we seek to stand out. In Japan, they seek to fit in.

These contrasting guides to personal behavior are not accidents of history. They are the inevitable product of our respective cultural heritages. I find many Americans seem to expect the Japanese to change, "to become more like us." I say, "Forget it." Four hundred years ago the famed Shogun Ieyasu Tokugawa made a simple declaration that still expresses a basic Japanese view; "All change is bad," he insisted. Fundamental change in that society will come only at a pace that would make a snail look like a speedster. Example: Early in this century the United States adopted Daylight Saving Time. The Japanese are just now "cautiously considering" it.

The foregoing observations on Japanese culture may strike some as "more than I wanted to know." Maybe so. Yet what may lay behind unfamiliar Japanese behavior can often be traced back to such cultural influences.

FAITH OR FORM?

Few subjects puzzle an outside observer more than the role, or non-role, of religion in Japan. As we know, Christians are admonished "to love one another." Though few Japanese are Christians (less than 2 percent), their personal behavior reflects more genuine togetherness affection than any other people with whom I am familiar. Shinto arches and Buddhist temples dot their landscape. But except for a few proselytizing sects, the hold of any faith on most of their populace seems tenuous at best. Many Japanese would tell me that Shintoism serves them for joyous occasions, such as weddings, while Buddhism is more often reserved for sad moments, such as funerals. Here again an impression emerges that the role of form exceeds reverence for substance.

"What do your people worship?" I asked a Japanese friend.

"We don't understand the term as you do," he replied, "but our main worship is ancestor worship."

"What do you believe in?" I asked another.

"We believe in ourselves, in Japanese people—some call it 'Japaneseness,'" was his answer.

Outsiders who hold beliefs in such things as a personal almighty God, salvation, life after death, and so on, will have trouble penetrating the essence of religion's role in the life of an individual Japanese.

Throughout my years in Japan, years that stimulated interest in standards of human behavior and societal values beyond anything I had previously known, I found myself constantly expanding my list of items where the East contrasts sharply with the West. However, since we can't escape one another these days, it is well that we know more about each other, especially about differences in cultures and customs. In dealing with unfamiliar cultures Churchill once made a shrewd observation. "One's logic is a poor guide to suitable behavior compared to local custom," wrote Sir Winston. In other words, our logic serves as a useful guide only within our own cultural framework. So if we would get along well with each other in this shrinking world it behooves us to be familiar with the way others slice the cultural melon.

Before concluding this chapter I thought I might offer a list of cultural contrasts—sharp contrasts between the American and Japanese perspectives (see table 5.1). The gap in these contrasts rarely is 180 degrees, but the difference is always more than normally significant. Some of these items have been the subject of earlier comment, some not.

TOGETHERNESS

Looking back, I remember when I took up residence in Tokyo I was prepared for a huge dose of culture shock. What I did not realize, however, was that along with that shock would come glorious new vistas of perception.

Table 5.1. Contrasting Cultural Concepts

American	vs.	Japanese
Substance	vs.	Form
Justice	vs.	Harmony
Rights	vs.	Relations
Individual	vs.	Group
"Stand out"	vs.	"Fit in"
Adversary	vs.	Consensus
Veracity	vs.	Loyalty
Guilt	vs.	Shame
Evil/Sin	vs.	Error/Mistake

For instance, in Japan I found I gained a wholly new appreciation of the role form can play in enriching one's life. Eventually, in a curious way, form seemed to merge with and even enhance substance.

Few who observe Japanese society can come away without noticing how uncommonly well their people get along with one another. They probably do this better than any other people of our time. To those of us in the world beyond their borders the Japanese people often seem almost distressingly fond of togetherness. Their familial bond is so strong they do just about everything in groups. Why this preference, even eagerness, to share each other's company? It seems to me that their careful observance of proper form in their relations with one another turns out to be a large part of a persuasive answer. If observing propriety of form can lead to greater harmony among men, I find it deserving of great respect. Few things are more needed in this fractious world.

NOTES

1. Two books may help: Arthur Golden's novel now made into a movie, *Memoirs of a Geisha* (New York: Vintage, 1997) and Liza Dalby's *Geisha* (Berkeley: University of California Press, 1998).

2. Chie Nakane, *Japanese Society* (Berkeley: University of California Press, 1970).

6

Negotiator Selection and Team Assignment

The initial step in business negotiations is often the selection of company representatives. Negotiators come from all ranks of firms, depending on the size and organization of the firms involved and the size and importance of the transaction. Selection of the best representative(s) can make or break a business deal. Diplomats often emphasize the importance of an individual representative's characteristics in international negotiations. A delegation's power is often more a function of the head delegate's personality than the economic power of the represented country. More than one American company has found that sending the wrong person to handle negotiations in Japan has led to failures.

We all have our own ideas about what makes a good negotiator. Long ago, Sir Francis Bacon told us to use "bold men for expostulation, fair-spoken men for persuasion, crafty men for inquiry and observation." Today, characteristics such as persistence, extroversion, a nimble tongue, a quick wit, or an affable demeanor come to mind. Such characteristics sound good, but do they really make a difference in business negotiations? Are they effective in Japan? Based on our discussion in the previous chapters, one would conclude that what makes a good bargainer in the United States may not lead to the best bargaining outcomes with Japanese clients. So whom do we send to Japan? What skills and personality traits should we look for in prospective representatives of our companies?

THE SCHOLARLY OPINION

Both social psychologists and professors of business administration in American universities have been involved in the investigation of negotiator traits and bargaining outcomes. However, they have attacked the problem in two different ways. Social psychologists have conducted hundreds of bargaining experiments (primarily using college students as subjects), looking for relationships between personal characteristics and outcomes of negotiation games. Meanwhile, business scholars in marketing departments of several major universities have looked for relationships between personality traits of sales representatives and sales performance. Table 6.1 lists the impressive (albeit incomplete) list of personality traits examined in both contexts.

Generally, the results of these numerous studies have been disappointing. In the majority of studies conducted in psychology departments and business schools, no systematic relationships have been found between negotiator characteristics and bargaining or sales performance. One study conducted by Richard Bagozzi at the Michigan Business School even revealed a negative relationship between verbal intelligence and sales performance. That is, contrary to what one might predict, the less intelligent sales representatives achieved higher sales performance!

We have considered the influence of the characteristics of American bargainers on the outcomes of negotiations with Japanese managers. In our studies at Ford and AT&T, Americans who were rated as better listeners and were more oriented toward relationship-building tended to be more successful with Japanese. Age similarity also seemed to be important. That is, Americans achieved better results when their ages better matched the ages of their Japanese counterparts.

Table 6.1. Bargainer Characteristics

Risk-taking propensity	Machiavellianism
Perceived focus of control	Rigidity of thinking
Cognitive complexity	Generalized self-esteem*
Tolerance for ambiguity	Task-specific esteem
Self-concept (positive or negative)	Extroversion/introversion*
Motives (need for power, affiliation, achievement)	Forcefulness
Generalized trust	Sociability
Cooperativeness	General intelligence
Authoritarianism	Education
Internationalism	Experience*
Flexible ethics	Age*

*Investigated using Japanese executives as subjects.

Finally, in a wide variety of communications studies similarity has been found to enhance interpersonal interactions. For example, one prominent researcher reported that in a study involving 125 insurance sales representatives and some 500 prospects, the more alike the salesman and prospect, the more probable the sale. Similarities in several social, economic, physical, personality, and communicational characteristics did make a difference in selling life insurance. And as we mentioned above, age similarity does seem to be important in Japanese-American negotiations. The explanation is that similarity promotes interpersonal attraction and ease of communication, and therefore, better negotiation outcomes. This view suggests that most Americans will have a difficult time in Japan because of the great disparity in cultural values and modes of communication. However, if American representatives can be found with values and personality traits similar to those of the Japanese, then perhaps better deals can be struck with companies across the Pacific.

KEY BARGAINER CHARACTERISTICS

So, whom do we send to negotiate in Japan? Our reading of the literature on negotiation, our management laboratory observations, our interviews with experienced bargainers, and our own experiences as negotiators in Japanese-American business transactions all suggest seven bargainer characteristics are particularly important in Japanese negotiations. They are:

1. Listening ability
2. Interpersonal orientation
3. Willingness to use team assistance
4. Self-confidence
5. High aspirations
6. Social competence
7. Influence at headquarters

Representatives with these qualities should be sought to fill temporary or more permanent positions in other countries. The seven key bargainer characteristics and the reasons for their importance are further described below.

Listening Ability

The ability to listen is crucial in any bargaining context. Negotiation is by definition a creative process. And creativity is enhanced by maximizing the pertinent information available, particularly including information about the client's or partner's needs and preferences. In order to achieve the most favorable bargaining solution for both sides, bargainers must be vigilant for subtle indications of clients' real interests. Also, good listening is the initial step in persuasion. Before trying to change the minds of those across the bargaining table, it is best to determine, through good questions and attentive listening, what the other side needs to know and what they want. There is little point in extolling the virtues of one's product when one's potential customer already believes it is the best available or when quick delivery is foremost in his or her mind. Finally, in international transactions one's listening abilities are put to the most difficult test—ascertaining meaning in the context of less than fluent English and different nonverbal vocabularies. Indeed, an excellent practice in international negotiation is "playing back" or repeating what one has been told to ensure clear understanding of key points.

Interpersonal Orientation

This characteristic includes two aspects. First, bargainers must attend to a client's or supplier's behavior; second, they must respond accordingly. Successful bargainers who have high interpersonal orientations adjust their bargaining approach according to the situation and the behavior of their bargaining partners. When clients take a competitive approach, bargainers behave competitively. When clients appear cooperative, bargainers respond in kind. Because negotiation styles differ from country to country (and person to person), your approach must be tailored accordingly.

Willingness to Use Team Assistance

This trait can make a substantial difference in international business negotiations. Expertise in technical details, financial matters, cultural considerations, and the all-important maintenance of business relationships is simply too much to expect of one person—even an American executive! Application engineers, financial analysts, interpreters, and foreign agents should be included and used when appropriate. The additional expense may be an important investment. Also, observation of negotiations can be a valuable training experience for younger members of an organization, even if they add little to the discussion. We are happy to report that in recent years increasingly American negotiators are adding members to their teams, thus enhancing both the expertise available and the teams' overall listening resources simultaneously.

Self-Confidence

The job of representative is one of the most difficult of all. Bridging the gap between companies and cultures can be exhausting work. Negotiations are being conducted not only with clients but also with the home office. Clients question your company's policies. Sales managers question the time and money you invest in building personal relationships, and so on. Self-confidence will be an important personal asset for those faced with situations of role ambiguity.

High Aspirations

High expectations regarding the business deal are key. One of the basic lessons of the hundreds of bargaining studies mentioned earlier is that bargainers who ask for more in the beginning end up getting more. Thus, given two otherwise equal executives, the one with higher aspirations is the better one to represent your interests. Over the years we have seen American negotiators improve in many of the ways recommended in our book. However, we still see our American clients making often making unnecessarily generous first offers to their Japanese counterparts. We still see substantial room for improvement in this area.

Social Competence

We mentioned the importance of personal relationships in business negotiations, and such transactions are very much a social activity. Social competence, the ability to get along with other people, not only smoothes the social contact points but also tends to encourage the flow of information from the other side of the table. Thus, better, more informed decisions can be made regarding the business deal.

Influence at Headquarters

This characteristic is vitally important in international negotiations. We mentioned above the difficulty of the international representative's job—bridging both organizational and cultural barriers. Many representatives we have interviewed suggest that the toughest part of business negotiations is selling the agreement to headquarters. Moreover, there is danger in presenting the other side's point of view too well—your own management might trust you less. In choosing a representative for negotiations in a foreign country, influence at headquarters is essential for achieving successful outcomes.

OTHER FACTORS

Personnel decisions regarding negotiations with Japanese firms therefore deserve special attention. We must add to the list of desirable characteristics.

Patience will be critical in Japan. Negotiations and decisions take longer—particularly the early stages of nontask sounding and information exchanges. Also, managers of quiet demeanor should be sent to Japan. By quiet we mean individuals who are good listeners and are comfortable with silence.

Another concern is ethnocentrism. We all suffer from this to a degree. But even those with the broadest views will be put to the test in Japan. Individuals harboring chauvinistic cultural attitudes will almost always do poorly in Japan, where mutual respect anchors all interpersonal contact.

LANGUAGE SKILLS

No bargainer characteristic is more important in Japan, yet more ignored, than the possession of Japanese language skills. A good example is Ford Motor Company, which used to send more than 1,000 executives to Japan every year to manage its various corporate alliances and ventures with Japanese firms. Ford now owns a controlling interest in Mazda and trades in component parts with a large variety of companies in Japan. Yet the company, still one of America's most global, has only a handful of American managers who can speak Japanese.

Moreover, proposals for Japanese partners are almost never translated—that's left up to the Japanese clients. One of Ford's primary strategic goals in allying with Japanese firms in the first place has been to gain technology. Yet conversations between Ford engineers and their Japanese counterparts are almost exclusively in English. Much of the key information is being missed because of a company-wide deficiency in Japanese language skills. And worse yet, Ford and almost all other major American firms are doing little about this problem. And, we do not intend to single out Ford on this issue—in fact, Ford does better on this dimension than most American firms.

Whenever we talk to groups of executives, we ask them what they're looking for in graduating business students. Almost always, the first thing mentioned is good communication skills. Letter and report writing and presentations to clients and internal groups are crucial parts of "making things happen" in the United States. In our business schools, we emphasize the development of such skills. We give our students instructions, practice, and feedback.

Now comes the paradox. As the markets of American companies become more global, why aren't managers asking for students with foreign-language skills? In American industry, at the present time, there is little payoff for fluency in Japanese. In fact, the lockstep curricula in most business schools almost preclude mastery of the language necessary to make things happen in a foreign country.

We used to be better at this. For example, in a course list bulletin from the University of Southern California Business School dated 1921—when American companies were taking over dominance of world markets from the British—of the forty-six classes offered, nine were international business-oriented. Listed were courses in commercial Spanish, French, German, and Chinese. In business school in 1921 we were teaching our students how to write a letter to a client in China *in Chinese*! It must have been important then. And it is clearly doubly important today.

Some of our undergraduates are recognizing that the world has changed from American economic dominance to broad economic interdependence. There have been major increases in enrollments in Japanese and Chinese language courses over the last few years. However, language training in this country still reflects history rather than reality. More students are taking Latin than Japanese! Even though France is our eighth most important market, more than ten times as many students take French as take Japanese.

Many American executives who lack fluency in foreign languages argue that English is the international business language. And when American firms dominated world markets during the second half of the last century, this was true. But now the Chinese can choose between American, Japanese, German, and even Korean suppliers. Indeed, the Koreans are spending millions of dollars on Chinese language lessons toward serving their growing trade with the People's Republic of China.

Perhaps the most important reason why foreign language skills aren't yet valued in American companies is a more personal one. By nature, we all like to hire and promote younger executives with skills and backgrounds similar to our own. "If foreign languages were not a part of my education, then the people I hire don't need those skills either. After all, I'm successful even though my Japanese vocabulary is limited to *konnichiwa* (Good day)."

MANAGEMENT IMPLICATIONS

Hiring young executives with language skills and foreign living experiences is crucial. But it's also never too late to gain something from language training yourself. Should you begin to study Japanese, you'll begin to have a greater appreciation for the deeper nuances of the culture. As soon as you learn that men say things differently from women, that sellers say things differently from buyers, you begin to understand how social rank influences not just conversational style but also all behaviors and thinking in Japan.

Finally, some may argue that language training is not worth an executive's valuable time. But if your business with your Japanese clients is important to your career, then you have an opportunity to both gain a personal competitive advantage and reap associated rewards by investing in Japanese-language training.

SELECTING THE TEAM

Now that we know what we're looking for in a negotiator to send to Japan, how do we measure these important personality traits? We have four options. First, the most frequently used personnel selection device is the interview. Prospective representatives might be asked to assess their own characteristics, and some factors may actually be assessed during the interview—listening ability, for example. Second, paper-and-pencil psychological tests are often used in employment and assignment decisions. However, we feel this approach is the least useful. Third, observation of the various characteristics during actual business negotiations is perhaps the best measure. Fourth, when field observations are not possible, as with new employees, role playing and observation are the next best methods of measuring personality traits and predicting future performance.

The next considerations are how many negotiators to send and what levels of management are appropriate? The "I can go it alone" style of American bargainers suggests sending one negotiator (usually middle management) with authority to sign. However, decisions regarding negotiation team composition must be made with consideration to the Japanese side.

A business negotiation team in Japan typically consists of the five following roles or positions:

1. *Shokai-sha* (trusted introducer)
2. *Sutaffu* (operational staff)
3. *Kacho/Bucho* (middle managers)
4. *Shacho* (chief executive officer)
5. *Chukai-sha* (mediator, often *shokai-sha*) (if necessary)

Shokai-Sha

The *shokai-sha*—literally, the person who introduces—is a neutral third party who makes initial contact with the courted party in a business deal in Japan. This third party introduction is absolutely necessary. The *shokai-sha* will often participate in the business discussion during the initial meeting (and perhaps the second one) and the last meeting, when the chief executives meet to give final, ceremonial approval to the deal. *Shokai-sha* may also help locate interpreters when necessary. For an American company courting a Japanese company, finding and using the appropriate *shokai-sha* is essential. An American firm being approached by a Japanese company will always be contacted initially by the *shokai-sha*.

There are several kinds of institutions in the United States and/or Japan that usually provide *shokai-sha* services and appropriate personnel. They are: (1) Japanese trading companies, (2) Japanese banks and international investment banking firms, (3) Japan External Trade Organization (JETRO), (4) American law and accounting firms, (5) the U.S. Embassy commercial representatives, (6) the American Chamber of Commerce in Japan, and (7) other specialized consulting firms such as Pacific Alliance Group. All provide excellent services, but each has special associated considerations.

Both Japanese trading companies and banks will be able to arrange introductions with only a limited group of Japanese companies—those in their "family" of companies. For example, Mitsubishi Trading Company or Mitsubishi Bank would not be appropriate *shokai-sha* for Hitachi, Inc., but would be appropriate for Mitsubishi Electronics, Ltd. If an American company wishes to determine which bank or trading company is appropriate, the *Yukashoken Hokokusho* (the Japanese equivalent of the American 10K Report) can be consulted online. Usually, the costs of the *shokai-sha* services will be cheaper with banks than with trading companies. That is, purchase of associated financial services when banks act as *shokai-sha* is usually less expensive than the commissions and other "pieces of the action" when trading companies participate.

American law firms and major accounting firms with Japanese practice divisions can also provide excellent *shokai-sha* services. The commissions associated with the former are generally higher but may be appropriate when substantial legal review is necessary. Major international banks with substantial operations in Japan may also provide *shokai-sha* services.

Finally, it should be noted that frequently two kinds of *shokai-sha* may be appropriate. That is, it may be best for operational level personnel of the *shokai-sha* firm to introduce operational level personnel of the two courting firms. And at the same time, the president of the *shokai-sha* firm should introduce the top executive officers.

Sutaffu

Once the proper introductions have been made, the work begins in earnest. *Sutaffu*, or operational level staff (personnel involved with the prospective deal on a day-to-day basis), meet to exchange information and hammer out concessions and agreements. Such meetings may occur frequently and over a long period of time until both sides are satisfied with the outcome.

Kacho/Bucho

The *kacho/bucho*, or middle managers, may attend operational staff level meetings but will seldom participate in the discussions and persuasive efforts. Occasionally, the middle managers will confirm concessions and decisions made during the other meetings. However, they will seldom make decisions at the negotiation table. Their function has been to listen and observe, not to persuade or decide. But we must note that the traditionally strict adherence to these prescribed roles appears to be fading some in recent years.

Shacho

Even in the recent past the *shacho*, or chief executive, has acted more as a ceremonial figure in Japanese negotiations. Ordinarily, they would be brought in at the final signing of the agreement. They were not involved in the discussions of details, nor did they make the decisions. Most importantly, chief executives of Japanese firms were not to be persuaded. Recall the previous description of the consensus decision making in Japanese organizations. Not only were persuasive tactics ineffective with top Japanese executives, they were considered boorish behavior.

Top Japanese executives tended to be included in initial meetings or at an intermediate stage to communicate the importance of the deal. But in neither case did they participate in substantive business talks. They had neither the knowledge of details nor the willingness to make a decision without consultation.

While strong vestiges of this traditional role of *shacho* can still be seen, now many Japanese CEOs take the "hands on" approach more familiar to most Americans. Still it is most worthwhile for negotiators from the States to look for some kind of blend of the new and old in the increasingly globalized Japan.

Chukai-Sha

The final participant or role to be played on a Japanese negotiation team is that of *chukai-sha*, or mediator. The job of the third-party *chukai-sha* is to settle disputes between the two negotiating companies. Rather than making threats and using other aggressive persuasive appeals, stalemated negotiators call in a *chukai-sha* when an impasse is reached. Often the *chukai-sha* role might be played by the *shokai-sha*. Traditionally Japanese law firms or most recently the local offices of American law firms may supply attorneys to fill this role.

The American style of negotiation is normally different. The formality and ceremony, the tight constraints of the well-defined roles, and the extra cost of third parties can seem like so much nonsense from the American perspective. But the best deal (and sometimes the only deal) will be made when American negotiation teams are assembled with full consideration given to the Japanese team's composition roles and bargaining process.

The first rule of negotiation team composition is to remember that, in Japan, talk flows horizontally across levels, not vertically between levels. Also, what is talked about varies from level to level. That is, when top executives are present, they talk to corresponding top executives about primarily nontask-related matters. Executives at other levels may be asked questions (with short answers expected), but the focus of such meetings is the development of personal relations at the top level. When only middle managers and operational staff are present, middle managers confirm decisions and commitments to corresponding middle managers. Or, middle managers listen while operational staff members exchange information and try to persuade one another. Given these circumstances, it is our recommendation that an American negotiation team should reflect the composition and behaviors of the Japanese team.

It should be noted that it is possible, when the Japanese firm is doing the courting, for an American middle manager to handle more than one role. Often, American managers pride themselves on having detailed information as well as decision-making authority. But a lone American negotiator will accomplish the most when he or she plays the appropriate role at the appropriate time. That is, persuasive tactics should be directed toward the Japanese operational staff. Only middle managers on the Japanese side should be expected to make commitments, and then only after separate consultation with their operational staff. And when the top Japanese executive is present, task-related discussions are completely inappropriate and ineffective. American negotiators can often get by using such a single-handed approach, but the better strategy is to include and use the three levels of executives in a well-planned and coordinated team effort with each executive playing the proper role.

There are two other important but more subtle reasons for including more than one American when bargaining in Japan. First, the image of the American negotiator is boosted if an assistant accompanies him or her to handle minor details. Second, it will almost always be to the American's advantage to establish an informal channel of communication between executives at lower levels. Things can and will be said by the lowest level Japanese that can't be said at the negotiation table. Such an informal channel of communication is best established using lower level executives on each side.

FINAL COMMENTS ABOUT TEAM SELECTION

A few years ago we were asked to take a look at AT&T's sales organization for marketing products and services to Japanese subsidiaries in the United

States. We found that the sales representatives who were calling on Toyota were calling on Nissan as well. This was a big mistake. Japan's two largest automakers are fiercely competitive with one another. And since a vendor must establish such a strong interpersonal tie with a Japanese client, having the same person call on both companies was fraught with danger. Managers in neither Japanese company would have truly trusted such a sales representative. So, we advised the managers at AT&T to organize their sales representatives targeting the Japanese subsidiaries in a different way—along the lines of the major groups of Japanese companies. At that point in time, much care had to be taken not to cross such Japanese industrial group lines when selecting negotiation teams and organizing the sales force.

But, we must also point out that because of the financial machinations associated with the 1990s economic downturn, many of the traditional *keiretsu* ties were broken via divestment. Now, more than at any time in the past one hundred years, partners and clients at the larger Japanese companies may be less concerned about this heretofore crucial consideration. However, it is still worthwhile to pay attention to the remaining *keiretsu* affiliations that are now readily discernable via the aforementioned *Yukashoken Hokokusho* report online.

Our final comment regarding negotiation team selection concerns interpreters. As we mentioned earlier, very few Americans speak Japanese. Thus, despite the disadvantages of using an interpreter, they are often a necessity. Particularly when substantive discussions begin, having your own interpreter will be important for two reasons. First, you will need to brief the interpreter before discussions begin. Second, you will need to sit with the interpreter after the negotiations end each day to assess results and the interests of the Japanese side. Without your own interpreter neither option is open to you.

The best interpreters will be a help in the negotiations not only by translating, but by communicating the meanings intended. (See boxes 6.1 and 6.2 for an idea of the difficulties of interpreting Japanese to English and vice versa.) Interpreters can hurt or help you, and generally you get what you pay for. Their fees vary depending on the level of technical knowledge and competence you require. But you can never spend too much money on interpretation services. Interpreters should be briefed on the background and terminology of the deal but not necessarily on your strategies. It must be remembered that interpreters are third parties. Even though they are paid by you they have different, personal motives.

The *shokai-sha* is perhaps the best source of information about selecting interpreters. Additionally, business information centers can provide references to the interpreters and interpreting companies. References such as the Japanese Yellow Pages also list major interpreting companies.

BOX 6.1. THE DEVIL'S TONGUE: MISUNDERSTANDING CAN CREATE BOTH OBSTACLES AND INSULATION

The first person pronoun "I" is a basic starting point: *eyo, je, ich, io, ya*. In Japanese, where nothing is that simple, the word has two dozen or more forms, depending on who is talking, and to whom, and the social relationship between them. An elderly man might refer to himself as *washi*, but his wife would say *watashi*, or, for that matter, *atakushi*, or *atashi*; their daughter might say *atai* and their son *boku*. Then there is *temae*, which means both "you" and "I." But the Japanese often evade these social difficulties by dropping all pronouns entirely.

The "devil's language" is the description generally attributed to St. Francis Xavier, the 16th century Jesuit missionary. Others have seen in the intricacies of the language a major influence on Japan's intellectual and artistic styles, even on its basic national character. Yet, sympathetic observers also believe that the language may represent a serious obstacle to Japan's functioning as a world power. According to former U.S. Ambassador Edwin O. Reischauer, "Japanese ideas are transmitted abroad only very weakly and through the filter of a few foreign 'experts'. . . Japanese intellectual life for the most part goes on behind a language barrier."

To cross that barrier, translators and interpreters are more necessary but less effective, since the Japanese language not only is difficult in itself but represents a quite different concept of speech. Anthropologist Masao Kunihiro notes: "English is intended strictly for communication. Japanese is primarily interested in feeling out the other person's mood." Misunderstandings are a constant hazard. At one top-level conference, for example, President Nixon asked for a cut in Japanese textile exports, and Prime Minister Sato answered, "Zensho shimaso," which was translated literally as "I'll handle it as well as I can." Nixon thought that meant, "I'll take care of it," but the Japanese understood it to mean something like "Let's talk about something else."

"Japanese can be made vague," says Paul Anderer, who teaches Japanese literature at Columbia University, "but the language is extraordinarily precise in determining who you are as you speak to someone else about what it is that you or that other person needs."

Source: John Greenwald, "The Negotiation Waltz," *Time*, August 1, 1983, 75.

CONCLUSIONS

By nature Americans prefer to "go it alone" in a business negotiation. However, even in the United States this is often not the best practice. There is much to be gained by a team approach. Listening, debating, maintaining

BOX 6.2. DIPLOMATIC INSIGHTS ON TRANSLATION PROBLEMS

It was James Schlesinger's first trip to Tokyo as U.S. Secretary of Defense. He was visiting for a series of meetings with a Japanese Defense Ministry official. The meetings went well, so a celebratory dinner was set for their final evening together. Protocol, of course, demands speeches on such occasions. So after coffee was served, the Japanese Defense Minister arose and treated us to an eloquent ten minutes of colorful remarks. Jim Schlesinger is not one to settle for second best on any occasion, so we wondered just how he might respond. We also wondered how his response might be handled by the evening's interpreter, a man of obviously limited skills.

So when the secretary rose to speak, we kept our ears well attuned. He led off with what might be described as a mixed aquatic metaphor. "This watershed evening," Jim began, "shall leave footprints on the sands of time." With that he stopped and turned toward the interpreter. Poor fellow! Completely baffled, his eyes wildly searched the room hoping someone would come to his rescue. Several of us, none more than moderately bilingual, pitched in with attempts to deliquify the secretary's metaphor. The process became so convoluted that the entire gathering eventually succumbed in a spirit of high hilarity. With good feeling and spasms of laughter abounding, a festive evening ensued.

Jim Schlesinger never did fully finish his remarks. And as we all learned, laughter needs no interpretation.

personal relationships, making calculations, and keeping track of technical information are all required at the negotiation table. Coordinated teamwork can accomplish such tasks more efficiently. And finally, there is the added social pressure of proper numbers—a simple and subtle consideration but an important one.

When meeting with Japanese clients, teamwork will be doubly important. Because the Japanese divide the labor of negotiation into clearly specified roles and functions, American negotiators will have to adjust their approach. This is particularly so when Americans travel to Japan. Finally, the individuals chosen to bargain with Japanese clients should have special characteristics—good listening skills, perhaps even Japanese-language skills, interpersonal orientation, patience, a broad worldview, and so forth. Teams and negotiators should be picked carefully for dealing with Japanese clients and partners. Selection decisions can easily make or break a trans-Pacific business relationship.

7

Negotiation Preliminaries

Once the best negotiation team has been selected, it is time to prepare for the meetings. These preparations include three aspects. First, training regarding Japanese negotiation styles is useful. Next, gathering information and planning strategies and tactics will be important. Third, manipulation of the negotiation situation may have a dramatic impact on the negotiation process and outcomes. The best negotiators on both sides of the Pacific manage such details with great care. To get the most out of business negotiations it is important to have every causal factor working in your favor. The time spent in careful planning and detailed adjustment of situational factors is an important investment.

TRAINING

Imagine yourself in 1945. An icy wind is blowing into the cockpit. You are all alone. The "divine wind" spirit doesn't exactly quiet your fear. It's a suicide mission.

This scene may not sound much like modern-day marketing, but it is a useful metaphor for what U.S. companies are doing today with some of our brightest young executives. They're sending them on suicide missions to Japan—kamikaze-style marketing.

A case in point is Jack Miller, a fast-track middle manager for a multimillion-dollar financial services firm. Aged thirty-five, with a degree from a top-rank American business school, he has tackled every tough job sent his way. So far.

Now the task is to drum up clients in the liberalizing Japanese market. The targets are large institutional investors. He has proved his ability to work wonders with similar clients in the United States. He even attended a week-long seminar called "Doing Business in Japan," and his corporation supports him by providing some expensive market research, arranging several appointments with local U.S. Commerce Department officials, furnishing a long list of contacts and appropriate letters of introduction.

His first two-week trip to Tokyo is seemingly a great success. He meets the "key" people in several of the firms and they sound interested. He sends the correct follow-up correspondence. Then the waiting begins. Four weeks. Three months. Six months. Another trip to "warm up" the contacts. Again they seem interested. He is encouraged. But again the weeks turn to months and still no business. Friendly talk, but no sales.

After a year or so, Jack Miller is given new responsibilities. The Japanese business just hasn't worked out. It wasn't his fault, but try to explain that to him. Now he has decided to change companies. He has failed at something, and, worse yet, he doesn't know why.

We'll tell you why. Despite all the company did to prepare him, he wasn't given the correct training and support. Consider for a moment how the Japanese prepare an executive for work in the United States market. Take, for example, Yoshihiro Ueda. English-language training started in grade school. He watched a lot of American television and movies. He received an undergraduate degree in economics from Tokyo University, then eight years' work experience, first in accounting, then sales, in the Yokohama branch office. By the age of thirty-two, he was sent for two years to an American business school for an MBA. Five years back in the Tokyo office, and then back to the United States to open his company's first office there. And most important, his company allowed him five years to succeed rather than the typical American approach of one year.

Mr. Ueda's company invested much more than $500,000 (tuition expenses and his salary) to train him to sell in the United States, to learn the American system. What's more startling, there are more than 10,000 Japanese like Mr. Ueda in the United States today selling Japanese products and services. They all have had similar training, representing investments of more than half a billion dollars by Japanese companies.

Many studies have noted the woeful state of American education in Asian languages and culture. At some point American business and governmental leaders will face the fact that we're suffering continual trade deficits with Japan (and other Asian nations) because we don't really know how to sell to them, because our armies of marketers are undertrained and unsupported by their companies. All this talk about "unfair" trade practices and congressional clamoring for protectionism won't make a dent in the trade deficit. If we don't do something to correct our own managerial deficiencies, then our marketing efforts in Japan will continue to be much less like a "divine wind" and much more like "hot air."

Ford Motor Company has offered its top executives a week's worth of programs on Japanese culture, business systems and strategies, and negotiation styles. (We designed the last program.) And the participants at Ford have found the material quite useful.

Unfortunately, Ford is one of the few major American companies making such a commitment to training its executives. But even Ford's innovative efforts are really just a first step toward increasing effectiveness in their Japanese partnerships and operations. We have advised them to begin to consider how their hiring practices—which, for example, place almost no emphasis on foreign-language skills—have not kept up with their increasingly global strategies. Training will help in the short run, but who will be running the global operations of American firms in 2020?

EFFICIENT PREPARATIONS

Any experienced business negotiator will tell you that there's never enough time to get ready. Given the typical time constraints of international negotiations, preparations must be accomplished efficiently. The homework must be done before bargaining begins. Toward the goal of efficiency in preparation and planning for bargaining with Japanese clients, we provide the following checklist:

1. Assessment of the situation and the people
2. Facts to confirm during the negotiation
3. Agenda
4. Best alternative to a negotiation agreement (BATNA)
5. Concession strategies
6. Team assignments

Assessment of the Situation and the People

It is only common sense to learn as much as possible about a potential client or partner before negotiations begin. All kinds of information might be pertinent depending on the nature of the contemplated deal. Various sorts of financial data and competitive information regarding American companies are available to other American firms. Much the same information is available about Japanese firms. For example, one can find distribution partners, *shokai-sha*, and financial and marketing data. The first step in preparing for many such negotiations is mining the critical information from several resources.

It should be clearly understood that knowing who you will be bargaining with in Japan is far more important than most Americans would assume. If you and your business associates step off the plane with no personal or professional perspectives on your Japanese counterparts, you can expect little success once the meetings begin.

In addition to the public sources of information about Japanese companies and executives, informal sources should be consulted. Other American companies that have dealt with the courted Japanese firm might be valuable sources of information. A final source of information specific to the prospective deal and the people involved will be the *shokai-sha*.

The last step is sizing up the probable goals and preferences of the Japanese side through the analysis of the various data using a Japanese perspective rather than an American one. In acquisitions, the Japanese tendency to focus on asset evaluations rather than potential cash flow streams, as is typical in America, and the often mentioned emphasis on long-term, gradual growth are Japanese modes of business reasoning that should be kept in mind. A comparison of automobile production in the United States and in Japan is most revealing of the difference in perspectives (figure 7.1). Notice the volatility in American production versus the slow, steady growth of Japanese production.

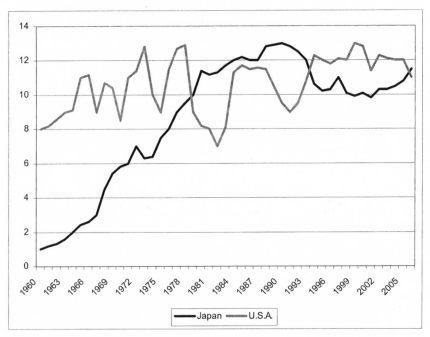

Figure 7.1.   Japanese and U.S. Motor Vehicle Production (millions of units)

Such differences persist in a wide variety of industries today. We compared thirty pairs of U.S. and Japanese companies—such as General Motors to Toyota, Kodak to Fuji, and Hitachi to GE—and found that the revenues of the Japanese firms were consistently more stable than those of their American counterparts.[1] All these figures reflect the basic view of Japanese business executives. As described in detail by Ouchi in *Theory Z* and Pascale and Athos in *The Art of Japanese Management*, the Japanese side will most likely be looking for stable growth over at least a ten-year period. Meanwhile, American companies and executives, looking at the same information, would be focusing on length of payback and profits in the first three years.

Once the file on the Japanese company is complete, it is time to evaluate carefully your own company's situation. The kind of economic analysis you have undertaken regarding the Japanese should be replicated regarding your own company. Without question the Japanese side will do the same, and you need to anticipate what they know about you. Finally, your own instructions from top management and your authority limits should be clearly understood. This latter aspect of preparations is often taken for granted, and lack of attention to this detail can cause serious problems during and after the negotiations. Frequently, American managers in the heat of a long negotiation will overstep their authority and make commitments that later must be retracted. "I'll take full responsibility," runs the cliché.

Facts to Confirm During the Negotiation

No matter how careful the analysis and how complete the information available, all critical information and assumptions should be reconfirmed at the negotiation table. As part of the preparations, a list of such facts should be discussed among the members of the negotiation team, and specific questions should be written down. We have found again and again that surprises (both pleasant and unpleasant) often surface as part of this confirmation of facts.

Agenda

Most business negotiators come to the negotiation table with an agenda for the meeting in mind. We feel it is important to do two things with that agenda. First, write out the agenda for all members of your negotiating team. Second, don't try to settle each issue one at a time. The latter recommendation goes against the grain of the typical American sequential approach. However, in any bargaining situation it is better to get all the issues and interests out on the table before trying to settle any one of them. This will be particularly true when the other side consists of representatives from a Japanese company.

You should understand that the Japanese bargainers will also bring with them a carefully considered agenda, and you may end up bargaining over agendas. The tendency will be for the Japanese side to be more flexible toward setting the order of topics but much less flexible about the choice of topics.

A Japanese agenda permits skipping around among selected topics. A safe strategy for the American side is to check beforehand with Japanese operational-level people about the agenda. However, there can be some value in surprise. We have witnessed American bargainers scrapping a previously agreed upon agenda, making the Japanese side scramble, and thus creating a major distraction, giving the American side time to regroup and reconsider thoughts and strategies. However, this tactic should be used with caution as it will result in great discomfort for the Japanese.

The Best Alternative to a Negotiated Agreement

Fisher and Ury, in their popular book, *Getting to Yes*, point out that an often skipped crucial aspect of negotiation preparations is a clear definition of the best alternative to a negotiated agreement, or BATNA. They suggest, and we agree, that negotiators and managers must spend time considering what happens next if the deal doesn't work out. "Is there another Japanese firm to court or should we just concentrate on our domestic business for now and try again later?" The BATNA sets the cutoff point where negotiations no longer make sense. But it is more than a simple bottom line; it is a kind of contingency plan. Moreover, your list of viable alternatives defines your power in the negotiation.

Concession Strategies

Concession strategies should be decided upon and written down before negotiations begin. Such a process—discussion and recording—goes a long way toward ensuring that negotiators stick to the strategies. In the midst of a long negotiation there is a tendency to make what we call "streaks" of concessions. The only way we have found to avoid this is careful planning and commitment before negotiation

Of particular concern is the American propensity to "split the difference." Never split the difference! Have specific reasons for the size of each concession you make.

Finally, you will notice very quickly that Japanese bargainers never make a concession without first taking a break. Issues and arguments are reconsidered away from the social pressure of the negotiation table. This is a good practice for Americans to emulate.

Team Assignments

The final step in negotiation planning is role assignments. We mentioned earlier the importance of the different roles in Japanese bargaining. Each American bargainer should understand his or her corresponding role. Other kinds of team assignments might include listening responsibilities, or monitoring the agenda or concession strategies. And perhaps roles should be adjusted to circumstances or over time.

MANIPULATION OF THE NEGOTIATION SITUATION

The second aspect of negotiation preliminaries is manipulation of the negotiation situation to your company's advantage. Some of the issues we raise in this section may appear trivial, but the most skilled negotiators and your Japanese clients always consider them. Particularly in a tough negotiation, everything should be working in your favor. If situational factors are working against you, it will be important before the negotiations begin to manipulate them. Also, management of situational factors may be important once the discussions have commenced. In the pages to follow we will consider seven situational factors that we feel are particularly important. They are:

1. Communications channels
2. Location
3. Physical arrangements
4. Number of parties
5. Number of participants
6. Audiences (news media, etc.)
7. Time limits

All seven factors are ordinarily set before negotiations begin. All can and should be manipulated to your advantage. Any one can make the difference between success and failure in business negotiations with executives from Japan.

Channels of Communication

Since the last edition of our book this is the area of greatest change in the conduct of Japanese/American commerce. The events of 9/11 and the increased risk of international travel in combination with broader acceptance of Internet usage, particularly in Japan, have dramatically changed the pace of negotiations. Now a business transaction that took three to six months and four or five trans-Pacific trips in the year 2000 takes just a couple of weeks and perhaps only two face-to-face meetings. Much more of the transaction can be conducted over the Internet and during teleconferences (both phone and with video). E-mail is particularly useful because the medium allows several team members to view the messages, allowing for clearer translations, careful and repeated readings, and therefore more accurate information exchanges. The medium also allows carefully thought out responses because of the time gaps inherent in cross–time zone usage. Of course, one of the new costs of trans-Pacific teleconferences is the sleep lost on one side or another. Still, most executives are happy to make the tradeoff between some late-night calls and a week's worth of jet lag. Recently, a negotiation on which we consulted required interactions among executives in Tokyo, Los Angeles, Charlotte, New York, and London. It's hard to calculate how much was saved in transaction costs—travel expenses and executives' time and health—because of the new technologies we were able to employ.

However, face-to-face negotiations with Japanese clients are always recommended, particularly for initial or potentially contentious meetings. Other channels of communication that might be used for negotiations in the United States are not used as much in Japan in such circumstances. As described earlier, the Japanese social system is built around almost continuous face-to-face contact. Too much of the important, subtly transmitted information can't be communicated in a letter, memo, fax, e-mail, telephone call, or even by teleconferencing. Moreover, it is much harder for Japanese bargainers to say no in the face-to-face situation. The social pressure and *wa* preclude negative responses, and these pressures are not so strong over the phone.

Location

The location of the negotiations is perhaps the most important situational factor for several reasons, both practical and psychological. Having the "home court" is an advantage because the home team has all its information resources readily available and all the necessary team members close by. Alternatively, the traveling team brings the minimum necessary resources, information, and players, and it stays in hotels. But perhaps a greater advantage the home team enjoys is psychological—a perception of power. If the other side is coming to you, that means you have something they want. You are in control of the scarce resource, whether it be a product or service (you're the seller) or access to a key market (you're the buyer). Smart negotiators will always try to hold negotiations in their own offices. Short of this, a neutral location is best.

The location factor will be even more important when dealing with Japanese clients or partners, for it communicates power much louder in Japan. Thus, in business dealings between Japanese we see a strong emphasis on getting to a neutral location, such as a restaurant or bar.

Let us assume for a moment that your Japanese clients and prospective partners play the cordial host and invite you to Japan. They may call on you initially in the United States to "bait the hook." However, they will be careful to mention that the visit to your offices was just incidental to other business. After such initial contact, you may be invited to Japan. "Kyoto is lovely this time of year, and while you're on the trip you might stop by our factory." The Japanese side will be very careful to manipulate the negotiation setting to their advantage. If you are clearly in the weaker position (that is, fewer alternatives to making the deal), then it will be best to go to Japan. But where power relations are more equal, the best response to a Japanese invitation is a counter invitation for their executives to visit the United States and your offices. A simple refusal to go to Japan would be inappropriate. Instead, a "come see Lake Michigan" approach is recommended. You may end up bargaining over location; however, this bargaining is best handled in a subtle and indirect manner.

In the event that neither side gives in to the other's suggestions, then it's time to suggest that negotiations be held in a neutral location such as Hawaii. It's not just the golf courses and beaches that explain why so many trans-Pacific business deals are struck in Honolulu. This neutral location, equally convenient to both parties and indicative of equal power relations, provides a place where both sides are subject to the same expenses, information, and time constraints. Both sides communicate, albeit subtly, that they have alternatives to bargaining; they don't *have* to travel to Japan, or *have* to travel to the United States. On the other hand, each side is confirming the other side's power by not holding out for a home court advantage.

In the event that you choose to travel to Japan, there are some things that can be done to reduce the Japanese home court advantage. One is to make arrangements for meeting facilities at your hotel (or your bank, or a subsidiary's office) and invite the Japanese executives to call on you. You might argue, "I've already made the arrangements and everything is all set," or perhaps you need to wait for an important phone call. This may not help much, but it may help some.

One final comment must be made about location of negotiations. Although restaurants, bars, and golf courses are all important locations for bargaining in Japan, the kinds of bargaining behaviors appropriate in these settings are very much limited. Generally, in these informal settings almost all talk is nontask sounding. One Japanese executive suggested that 98 percent of the conversation has to do with sports, politics, and family, while only 2 percent deals with business. Usually, the task-related matters are discussed indirectly, very briefly, and toward the end of the evening, after a few drinks.

For example, an American CEO and his associates were visiting Japan to meet with his Japanese partners' companies and negotiate an increased level of import-export business. The day after their arrival in Tokyo, they visited retail stores with which they deal. Later, the Americans graciously accepted the Japanese negotiator's invitation to dinner at a plush Japanese restaurant overlooking the beautiful garden of the Hotel New Otani in Tokyo. Dinner was elaborate, including more than fifteen dishes with the flavor of spring. At the end of dinner the chef brought in a huge birthday cake to celebrate the CEO's birthday. All of the Japanese businessmen sang a happy birthday song in Japanese. Blowing out the candles and gift-giving marked the end of the evening. As all the members were ushered toward the exit, one negotiator pulled his American counterpart to the side and whispered the amount of exports and imports the Japanese were willing to approve.

Physical Arrangements

Once the negotiation site has been agreed upon, then comes the question of specific physical arrangements. American bargainers should understand that the physical arrangements of the bargaining room will be much more important and will communicate far more to Japanese executives. Americans value and feel comfortable with informality. Japanese value and feel comfortable with formality. If you travel to Japan, the Japanese will manage the physical arrangements of the negotiations (that is, unless you make the arrangements). The formal seating arrangement by rank is modeled in figure 7.2. The only advice we have for Americans in such situations is to ask the Japanese where to sit. They will have a specific arrangement in mind, and if you ignore their arrangement they will feel uncomfortable.

If the Japanese are calling at your offices, then we recommend setting the physical arrangements to make them feel comfortable and more cooperative. If you wish to communicate that you are interested in the prospective business deal, then the most appropriate atmosphere will be a comfortable living room setting without desks or conference tables. Many chief executives have such furnishings in their offices, and for more reasons than one, a brief nontask encounter with the American CEO may be the appropriate first step. For companies that have frequent visits by Japanese clients, a specific room should be set aside and furnished as described.

Given that you wish to greet the Japanese visitors as honored guests, they should also be seated appropriately. But what is the "best seat in the house" to an American may not be the best seat from the Japanese perspective. Two

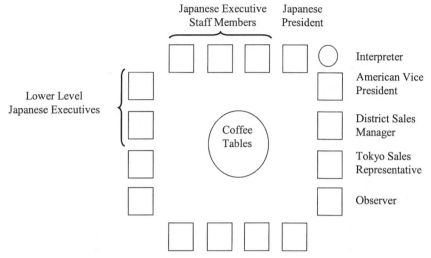

Figure 7.2.   Seating Arrangement at the *Aisatsu*

criteria are important to the Japanese: (1) distance from the door, and (2) location of the center of focus in the room. The top Japanese executive will feel most comfortable seated furthest from the door and framed by the focal object, which is usually a window with a view or a large painting. In most American meeting rooms these criteria are complementary; the focal point is furthest from the door. This is also done at dinners and other business-related functions. We recommend place cards as an easy way to avoid a faux pas. Finally, if a couch is in the room, it will be best to sit the Japanese client there, by himself, because size of the chair is another signal of status.

Number of Parties

In many trans-Pacific business deals, more than two companies are involved. Often, in addition to a buyer and a seller there are other involved suppliers, engineering consulting firms, banks, trading companies, and government officials. For example, in joint venture talks between Toyota and GM, not only was the general trading firm that acted as *shokai-sha* involved but also the United Auto Workers, the Federal Trade Commission, and numerous other local governmental bodies. Another example is that of Safeway's investment in Allied Import Company (AIC), where six parties were involved in the contract-signing ceremony—Safeway, AIC, and four of the AIC member companies. Generally, the more parties involved, the more complex and more difficult the negotiations. Despite such common sense, our American impatience often leads us to try to get everyone together and hammer out an agreement. Such attempts almost always end in frustration. It is our recommendation that negotiations include as few parties as possible—hopefully just representatives of the two primary companies. If more than one other party is involved we recommend a *nemawashi* approach, which includes meeting with the separate parties individually before calling everyone together.

Occasionally, there may be some benefit to meeting with all parties in the early stages—as when everyone except the client agrees with you. But such circumstances will be rare, particularly when other Japanese companies are involved. You should be aware that Japanese companies will try to use this approach. In response you should always ask who is going to be involved and why. If you feel the reason is insufficient, you might suggest that things may be "simpler" without them. Alternatively, if you plan to bring along a third party, you should let the Japanese know ahead of time and be prepared with a good explanation.

Number of Participants

In negotiations, Americans are almost always outnumbered by Japanese. We consider this to be a serious disadvantage. In the previous chapter we mentioned the importance of finding out whom the other side is sending and then putting your team together in response. Moreover, you shouldn't hesitate to include additional members on your team such as financial or technical experts. The extra expense may be a wise investment.

You should also appreciate how important numbers are to your Japanese counterparts. They will bring along technical specialists and younger non-participants for on-the-job training. They will make one person responsible for carefully observing your nonverbal and verbal responses to their proposals; that person's evaluation and comments will appear in a written report. Since a committee will make the decision, they will bring along a committee of deciders.

In addition to bringing along extra team members, the relative numbers can be manipulated in other ways. We have heard of Chinese negotiators who, when faced with large numbers of visiting Japanese negotiators, purposefully delayed progress. As a result, some of the other side's team returns home and the difference in numbers is reduced. We don't suggest you use such tactics, but you should be aware that they may be used against you.

Finally, it is possible to include too many people on your side. One such case regarded a prospective franchise agreement between a major chain of American restaurants and a Japanese investment group. The executive vice president and corporate counsel for the U.S. company was in charge of the American team. Because of his concern for the best contract, he included an attorney in Japan in addition to his corporate lawyer in the United States. The Japanese became concerned with the legal aspects of the negotiation and decided to hire a Japanese attorney of their own. Thus, four lawyers, including the executive vice president, were involved. With so many legal opinions, the situation soon turned sour and the Japanese backed out of the discussions.

Audiences

In any particular business deal there might be a number of audiences that could exercise influence on the negotiation outcomes. The GM-Toyota joint venture is a case in point. Consider how many audiences existed:

1. Other suitors—Ford (jilted by Toyota earlier), Chrysler (a strong critic)
2. Governmental agencies—FTC (antitrust), Congress (trade barrier saber rattling), Commerce Department and U.S. Trade Representative, California and local municipal governments
3. The public
4. United Auto Workers
5. Related competitors—Ford, Chrysler, American Motors, Nissan Toyota Motor-Sales USA, and GM subsidiaries

Now consider how the two companies might have manipulated these various audiences to their advantage. All the audiences had an interest and a stake in how the GM-Toyota talks continued, and certainly some were manipulated through selective leaking of information.

We know such manipulations do occur in deals between Japanese companies and between American companies. We are familiar with at least two cases in which information was deliberately leaked to the news media to pressure the other negotiating party to agree to the terms of the proposal. It is difficult for the other party to say no to an already publicized agreement. However, extreme caution is advised in this area. Often, the action by one party may result in mistrust and a breakdown in the negotiations. Such was the result in one of the two cases. In particular, trying to influence negotiations through leaking information to a foreign press (that is, Americans in Japan or vice versa) is quite risky.

You should anticipate that Japanese clients or partners may manipulate audiences for their own advantage, particularly Japanese audiences with which they are more familiar. You should also be aware of audience reactions that may help you, and you should know how to elicit such reactions when appropriate.

Finally, as many trans-Pacific negotiations hold important implications for stock valuations in both countries, announcing agreements must be carefully orchestrated. Time of day, day of week, and across time zone coordination can be pertinent considerations, with Friday press releases allowing for Monday morning newspaper stories.

Time Limits

If location is not the single most important aspect of the negotiation situation, then time limits are. Generally, the side that has more time *and knows it* is in a stronger bargaining position. The side with less time is forced to make concessions in order to move the other toward agreement. The use of time can be a powerful bargaining tool.

Ordinarily, time constraints are established by factors beyond the control of negotiators. On the selling side, orders must be secured to keep the factory busy, the expenses of foreign travel are substantial, other customers must be called on, quotas must be filled, and the home office management is in a hurry. Likewise, purchasers must bargain with other suppliers of complementary goods. Purchases must be made before other buyers come on the scene. Purchases must be made according to complex time schedules and before profits can be made from associated operations. Circumstances and company goals set time limits for practically every kind of negotiation and for buyers and sellers alike. Negotiators should try to determine beforehand what the other side's time constraints are. Hopefully, theirs will be shorter than yours. But in any case negotiators can manipulate time limits, or at least the perception of time limits, to their advantage.

Japanese bargainers have a big advantage when it comes to manipulation of time limits—an American's internal clock apparently ticks much faster and much, much louder. Impatience is perhaps our greatest weakness in international negotiations. We're interested in quick action and immediate results. In contrast, the Japanese executive tends to take a more careful approach to business transactions. Long-term steady growth is valued over short-term fantastic results. It is much more difficult to rush a Japanese decision by imposing a time limit because (1) the consensus approach generally takes longer, and (2) the Japanese would rather make no decision than a bad one. Alternatively, most Americans would rather risk a bad decision than let a potential opportunity slip by.

Americans in Japan can also manipulate the Japanese side's perception of their time limits by making hotel reservations for longer or shorter periods than expected. Most foreign clients will check the length of your hotel reservations as part of their prenegotiation preparation. Your reservations will influence their behavior. Upon your arrival, you will also be asked how long you expect to stay in Japan. Negotiators should be aware that something simple like a hotel reservation communicates much, and this channel of communication should be used to your advantage, not theirs.

Another factor related to the timing of negotiations is Japanese holidays (see table 7.1). Negotiations might be scheduled to use the holidays as a lever.

Table 7.1. Public Holidays in Japan

Date	Name of the Day
January 1	New Year's Holiday
The second Monday of January	Coming-of-Age Day
February 11	National Foundation Day
March 21	Vernal Equinox Day
April 29	Greenery Day
May 3	Constitution Memorial Day
May 4	National Holiday
May 5	Children's Day
The third Monday of July	Maritime Day
The third Monday of September	Respect for the Aged Day
September 23	Autumnal Equinox Day
The second Monday of October	Health and Sports Day
November 3	Culture Day
November 23	Labor Thanksgiving Day
December 23	The Emperor's Birthday

Such tactics are often used by foreign business people against Americans—purposefully scheduling talks right before Christmas, for example.

Finally, in some circumstances it may be possible to impose time limits on Japanese negotiators by setting deadlines. For example, we have heard of one American capital equipment supplier who told his Japanese clients that "beginning on Monday, for every day you delay your decision the price goes up $10,000." So on Monday the price was $100,000, Tuesday $110,000, and they bought on Wednesday at $120,000. Such a story is entertaining but we recommend avoiding such threats and deadlines. The only reason the American got the order is because the Japanese had no alternative *at that time.* There is no doubt that the American's threats precluded a long-term relationship and any future orders. The imposition of time limits should only be used in extreme circumstances and should be accompanied with an explanation. Even a comment such as, "When can we expect to hear from you?" can translate into Japanese as inappropriate impatience. It is probably best to say nothing at all. American bargainers should understand the Japanese decision process, anticipate that things will move more slowly, and plan accordingly.

A FINAL NOTE ON HOW THE U.S. GOVERNMENT CAN HELP

When a U.S. business enterprise contemplates an initial venture in Japan or any other nation, it faces many a circumstance that lies outside the sphere of its familiarity. To start with, it must become schooled in any applicable federal regulations including tax regulations and such. It must also become familiar with any diplomatic conundrums that may pertain.

Table 7.2.   Useful Websites to Aid in Preparations for Negotiation

Central Bank	www.boj.or.jp/en/index.htm
Daiwa Securities	www.daiwa.co.jp
Finance Ministry	www.mof.go.jp/english/index.htm
Japan External Trade Organization (JETRO)	www.jetro.go.jp
Japanese Company Handbook	www.toyokeizai.co.jp/english/jch
Japanese Statistics Bureau	www.stat.go.jp/english/index.htm
Nikkei	www.nni.nikkei.co.jp
Nikko Securities	www.nikko.co.jp/SEC/e_home.html
Nomura Securities International	www.nomurany.com
Sumitomo Bank Capital Markets	www.smbc-cm.com
Websites of 715 leading Japanese firms	www.toyokeizai.co.jp/english/e_link/index.html

This information is available from many sources (see table 7.2 for suggestions). Some may choose to start with the country desk at the State Department. (The Japan desk can be reached by phone at 202-647-2913.) Other sources include the Japanese Embassy in Washington and the American Embassy in Tokyo. The American Chamber of Commerce in Tokyo is an exceptionally active and responsive organization. Armed with information from these or other sources, a U.S. business can proceed with some confidence.

A complicated question sometimes arises at this juncture. Beyond seeking basic information, should the enterprises also seek "help" from government offices? Unfortunately, the answer here must be, "It all depends." Let us examine some ingredients that lead us to this inconclusive conclusion.

As we know, help from any source can come at a price—in the loss of privacy, in intentions revealed, or even in the creation of reciprocal obligations. The relationship between business and government in foreign economic affairs has had a checkered history that needs understanding. In the early post-WWII period, many an American company sought to launch its ventures into new lands with little planning or preparation. Mistakes—costly and awkward mistakes—were made. Indifference to local customs and practices not only led to failures but to serious international relationship problems for our government. Accordingly, government became concerned that an ill-planned venture could create a foreign relations problem. Business, in turn, often saw government wariness as hostile to its ambitions. Both views can now be seen as overreactions.

Happily, this era and these attitudes are now pretty well behind us. In these days of galloping economic globalization, both parties have found they can no longer remain indifferent to the other's needs and interests. America obviously cannot afford to be a loser in the globalization race that becomes the common denominator.

Meanwhile, at an operating level a delicate question requiring careful judgment exists. How much help can our government provide an individual company without being accused of competitive favoritism? In the arena of private sector/public sector affairs, favoritism can become a damaging word. When it arises, both parties can lose and lose badly.

So where does this worrisome talk about help from government sources leave a company with foreign aspirations? We believe the best counsel comes down to this: Use it but don't abuse it. Interesting cases in point are those described in chapter 12 about government interventions in the negotiations regarding both the rice and beef trade.

NOTE

1. Cathy Anterasian, John L. Graham, and R. Bruce Money, "Are U.S. Managers Superstitious about Market Share?" *Sloan Management Review*, Summer 1996: 67–77.

8

At the Negotiation Table

The best negotiators in the world are the Japanese—they will spend days
getting to know their opponent. The worst are the Americans—they think
things work everywhere like they do in the United States.

—Sanfrits LePoole, Dutch expert on international negotiations

The most difficult aspect of an international business negotiation is the actual conduct of the face-to-face meeting. Assuming that the appropriate
people have been chosen to represent your firm, and that those representatives are well prepared, and that the situational factors have been manipulated in your favor, things can still go wrong at the negotiation table. Obviously, if these other preliminaries haven't been managed properly, then
things will go wrong during the meetings.

In chapter 3 we mentioned four stages of business negotiations: (1) nontask sounding, (2) task-related information exchange, (3) persuasion, and
(4) concessions and agreement. We pointed out that international business
negotiations all over the world tend to follow this sequence of events. We
also suggested that some of the major differences between the American
and Japanese negotiation styles regard the importance of and time spent on
each of the four steps. Our presentation of recommendations regarding the
face-to-face meetings with Japanese clients is ordered according to these
four stages typical in most business negotiations.

NONTASK SOUNDING

Americans always discuss topics other than business at the negotiation table. But we're quick about it. We move the discussion to the specific business at hand usually after five or ten minutes. There is a purpose, beyond friendliness and politeness, to this preliminary talk. Before getting to the business at hand it is important to learn how the other side feels this particular day.

We also learn how to communicate to our clients by learning about their backgrounds and interests. To the extent that people's backgrounds are similar, communication can be more efficient. Engineers can use technical jargon when talking to other engineers, golfers can use golfing analogies, family men and women can compare the cash drain of a fledgling business unit to putting kids through college.

During these initial stages of conversation we also make judgments about the people with whom we will be dealing. Can he be trusted? Will she be reliable? How much power does he have in his organization? Are they in a receptive mood today? Is now the right time to ask for something? Such assessments are made before business discussions even begin.

Perhaps this sounds like a lot to accomplish in five to ten minutes, but that's how long it usually takes in the United States. Not so in Japan. The goals of the nontask sounding are identical, but the time spent is far longer. In the United States we depend on our lawyers to get us out of bad deals if we've made a mistake in sizing up our clients or vendors. In Japan lawyers aren't used for such purposes. Instead, Japanese executives spend substantial time and effort in nontask sounding so that problems requiring lawyers don't develop later. (See box 8.1 for insights on nontask sounding based on James Hodgson's experiences as U.S. Ambassador to Japan.)

Nontask Sounding for Top Executives

The role of top executives in Japanese negotiations is often more ceremonial. Usually they are brought into negotiations only to sign the agreement after all issues have been settled by lower-level executives. On occasion, top executives are included earlier in the talks to communicate commitment and importance. In either case, their main activity is nontask sounding.

Getting top American executives to understand the importance of nontask sounding and make these adjustments in their behavior may be difficult. One successful way has been to supply them with a list of appropriate questions to ask during the *aisatsu* and other such meetings. (See box 8.2 for a hypothetical example of such a list.)

The questions and topics can be assembled using information from the *shokai-sha* or the Japanese companies themselves. Many Japanese firms have

BOX 8.1. DIPLOMATIC INSIGHTS ON TIMING

"Strike while the iron is hot." In negotiations, the iron is hot when the other party appears in a particularly receptive mood. During my diplomatic years in Japan, I saw how convincingly this truism works in practice. In the fall of 1974, at our embassy, we Americans were wrestling with an issue on which we knew it would be exceedingly difficult to bring the Japanese around to our point of view. So we postponed negotiations on the subject until after President Gerald Ford's scheduled November visit. Being the first ever American presidential visit to that country, the event had the effect of putting the Japanese in a particularly buoyant mood toward the United States. Capitalizing on that mood, we proceeded to reach a favorable agreement quickly on the controversial issue. Later a Japanese minister told me that while there was much in the agreement his country didn't care for, the Japanese thought it would be unseemly in the prevailing atmosphere to resist our position. Yes, it is wise to remember that the emotional tone at the negotiating table can ease, make, or break a negotiation.

resumes on hand that contain key personal information of top executives for such purposes. The Japanese will also want the *aisatsu* and associated top-level meetings to go smoothly. The conduct of such meetings is critical in Japan, and surprises at this stage are best avoided.

Another way to induce top American executives to behave properly is to emphasize that in Japanese conversation, what is said is not as important as how it is said. The Japanese top executive is making gut-level judgments about the integrity, reliability, commitment, and humility (if the Japanese is considerably older or his company is more powerful) of his American counterpart. Moreover, from the American perspective, the content of the talk—the words and verbal information—may seem inane. But from the Japanese point of view the content of the talk—the nonverbal messages and feelings conveyed, the *wa*—will be critical.

A few other details regarding nontask sounding at top levels should be mentioned. First, business cards may or may not be exchanged. The American executives should be prepared with cards in Japanese and should exchange them if the other side offers. However, when presidents of companies meet, business cards often are not required. In such cases, American presidents should be very familiar with their Japanese counterparts in advance. Second, small gifts are appropriate. Examples are pens, ties, or desktop ornaments, all with your company's logo. Anything that cuts (scissors, letter openers) and handkerchiefs should not be given, as such items symbolize the severing of relationships in Japan. The thought is what counts in this exchange of gifts, and very expensive gifts are unnecessary and actually

BOX 8.2. HYPOTHETICAL AGENDA
FOR TOP EXECUTIVE NONTASK SOUNDING

Date and Time: April 25, 11:00. a.m.
Meeting with: Mr. Ishiro Matsuyama, Senior Councillor of the Mitsuichi Bank
Location: Mitsuichi Bank Headquarters, Otemachi, 1-Chome, Chiyoda-ku, Tokyo

Purpose of Visit:
Courtesy call and to thank him for the kind introduction to the chairman and the president of ABC Corporation

Suggested Topics:
Thank him for sharing busy time with us.
Talk about bamboo jogging board Mr. Suzuki, chairman of Mitsuichi Bank, California subsidiary, gave. Mr. Matsuyama also uses it.
Report to him that a former ambassador to Japan and a mutual friend fully recovered from a recent illness to the point that he can play golf again.
Report to him how the meeting proceeded at ABC Corporation Headquarters, and thank him for his junior executives' support. (Names of junior executives: Mr. Suzuki and Mr. Ikeyama, California subsidiary, Messrs. Kojima and Ohmori of Mitsuichi Bank, Kyoto Branch.)
Ask him about his reaction to the recent acquisition of Union Bank by the Japanese bank.
Ask when he is scheduled to visit Los Angeles again. Promise to play golf with him during his visit. Invite him to visit Los Angeles during the Los Angeles Open Golf Tournament with a lot of Japanese yen to spend.

Background Information:
You met with Mr. Matsuyama last year when you were invited by MITI (Ministry of International Trade and Industry) and JETRO (Japan External Trade Organization). That meeting was arranged at the U.S. Ambassador's suggestion. The ambassador was willing to provide a letter of introduction to Mr. Matsuyama.
Two days ago Mr. Matsuyama visited the chairman of ABC corporation to introduce you and your profile.

inappropriate, even for presidents of Japanese firms. Third, a vague or implied reference to the future business relationship is appropriate toward the end of the *aisatsu*. It should be remembered, however, that indirectness and vagueness are key. Comments such as the following are appropriate:

1. "We would be glad to be of assistance to you in any way in the future."
2. "We pride ourselves in our high-quality products and we hope you share our views."

3. "Your company and our company appear to share some common goals."

Alternatively, comments as substantive as the following are inappropriate, even boorish, from the Japanese perspective:

1. "I hope you will consider our firm for your advertising services in the United States."
2. "A distribution agreement involving our two firms would prove profitable for both."
3. "If we can come to some agreement on the tough question of price, then the rest of the issues are minor."

Finally, when high-level meetings are held in the United States, we recommend the Japanese approach. Top-level Japanese executives will not be prepared to bargain and will not be persuaded, even when in the United States. It's simply not their role. When American hosts wish to demonstrate the importance of the visit and the deal, we advise sending a limousine to pick up the Japanese party at their hotel. The initial meeting between top executives should not be held across a boardroom table, and certainly not across the American executive's desk. Rather, a more comfortable, living room atmosphere is preferable.

Nontask Sounding for Lower-Level Executives

In the United States business relationships are typically established using the following procedures: first, a letter of introduction; then a phone call for an appointment; then a meeting at the client's office (including five to ten minutes of nontask sounding followed by the business proposal); and perhaps lunch, with more business talk. Almost always, after five to ten minutes of nontask sounding, an American client will ask, "Well now, what can I do for you?"

In Japan the typical routine goes something like the following. The initial appointment will be set up and attended by the *shokai-sha*. The Japanese client will invite the American party, including the *shokai-sha*, for a late afternoon meeting at the Japanese firm's offices. There the Americans will meet the concerned operational level personnel for a chat that does not include business talk or proposals. The same topics appropriate for the *aisatsu* are appropriate here, but business is not to be discussed yet. At around 6:00 p.m. the Japanese will suggest dinner or perhaps a drink at a favorite *izakay* (Japanese-style pub). Ordinarily, they will pick the restaurant and pick up the tab. Americans won't have a chance to fight for the bill because they will never see one. Business talk will still be inappropriate. Before the mid-1990s the next stop would have been more drinking at an outrageously expensive Ginza nightclub. There, more nontask sounding, including sharing drinks and conversation with the bar hostesses, would have been the bill of fare. These sessions ordinarily went on past 11:00 p.m. Now, evenings end earlier and Japanese executives have healthier livers. In any case, throughout this first afternoon and evening of introductions, only vague and indirect references to a future relationship may be made, but we advise they be mentioned only in response to similar comments by the Japanese. As in the *aisatsu*, the Japanese will be looking for integrity, sincerity, a cooperative attitude, and *wa*. Economics will come later. If things have gone well on this first day, future meetings will be scheduled.

Other minor considerations: Business cards will be required and small gifts (exchanged before leaving the offices) will be appropriate. For meetings in the United States, setting and formality will be marginally less important for operational-level executives, but not much less. Particularly when the Japanese firm is the one courted, more of a Japanese approach— longer periods of nontask sounding including dinner at a very good restaurant or at your home—is advised.

TASK-RELATED EXCHANGE OF INFORMATION

Only after the nontask sounding is complete and the *wa* is established should business be introduced. American executives are advised to let the Japanese signal when the task-related exchange of information should start. Typically, such signals will be given after tea or coffee has been served and may include a statement such as, "Can you tell me more about your company?" or, "Tell me, what has brought you to Japan?"

A task-related exchange of information implies a two-way communication process. However, it has been the observation of several authors that when Americans meet Japanese across the negotiation table, the information flow is unidirectional—from the American side to the Japanese. In the paragraphs to follow we will recommend actions for American bargainers that will help them to manage efficiently the give-*and*-take of information.

Giving Information

The most obvious problem associated with providing information to Japanese clients will be the language. It is true that many more Japanese executives can speak and understand English than Americans Japanese. English is, after all, the international language of business and technology. However, Americans should be careful of misunderstandings arising from the Japanese side's limited knowledge of English. Confusion can result when Japanese executives, because of politeness, indicate they understand when in fact they do not. When any doubt exists Americans should use visual media (slides and brochures) and provide copious written support materials and an interpreter if the Japanese side hasn't provided one. Even when the Japanese side does provide an interpreter, there may be critical stages of the negotiations when your own interpreter should be included on your negotiation team.

In the *Harvard Business Review*, Howard Van Zandt made several recommendations regarding the use of interpreters in business negotiations. However, now higher quality interpreters are available and a few of his recommendations simply don't apply. (Box 8.3 includes all of his recommendations and our dissenting comments.) If interpreter problems do surface during your negotiations you should make a change. But be certain the replacement is a definite improvement. More than one interpreter change can cause serious disruptions of the negotiations. Finally, you should be aware that interpreters are available who specialize in business, engineering, or government, and an appropriate one should be selected for your negotiation.

In response to complaints by numerous U.S. telecommunications suppliers, Nippon Telephone and Telegraph (NTT) opened a purchasing office in New York City. NTT also agreed to accept proposals in English for the first time, thus seemingly opening the door a bit wider for American participation in the fast growing telecommunications market in Japan. However, imagine for a moment that you are a Japanese executive, trying to choose between two competitive offerings. One is written in your native language, and the other is written in a foreign language. Which proposal will you "like" better? Which company will you choose as a vendor? Proposals for Japanese clients should be written in the Japanese language. Perhaps you can get by with technical or engineering details in English, but the sections that will be reviewed and evaluated by upper Japanese management must be written in their native language. We've heard more than once that translation of documents is expensive and takes time. But would you rather have your client spending his time reading your proposal in his second language? And how expensive is losing your next deal to a more conscientious competitor?

Once you are comfortable with the language situation, you can turn your attention to more subtle aspects of giving information to the Japanese. The first of these has to do with the order of presentation. In the United States we tend to say what we want and explain the reasons behind our request only if necessary. That's why the task-related exchange of information goes so quickly. This isn't the Japanese way. Recall the description of the *naniwabushi* in chapter 4—long explanation followed by the request followed by expressions of sorrow for the request. Given this mode of operation, it is

BOX 8.3. VAN ZANDT'S RECOMMENDATIONS REGARDING INTERPRETERS (AMENDED BY AUTHORS)

1. Brief the interpreter in advance about the subject and give him a copy of the presentation to study and discuss.
2. Speak loudly, clearly, and slowly. (Some Americans try to talk with a cigar in the mouth—an egregious mistake.)
3. Avoid little-known words, such as "arcane," "heuristic," or "buncombe."
4. Maintain a pleasant attitude.
5. Explain each major idea in two or three different ways, as the point may be lost if discussed only once.
6. Do not talk more than a minute or two without giving the interpreter a chance to speak.
7. While talking, allow the interpreter time to make notes of what is being said.
8. Assume that all numbers over 10,000 my be mistranslated. Repeat them carefully and write them down for all to see. The Japanese system of counting large sums is so different from that of the West that errors frequently occur. Also, the number billion should be avoided, as it means 1,000,000,000,000 in Europe, and 1,000,000,000 in the United States.
9. Do not lose confidence if the interpreter uses a dictionary. No one is likely to have a vocabulary of 40,000 words in each of two languages, and a dictionary is often essential.
9. (Amended) We disagree. Having to use a dictionary is a sign of potentially serious problems.
10. Permit the interpreter to spend as much time as needed in clarifying points whose meanings are obscure.
10. (Amended) If the interpreter is spending more time than you in talking, then he is doing more than translating. This may help or hurt you.
11. Do not interrupt the interpreter as he translates. Interrupting causes many misunderstandings, usually.
12. Do not jump to conclusions, as Japanese ways of doing things are often different from what foreigners expect.
13. Avoid long sentences, double negatives, or the use of negative wordings of a sentence when a positive form could be used.
14. Don't use slang terms, as, for example, "If you will let me have half a 'G' at six bits a piece, it'll be gung ho with me." Rather, state simply, "I want 500 at 75 cents each."
15. Avoid superfluous words. Your point may be lost if wrapped up in generalities.
16. Try to be as expressive as possible by using movements of hands, eyes, lips, shoulders, and head to supplement words.
17. During meetings, write out the main points discussed; in this way both parties can double-check their understanding.

18. After meetings, confirm in writing what has been agreed to.
19. Don't expect an interpreter to work for over an hour or two without a rest period. His work is exhausting and a nervous strain.
20. Consider using two if interpreting is to last a whole day or into the evening, so that when one tires the other can take over.
20. (Amended) This is only true in cases of "simultaneous" translation, as opposed to the usual "consecutive" translation used in most business transactions.
21. Don't be suspicious if a speaker talks for five minutes and the interpreter covers it in half a minute. The speaker may have been wordy.
21. (Amended) Be suspicious. This can be a sign that the interpreter is fatigued or simply not paying attention.
22. Be understanding if it develops that the interpreter has made a mistake. It is almost impossible to avoid making some errors, because Japanese and European languages are so dissimilar.
22. (Amended) Mistakes are a sign of the interpreter's incompetence. Often in major negotiations, minor mistakes can result in the breakdown of the negotiation.
23. Be sure the Japanese are given all the time they want to tell their side of the story. If they hesitate, ask the interpreter for advice on what next to say or do.

Source: Howard Van Zandt, "How to Negotiate in Japan," *Harvard Business Review* (November–December 1970): 45–56.

not surprising to hear the American executive's complaint about the thousands of questions the Japanese ask. The Japanese expect long explanations. Thus, Americans should be prepared with detailed information to back up their proposal. Appropriate technical experts should be included on negotiation teams; their contribution will be required. Finally, we recommend a Japanese style of presentation. Background and explanations should be presented first, and only toward the end should the actual request or proposal be made. Such an approach will take longer, but it will obtain better results with Japanese clients.

It should be noted that we do not recommend the third step of *naniwabushi*, the *urei*. Such an expression of sorrow requires subtle nuances and special circumstances to be effective. *Urei* attempted by even the most informed and experienced American negotiators will appear completely out of context and, therefore, insincere. In any case, most American negotiators would view such behavior as going too far.

Another reason for the many questions the Japanese ask has to do with their consensus decision-making style. Several people on their side may ask for the same information or explanation. Most Americans find this repetitive questioning irritating and even insulting: "Didn't they believe me the first time?" But such tactics should be viewed in light of the Japanese decision-making process, in which everyone must be convinced. You should also realize that interrogation may be a tactic to make sure your explanation holds up under close scrutiny. Therefore, we recommend patience and the kind of detailed preparations necessary to prevent inconsistent answers.

Clearly then, communicating your bargaining position, your company's needs and preferences, will take longer in Japan. Language problems and required explanations will require more meetings, involving more of your people (technical experts) and more of theirs. We strongly recommend patience with this process and the anticipation of increased time and money spent at this stage. But at some point American bargainers will have to terminate such questioning. While answering a thousand questions may be tedious but necessary, answering two thousand questions may not be productive. We suggest the following tactics for ending the Japanese side's questions:

1. Summarize your previous answer after such statements as the following: "I already gave that information to Suzuki-san yesterday, but to reiterate . . . ," or, "That's the same question we talked about before, but I'll go over it again."
2. Offer to write down the requested information so that it may be shared with all concerned Japanese executives.
3. Generally, a repeated question should be answered the second time in about three minutes. The third time it's asked the answer should be a one-minute summary. If the same question is asked a fourth time, it's probably a persuasive tactic and not information gathering. The appropriate response is then silence or a change of subject.

You should recognize one other thing about Japanese questions. The Japanese understand, and even expect, that some questions cannot be answered. But they will go ahead and ask them anyway. This is in sharp contrast to the American practice of only asking questions that will be answered. That is, if an American manager asks a question and doesn't get an answer, he often gets upset. This is not necessarily the case with the Japanese.

We have heard of Japanese bargainers in Tokyo asking their New York office to verify price quotes with your New York office. In Japan, as well as in the United States, this is pushing the questioning too far. We suggest expression of your company's irritation through your informal communication channel or, if necessary, at the table using a more tactful approach such as, "Let's consolidate our channels of communication and not involve my

New York office. I am representing my firm here and what New York has to say doesn't pertain."

Finally, we recommend that American bargainers guard against the tendency of making concessions during this exchange of information. We have found that often American negotiators, impatient with the process, will actually make concessions during this second stage of negotiations, before they have even determined the Japanese negotiator's position, needs, and interests. It will take great patience indeed to avoid the natural urge to get to the third stage, persuasion, by making concessions in the hopes that the Japanese will reciprocate.

Getting Information

Hopefully, your Japanese clients will be courting your business. In such a situation they will be the ones making proposals and supplying you with more information than you probably want. But should your firm be initiating the contact or trying to make the sale, expect great difficulties getting feedback to your proposals. If you ask a group of Japanese executives what they think of your price quote and proposal, they will invariably say, "Oh, it looks fine." They will respond in such a manner even if they think it stinks.

Let's review the reasons behind this seemingly unfathomable behavior. The first regards consensus decision making. No Japanese, especially the boss, feels qualified to speak for the group before a consensus has been reached. Second, the Japanese executive wishes to maintain the *wa*; from his point of view a negative, albeit honest, answer at the negotiation would disrupt the harmony established. Finally, American executives are unable to read the subtle, nonverbal, negative cues that accompany the "Oh, it looks fine." Another Japanese executive would read the nonverbal message that "it stinks," but even the most experienced Americans won't be able to process this implied message.

Just as Japanese executives speak a different language, their nonverbal behaviors also have different meanings. We have found in both simulated and real business negotiations that the Japanese conversational style includes much less eye contact than does the American one. When Americans bargain with the Japanese this difference seems to cause problems for both sides. Japanese report discomfort at the "aggressive staring" of the Americans. Americans suggest that something must be wrong because the Japanese "won't look me in the eye." Eye contact and eye movements, ordinarily a source of information about others' feelings, don't communicate well across cultural barriers.

In the United States, another key source of information regarding your client's reaction to your proposals is his or her facial expression. Most of us process such information unconsciously, but we all do pay attention to this channel. Indeed, many American executives report great frustration because of the Japanese negotiator's "poker face." However, we have found by studying videotapes of simulated business negotiations that there appears to be little difference between Japanese and Americans in the quantity of facial expressions. The "inscrutability" of the former has more to do with the timing and cultural rules for facial expressions than with intentionally trying to keep negotiating partners in the dark. (See box 8.4 for one author's explanation of such rules for facial expressions in Japan.)

These are the reasons why in our interviews we have heard very experienced Americans report, "I make deals all over the world. And everywhere I go I can pretty much tell where I stand with my clients. Everywhere, that is, except Japan." So, how can Americans get at the *honne*, or true mind of the Japanese negotiators? The *tatemae* (official stance) of the negotiation table often isn't very helpful. The only way Americans can be privy to the *honne* is through an informal channel of communication. And this informal chan-

BOX 8.4. THE JAPANESE SMILE

A Japanese can smile in the face of death, and usually does. . . . There is neither defiance nor hypocrisy in the smile; nor is it to be confounded with that smile of sickly resignation which we are apt to associate with weakness of character. It is an elaborate and long cultivated etiquette. It is also a silent language. But any effort to interpret it according to Western notions of physiognomical expression would [not be successful].

[The] first impression is, in most cases, wonderfully pleasant. The Japanese smile at first charms. It is only at a later day, when one has observed the same smile under extraordinary circumstances—in moments of pain, shame, disappointment—that one becomes suspicious of it. Its apparent inopportuneness may even, on certain occasions, cause violent anger. . . . The Japanese child is born with this happy tendency, which is fostered through all the period of home education. . . . The smile is taught like the bow; like the prostration; . . . But the smile is to be used upon all pleasant occasions, when speaking to a superior or to an equal, and even upon occasions which are not pleasant; it is part of deportment. The most agreeable face is the smiling face; and to present always the most agreeable face possible to parents, relatives, teachers, friends, well-wishers, is a rule of life. . . . Even though the heart is breaking, it is a social duty to smile bravely.

Source: Lafcadio Hearn, *Glimpses of Unfamiliar Japan* (Boston: Houghton Mifflin, 1894), 656–683.

nel can only be established between and through the lowest levels of the negotiation teams. This is perhaps the primary reason for including lower level executives on your negotiation team. It will be almost impossible for one American to handle both the formal communication at the negotiation table and the informal communications after hours.

Management of this informal channel of communication will be critical for efficient and successful negotiations, and therefore an important yet delicate undertaking. Your lowest-level bargainer should be assigned the task of establishing a relationship of trust with an operational-level manager on the Japanese side during the nontask sounding activities. The *shinyo* is critical. During the task-related exchange of information, indeed throughout the negotiations, time should be spent after hours nurturing this relationship. Such a relationship can be initiated by simply asking the selected Japanese executive out for a drink, "to solve our companies' problems." The Japanese side will also be looking to open such a channel of communication, and the American side should be alert for such overtures.

At first, all this may appear a bit sneaky and even unethical to the American reader. It seems the opposite of laying your cards on the table. But it makes perfect sense from the Japanese perspective. The *honne* can be communicated without risk through a low-level executive, who makes no commitments as he or she speaks and who saves the face of the American managers and preserves the *wa* between the higher-level negotiators. This may seem a monumental waste of time to an American, but we have learned through experience that negotiations with Japanese proceed smoothly when this informal channel of communication is managed properly.

Once this informal channel of communication has been opened, it will be used for aggressive persuasive tactics and for assessing how each side really feels about the involved proposals and the arguments. Such information will be communicated after hours over drinks, in restaurants and *izakaya* (pubs). It will emanate from and be transmitted to all members of the negotiation team. But despite the fact that everyone knows about this "behind-the-scenes" channel of communication, it is critical that it remain just that. Any reference to such a channel (e.g., "Suzuki-san told Mr. Smith last night that . . .") will lead to immediate dismissal of Suzuki-san from the negotiations and, thus, elimination of the "leak."

As an example of how important this informal channel can be, we tell the following story. One large American firm that we have worked with sought to acquire a smaller Japanese firm. Talks between executives of the two companies had not been fruitful. Although the Japanese executives showed initial interest in the deal, and the American firm had a final proposal ready, the Japanese seemed hesitant. The American side decided on a wait-and-see strategy and nothing happened for almost six months. Then a lower-level manager of the American firm received a call from an acquaintance in the Japanese firm, asking for an appointment. Over a drink the Japanese explained why there were delays: "I have something to tell you that just couldn't be talked about by my boss to your boss. . . ." And he went on to explain the primary problems from the Japanese point of view—the acquisition price and the renaming of the company. Once out in the "open," the companies were able to deal with both issues. But the Japanese side simply felt it inappropriate to use a formal communication channel at the negotiation table to voice such objections to a higher-status buyer and potential owner.

One final point should be made about the task-related exchange of information. Often, one negotiation team member will be assigned note-taking responsibilities only. Another common practice is to tape-record meetings, ordinarily with the other side's permission. The intent is to have the tapes available for careful review later. Americans may also wish to tape the meetings. At the very least notes should be taken during the meeting. We have found it useful to keep a tally of the topics of Japanese questions. That is, if the Japanese ask about delivery schedules six times and service contracts only twice, then they are signaling the importance of delivery.

In the event that an informal channel of communication cannot be established between lower-level members of each firm's negotiation team, then the *shokai-sha* or *chukai-sha* can be used in such a way. Perhaps they will be able to set up the necessary relationship by inviting the two appropriate lower-level executives out for dinner. However, this option should be exercised only as a last resort because of the added communication problems associated with a less involved third party and because it is best to keep *shokai-sha* and *chukai-sha* in reserve. That is, if *shokai-sha* and *chukai-sha* fail, then the business IS over.

PERSUASION

We hope that it is evident from the above discussion that in Japan there is not a clear separation of the task-related exchange of information and persuasion. The two stages tend to blend together as each side more clearly defines and refines its needs and preferences. So much time is spent at this task-related exchange of information that little is left to "argue" about during the persuasion stage. Indeed, Robert March reports that Japanese negotiators tend to prepare for negotiations in a way very different from Americans:

> They developed defensive arguments with no consideration of persuading or selling or converting the other side. Nor did they consider what the other side

might be thinking or offering, nor of anticipated strategies, nor of any concession strategies.

A strong consensus was reached based on the arguments supporting their
position after the leader had reviewed these and everyone had noted them
down. There was strong group cohesion.

However, from the American perspective persuasion is the heart of a negotiation. In America we have a wide range of persuasive tactics that can be
and often are employed to change our clients' minds. Researchers at the Kel-
logg School of Business at Northwestern University have come up with a list
of such persuasive tactics (see table 8.1).

We have observed Americans using all such persuasive tactics. Perhaps the
most interesting example of differing reactions of Japanese and Americans
is in the use of "veiled" threats. We know of one American firm putting a
"dog" business unit up for sale. They solicited bids from several American
buyers whom they thought might be interested. However, only one
takeover proposal was received. When the managers from the one interested company called on the executive in charge of the sale, they met in the
executive's office. When substantive discussions began, that executive was
careful to search through what appeared to be a stack of competitive proposals on his desk for the pertinent proposal. Thus, a subtle bluff or threat
was made, "If you don't make some concessions, we'll talk to someone
else." Those imaginary competitive proposals were never discussed, but the
buyer did make concessions.

Be aware that the use of some of these tactics with Japanese clients would
signal the end of bargaining. During a similar acquisition negotiation one
of our Japanese clients called on an executive vice president of the American selling firm. The American "happened" to have a letter from another
possible buyer (the colorful logo on the letterhead was easily recognizable)
on his desk. Another veiled threat, a bluff, or an accident? We don't know.
Neither the letter nor other buyers were discussed. We do know, however,
that the Japanese interpreted the letter on the desk as a threat and thereafter
refused to consider dealing with that American company. Even a veiled
threat is too strong a tactic to use with Japanese buyers.

Another important factor in Japan is the context in which specific tactics
are used. Box 8.5 presents a list of persuasive tactics appropriate in Japan.
At the negotiation table, bargainers are limited to the use of questions, self-
disclosures, and other positive influence behaviors. Aggressive influence
tactics, which can only be used by negotiators in higher power positions,
should be communicated through the low-level, informal communication
channel. And even then, only subtle and indirect threats, commands, and
so on, are appropriate. So this informal channel of communication is doubly important from the American perspective. First, it provides a method of

Table 8.1. Persuasive Tactics

Positive Influence Tactics	Aggressive Influence Tactics	Information Exchange Tactics
Promise A statement in which the source indicates his or her intention to provide the target with a reinforcing consequence, which the source anticipates the target will evaluate as pleasant, positive, or rewarding. "If you can deliver the equipment by June 1, we will make another order right away."	**Threat** Same as promise, except that the reinforcing consequences are thought to be noxious, unpleasant, or punishing. "If you insist on those terms, we will have to find another suitor for our company."	**Commitment** A statement by the source to the effect that his future bids will not go below or above a certain level. "We will deliver the equipment within three months, and at the price we originally quoted."
Recommendation A statement in which the source predicts that a pleasant environmental consequence will occur to the target. Its occurrence is not under the source's control. "If you keep the company name after the acquisition, then your present customers will stay with the company."	**Warning** Same as recommendation, except that the consequences are thought to be unpleasant. "If we can't get together at this stage, few other companies will be interested in your proposal."	**Self-Disclosure** A statement in which the source reveals information about itself. "My company now requires an ROI of at least 15 percent during the first year."
Reward A statement by the source that is thought to create pleasant consequences for the target. "This negotiation is progressing smoothly because you have prepared well."	**Punishment** Same as reward, except that the consequences are thought to be unpleasant. "You can't possibly mean that. Only a fool would ask for such a high price."	
Positive Normative Appeal A statement in which the source indicates that the target's past, present, or future behavior was or will be in conformity with social norms. "Lowering your price in light of the new information will	**Negative Normative Appeal** Same as positive normative appeal, except that the target's behavior is in violation of social norms.	

Positive Influence Tactics	Aggressive Influence Tactics	Information Exchange Tactics
demonstrate your interest in good principles of business.	Command A statement in which the "source suggests that the target perform a certain behavior. "It's your turn to make a counteroffer."	Question A statement in which the source asks the target to reveal information about itself. "Why are you asking for such a high royalty payment?"

more accurately reading Japanese clients, and, second, it makes available to American bargainers persuasive tactics that would be completely inappropriate during the formal talks.

To sum up, if an impasse is reached with Japanese clients, rather than trying to persuade in the usual American manner, we recommend use of the following nine persuasive tactics, in the following order and in the following circumstances:

1. Ask more questions. We feel that the single most important advice we can give is to use questions as a persuasive tactic. This is true not only in Japan, but anywhere in the world, including the United States. In his book, *The Negotiating Game*, Chester Karrass suggests that sometimes it's "smart to be a little bit dumb" in business negotiations. Ask the same questions more than once—"I didn't completely understand what you meant. Can you please explain that again?" If your clients or

---

BOX 8.5. PERSUASIVE TACTICS APPROPRIATE FOR NEGOTIATIONS WITH THE JAPANESE

At the Negotiation Table
1. Questions
2. Self-disclosures
3. Positive influence tactics
4. Silence
5. Change of subject
6. Recesses and delays
7. Concessions and commitments

Informal Channels and Buyers Only
1. Aggressive influence tactics

potential business partners have good answers, then it's perhaps best if you compromise on the issue. But often, under close scrutiny, their answers aren't very good. And with such a weak position exposed they will be obligated to concede. Therefore, questions can elicit key information and can be powerful persuasive devices.

2. Reexplain your company's situation, needs, and preferences.

3. Use other positive influence tactics.

4. If you are still not satisfied with their response, try silence. Let them think about it and give them an opportunity to change their position. However, you should recognize that the Japanese are the world's experts at the use of silence. If silence is a tactic you find difficult to use, you should at least be aware that your Japanese clients will use it frequently.

5. If tactics 1 through 4 produce no concessions, it will be time to change the subject or call a recess or for a change of venue, and put to work the informal communication channel. But rather than going directly to the more aggressive tactics, we recommend repeating the first four tactics. The questions and explanations may expose new information or objections that couldn't be broached at the negotiation table. Recently we have seen more Americans and Japanese asking for breaks in face-to-face meetings. This is a good trend. We know from our studies of negotiations as creative activities that breaks, particularly those that allow for contemplation of problems overnight, often result in new perspectives on problems and novel solutions wherein both sides benefit.

6. Aggressive influence tactics may be used in negotiations with Japanese only at great risk and in special circumstances. First, they should only be used via the informal channel, and even then they should be used in the most indirect manner possible. Rather than saying, "If your company can't lower its price, then we'll go to another supplier," it would be better to say, "Lower prices on the part of your company would go a long way toward our not having to consider other options available to us." Second, they should be used only when the American company is clearly in the stronger position. Even in these two circumstances, use of such aggressive persuasive tactics will damage the *wa*, which may in the long run be to your company's disadvantage. If power relations ever shift, the Japanese will be quick to exploit the change in events. However, if the American side exercises restraint and maintains the *wa*, then if and when power relations shift, the Japanese side will consider the American company's interests.

This latter point is difficult for most Americans to believe. But we have witnessed Japanese executives behave in this way several times. For example, several years ago International Multi-Food Company

(IMFC) sold franchise rights for a Mr. Donut chain to Duskin, Ltd. in Japan. Initially, IMFC provided the know-how (operations and marketing) for a successful venture in Japan. Since then, Duskin has turned Mr. Donut into the largest doughnut chain in Japan. Indeed, the franchise revenues from Duskin now exceed the total profits IMFC makes from its U.S. operations. When IMFC executives later met with Duskin to renegotiate the franchise agreement, they anticipated substantial changes in the agreement to reflect the change in power relations. An American franchisee would certainly demand such an adjustment. However, because IMFC had been careful to maintain *wa* with the Japanese clients initially, the president of Duskin suggested only minor revisions to the agreement.

7. If tactics 1 through 6 have not produced Japanese concessions, we suggest the use of time to enable them to consider new information and to reach a consensus (#5 above is relevant here as well). The Japanese rarely make concessions immediately following persuasive appeals because everyone involved in the decision must be consulted and must agree. Unfortunately, time is perhaps the most difficult tactic for American bargainers to use. We're in a hurry to solve the problem and settle the deal. "Letting things hang" goes against our nature. But it may be necessary. And hopefully, they will run into their time limits before you run into yours. Also, use of this tactic will require the cooperation and understanding of your home office.

   It should be remembered that the Japanese are skilled in the use of time as a persuasive tactic. Consensus decision making and the long-term approach to business deals seems to enhance the effectiveness of tactical delays for Japanese bargaining with Americans.

8. The next persuasive tactic to use is asking the *chukai-sha* or *shokai-sha* to arbitrate your differences. Let them call your clients and meet as a go-between. We have seen *chukai-sha* successfully settle otherwise irreconcilable differences. For example, a major West Coast retailer contacted an American accounting firm for *shokai-sha* services. They wished to be introduced to a Japanese sushi-bar chain that would participate in a "Japan Fair" promotion they had planned for several of their southern California stores. The *shokai-sha* introduced the vice president of the retail chain to the appropriate executives of one of Japan's largest sushi chains and negotiations began. However, the Japanese seemed hesitant despite the several advantages of participation offered by the American company. They considered the expense of sending operational managers to the United States not worth the benefits of participation. So the somewhat exasperated American executives requested *chukai-sha* services. The *shokai-sha/chukai-sha* acted as a mediator and presented again the benefits of the proposal-promotion and market research in

the United States and use of the trip to Los Angeles as a reward for employees. Through the persuasive efforts of *chukai-sha* the deal was finally struck. However, serious consideration should be given to making concessions yourself before calling in *chukai-sha*. Third-party
arbitration will ordinarily work only once.

9. Finally, if all else fails, it may be necessary to bring together the top executives of the two companies in the hope of stimulating more cooperation. However, such a tactic may fail, particularly if negative influence tactics have been used in the past. A refusal at this stage means
   the business is finished.

To conclude our discussion of persuasive tactics, we want to emphasize
the importance of our recommendations. A mistake at this stage, even a minor one, can have major consequences for your Japanese business. American managers will have to be doubly conscientious to avoid blunders here
because the Japanese style of persuasion is so different and apparently cum-
bersome. Remember that the Japanese are looking to establish a long-term
business relationship of mutual benefit. Threats and the like don't fit into
their understanding of how such a relationship should work. You should
also recognize that we are recommending adoption of a Japanese approach
to persuasion when bargaining with Japanese clients and business partners.
We realize it takes longer, but in the end you and your company will benefit by such an approach. Finally, smart American negotiators will anticipate
the Japanese use of the nine persuasive tactics just described.

Finally, see box 8.6 for Jim Hodgson's views about diplomatic persuasion.

CONCESSIONS AND AGREEMENT

The final stage of business negotiations involves concessions, building toward agreement. Negotiation requires compromise. Usually, both sides give
up something to get even more. But the approach used for compromise dif-
fers on each side of the Pacific.

American managers report great difficulties in measuring progress. After
all, in America you're half done when half the issues are settled. But in Japan
nothing seems to get settled. Then, surprise, you're done. In Richard Nisbett's wonderful book, *The Geography of Thought*,[1] he distinguishes between
Western and Eastern thinking patterns. That is, Americans tend to break up
a complex problem into pieces, solve each, and the final solution becomes
a sequence of smaller solutions. Japanese will take a more comprehensive
approach, discussing all issues at once and jumping around among the various issues, before reaching an agreement on all simultaneously.

BOX 8.6. DIPLOMATIC INSIGHTS ON PERSUASION: THREE APPROACHES TO PERSUASION

Confrontation

The confrontation approach is brutally direct. Quite simply it involves using whatever power leverage you have to the maximum in an endeavor to bring the other party around to your demands. This stance is normally employed only when it is expected that no relationship with the party across the table will exist following the negotiation.

Compromise

Compromise reflects a "split the difference" approach to all issues at stake in the negotiations. It has the virtue of often producing agreement, but it leaves both parties dissatisfied, usually just awaiting the next negotiating session when they anticipate being able to force stronger concessions. It does little to enhance goodwill between the parties.

Integration

Integration as a concept is less well understood, though it is often put into practice. It involves a careful mutual examination of the common interests that exist between the parties and then settling issues in a way that best reflects the commonality of those interests. At times, surprisingly, all matters at issue can be resolved with this approach. Admittedly, however, more often an issue or two will lack real commonality of interest. When this happens, compromises may prove necessary, but only compromises on such issues. As a general approach, I have found this integration concept to be exceptionally useful. The very process of mutual examination of common interests on issues serves to soften negative attitudes, to dispel what may have been an adversarial climate, and to create a spirit of willingness to compromise fairly on what issues remain. I have found most successful negotiators employ something like this process, even if they are unfamiliar with its philosophical underpinnings. It passes the ultimate pragmatic test—it works.

Leave Something on the Table

In most business negotiations there exists a further objective beyond merely reaching an agreement. The agreement should be reached in such a way as to assure a continuing good relationship between the parties. Amity is not served by driving the other fellow to the wall. It may even prove wise on occasion, as is said, "to leave something on the table," particularly when the other fellow needs that something worse than you do. A fund of goodwill can often be bought with a little grace in such circumstances.

(continued)

BOX 8.6. DIPLOMATIC INSIGHTS ON PERSUASION: THREE APPROACHES TO PERSUASION (*continued*)

Don't Threaten

Experience has taught me that probably the worst mistake negotiators can make is this: they try to use power they don't have. Bluffing may have its place at the poker table, but it can prove ruinous at the bargaining table. Idle threats will probably turn out to be just that—idle. Further, never make a proposal you would not be prepared to live with. I have seen such proposals made in the considered belief that they would never be accepted. When, strangely enough, they were accepted, the result was chagrin, a bargaining gambit exposed, and an objective sacrificed.

Keep Reserve

Next, always try to keep something in reserve, especially when engaged in critical negotiations. Have available alternate courses of action. Should you find your negotiation stuck on dead center, don't just continue to rehash the same old stuff. Introduce a new element such as calling in new participants from either side or both sides, creating new subcommittees, or even convening at another physical site. Surprisingly, even though such a move may seem to make no particular sense, it can, at times, trigger an attitudinal change or provide a face-saving reason for a position change by one or both parties.

Two negative consequences occur because of such differences: (1) Americans often become exasperated, even angry, because the Japanese seem to be bringing up issues they thought to be already settled ("Why are you asking about delivery again?); and (2) often Americans make unnecessary concessions right before agreements are announced by the Japanese. In the latter case, we know of an American retail goods buyer traveling to Japan to buy six different consumer products for a large chain of discount department stores on the West Coast. He told us that negotiations for his first purchase took an entire week. In the United States, such a purchase would be consummated in an afternoon. So by his calculations, he expected to have to spend six weeks in Japan to complete his purchases. He considered raising his purchase prices to try to move things along faster. But before he was able to make such a concession, the Japanese quickly agreed on the other five products in just three days. This particular businessman was, by his own admission, lucky in his first encounter with Japanese bargainers.

This American businessman's near blunder reflects more than just a difference in decision-making style as Nisbett describes above. More fundamentally, American and Japanese goals for negotiations are different as well. That is, to the American, a business negotiation is a problem-solving activity, the best deal for both parties being the solution. To a Japanese businessperson, a business negotiation is a time to develop a business relationship with the goal of long-term mutual benefit. The economic issues are the context, not the content, of the talks. Thus, settling any one issue really isn't important. Such details will take care of themselves once a viable, harmonious business relationship is established. And, as happened in the case of our retail goods buyer, once the relationship was established—signaled by the first agreement—the other "details" were settled quickly.

American bargainers in Japan should expect this holistic approach and be prepared to discuss all issues simultaneously and in an apparently haphazard order. Progress in the talks should not be measured by how many issues have been settled. Rather, Americans must try to gauge the quality of the business relationship. Important signals of progress will be:

1. Higher level Japanese executives being included in the discussions
2. Their questions beginning to focus on specific areas of the deal
3. A softening of their attitudes and position on some of the issues "Let us take some time to study this issue. . . ."
4. At the negotiation table, increased talk among themselves in Japanese, which may often mean they're trying to decide something
5. Increased bargaining and use of the lower level, informal channel of communication

In chapter 7 we discussed the importance of a documented concession strategy prepared before negotiations begin. Americans need to follow such strategies with care. Trading concessions with Japanese bargainers will not work because they view nothing to be settled until everything is settled. We advise making no concession until all issues and interests have been exposed and fully discussed. Then concessions should be made, on minor issues first, to help establish the relationship.

Concessions should not be decided upon at the negotiation table. Rather, Americans are advised to reconsider each concession away from the social pressure of the formal negotiations. This again is a Japanese practice. Because of the nature of the consensus decision making, you will find the Japanese having to "check with the home office." It is a negotiation practice that Americans will do well emulating, particularly in Japan. Having limited authority can be an important check on concession making.

MINOR DISTRACTIONS

Before closing our discussion of the process of business negotiations, it is important to mention briefly three Japanese behaviors that will seem rude to American bargainers but are nothing more than common habits for Japanese executives. First, the Japanese will often break into side conversations in Japanese. Ordinarily, the purpose of this side conversation is clarification of something Americans have said. Second, often Japanese executives will enter or leave negotiations in the middle of your comments. This reflects their busy schedule and a different view of "meeting etiquette." Finally, it can be particularly disturbing to be talking to a group of Japanese and discover that one, perhaps even the senior executive, is "listening with his eyes shut." (This is the Japanese description for sleeping during meetings.) Again, this shouldn't be taken personally; it simply reflects a different view of appropriate behavior at meetings. Further, sleeping senior Japanese executives can also be signaling that they are comfortable with how things are going—if they are not comfortable, they will remain quite alert.

NOTE

1. Richard Nisbett's book, *The Geography of Thought* (New York: Free Press, 2003), is an important read for anyone involved in East/West commerce.

9

After Negotiations

Once verbal agreements have been reached it is time to consider what follows the negotiations. In the United States executives talk of "concluding business deals." In Japan executives speak of "establishing business relationships." We've already discussed how such differing views influence negotiation processes. Now we will turn to the subject of how they influence post-negotiation procedures.

CONTRACTS

Since the 2000 edition of our book, Japanese firms have pretty much embraced the American approach to written contracts. But, it is worthwhile to briefly review the Japanese perspective and practices from the end of the last century toward better understanding the background of their present policies.

Contracts between American firms are often longer than one hundred pages and include carefully worded clauses regarding every aspect of the agreement. American lawyers go to great lengths to protect their companies against all circumstances, contingencies, and actions of the other party (see box 9.1). In the contract presented in box 9.1, conditional phrases such as, "If . . .," "In the event . . .," and "Should . . .," were used more than fifty times. The best contracts are the ones so tightly written that the other party would not think of going to court to challenge any provision. Our adversarial system requires such contracts.

In Japan, as in most other countries, legal systems have not been depended upon to resolve disputes. Indeed, the term "disputes" doesn't reflect

BOX 9.1. EXCERPTS FROM
AN AMERICAN-STYLE CONTRACT

14.1

Should any circumstances preventing the complete or partial fulfillment by either of the parties of the obligations taken under this contract arise, namely: fire, floods, earthquake, typhoon, epidemics and other actions or force of nature, as well as war, military operations of any character, prohibitions of export or import, the time stipulated for the fulfillment of the obligations shall be extended for a period of equal to that during which such circumstances will remain in force.

14.2

If these circumstances continue for more than six months, each of the parties shall have the right to refuse in full or in part from any further execution of the obligations under this contract and in such case neither of the parties shall have the right for reimbursement of any possible damages by the other party.

14.3

The party for whom it becomes impossible to meet its obligations under this contract shall immediately advise the other party as regards the commencement and cessation of the circumstances preventing the fulfillment of its obligations.

14.4

The delayed advice of the commencement or cessation of *force majeure* circumstances exceeding 15 days will deprive the party of the right to refer to these circumstances at a later date.

how a business relationship should work. Each side should be concerned about the mutual benefits of the relationship, and therefore should consider the interests of the other. Consequently, in Japan written contracts traditionally were very short (two to three pages), were purposefully loosely written, and primarily contained comments on principles of the relationship (box 9.2). From the Japanese point of view, the American emphasis on tight contracts was tantamount to planning the divorce before the marriage. Klaus Schmidt puts it well:

> The Japanese are now used to complying with American contract requirements, but the underlying cultural differences still influence basic views about relationships and dispute handling. Japanese still feel that agreements require seasoning and maturity; as people work together, understandings become clearer

BOX 9.2. A SAMPLE TRADITIONAL
JAPANESE-STYLE CONTRACT

Article 1:

This agreement is made this 4th day of October 1989 between "A" located in Tokyo, and "B" located in Shibuya-ku Tokyo, to maintain mutual prosperity and coexistence and lasting amicable relations.

Article 2:

B shall continuously develop products based upon all of B's copyrighted materials or designs, and actively conduct sales of such products in Japan and other nations. A shall not, without B's consent, have third parties in the aforementioned areas develop products based upon any of A's copyrighted materials or designs, provided, however, that this limitation shall not apply to written materials.

Article 3:

B may register designs to protect B's rights against third parties.

Article 4:

The content and proofreading of the said copyrighted materials shall be the responsibility of A.

Article 5:

The costs required for the writing of the said copyrighted materials shall be borne by A, and the costs of producing, selling and advertising shall be borne by B.

Article 6:

As a royalty for the production of A's copyrighted materials and designs, B shall pay A 3 percent of the cost thereof.

Article 7:

With A's consent, B shall have the right to have third parties produce totally or partially products based upon A's copyrighted materials or designs. In such cases, B shall pay A the royalty set forth in Article 6.

Article 8:

In the event that either A or B suffers damages due to violation by the other party of the terms set forth in this contract, the first party may claim damages.

Article 9:

Two identical counterparts are to be prepared, signed and sealed to evidence this contract, whereupon each party shall retain one copy.

A: _____

B: _____

Source: Graham and James, Attorneys.

and increasingly advantageous to both partners. As relationships and conditions change, the assumption is that performance expectations ought to change. Flexibility, adjustment, and pragmatics, then, dominate the execution of long-term contracts.

Despite the relative sameness in legal documents, you must also realize that the legal system works much differently in the two countries. The best measure of this difference is reflected in the amazing statistics in figure 9.1. America is clearly the most legalistic society on the planet with more than 300 lawyers per 100,000 people, while Japan is one of the least with about 20 lawyers per 100,000. The Japanese government is trying to address this relative "shortage" of attorneys by opening sixty-eight Western-style law schools at universities across the country. They hope to double the numbers of home-grown attorneys by 2018. But, their ambitious goal to grow from the current 23,000 to 50,000 then will still not come close to the one million lawyers in America now.

Thus, contracts in Japan do not fulfill the same purposes as they do in the United States even though they appear quite similar in form.

So what form should a contract between a Japanese and an American firm take? There is no simple answer. It may have to be negotiated. It depends somewhat on the size and importance of the agreement and the size and experiences of the firms involved. Generally, larger deals justify the extra expense of including legal review by both Japanese and American lawyers. Large Japanese firms with histories of American contracts will understand

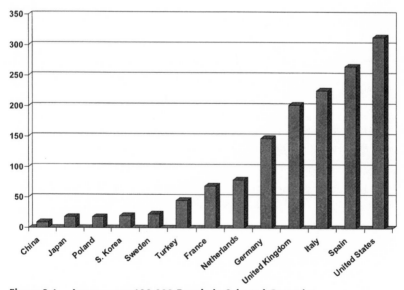

Figure 9.1. Lawyers per 100,000 People in Selected Countries

the Americans' need for detailed contracts. Some Japanese, recognizing the increasing frequency of litigation between U.S. and Japanese firms, will specify the American approach. It is the executives of smaller Japanese firms, inexperienced in the ways of Americans, who may become uncomfortable when faced with lengthy, fully detailed contracts. In these cases, it will be particularly important to explain the necessity of the legal review and detailed contract. However, you should realize that even with the most complete explanation not all Japanese executives will understand.

An American style contract will also cause considerable delays in signing. Japanese lawyers will tediously consider every detail. One rule of thumb suggests that every clause takes an entire day. Thus, something your legal counsel ordinarily reviews in three days will take considerably longer in Tokyo.

It is difficult for us to make general recommendations regarding contracts. Many American executives of even the largest firms have been satisfied with a "compromise" contract when strong, long-standing personal relationships are involved. Indeed, Ford and Nissan produced and sold the very successful Villager/Quest minivan, even though a final contract remained unsigned. But each case is different. It is important that you and your firm push for the kind of contract you feel is necessary. Also, your legal counsel should be consulted on this issue.

SIGNING CEREMONIES

Informality being a way of life in the United States, even the largest contracts between American firms are often sent through the mail for signature. Here, ceremony is considered a waste of time and money. The Japanese are again moving in the direction of Western standard practices and with increasing frequency we see contracts signed will little ceremony, by fax or electronically. But still, as you might guess, when a major agreement is reached with a Japanese client or partner, some Japanese will appreciate the top executives involved to meet and sign the contract with ceremony. We recommend American firms give consideration to this different tradition. Below, a contract signing ceremony of the traditional sort is described involving the CEO of Safeway Stores and the president of Allied Importing Company (AIC) of Japan.

The presidents of each of the four retailers that made up the AIC consortium and the president of the joint venture flew to San Francisco for the signing ceremony. They and their staffs arrived at Safeway headquarters in Oakland at 3:00 p.m. (chauffeured from San Francisco) and were escorted to a large meeting room on the executive floor. Once everyone had arrived, the American CEO made a brief speech welcoming all and expressing pleasure at the agreement. His Japanese counterpart also made a speech echoing the American's remarks and thanking the hard-working negotiators on both

sides. The four company presidents also came prepared to deliver similar remarks, but the staffs negotiated the agenda to preclude this sort of ceremony,
which surely would have been necessary in Japan.

After the greetings all six executives seated themselves, according to a pre-
arranged ranking, for the actual signing. Gold Cross pens with the Safeway
logo were supplied by the Safeway staff for the signing and to serve as gifts
for the Japanese executives. During the signing, pictures were taken by a
professional photographer and two members of the Japanese staff.

Following the signing, gifts were exchanged. The Safeway staff produced
decorative pieces of redwood, explaining that the gifts symbolized California and long-term business relations (California redwood is noted for its
durability)—a thoughtful choice. One minor problem did occur. After the
gift giving, the Japanese insisted on toasting the deal with champagne. So
Safeway staff members arranged for Christian Brothers champagne and
glasses. This was the very first time alcoholic beverages had been consumed
in the corporate offices at Safeway.

HEADQUARTERS' ASSESSMENT OF THE AGREEMENT

Often U.S. negotiators return to company headquarters with an agreement,
only to receive a mixed greeting. Executives at several companies have told
us, "The second half of the negotiation begins once I return to the home office." Headquarters, unaware of the requirements of business negotiations
in Japan, will ask, "What took so long?" Ordinarily, all compromises and
concessions have to be explained and justified in detail. Moreover, commitments requiring specific management actions must be delegated and ordered. All this can slow implementation and performance of the contract.
In the worst cases, when negotiator and home office communications have
been poor, negotiators have been required to renege and start over. When
this occurs, the Japanese client or partner will either bypass this executive,
who has lost face, and talk to those considered the real decision makers or
decline further discussion, thus ending the relationship.

In Japan, as you might expect, everyone is pleased with negotiation outcomes. No one is blamed for shortcomings in the deal because all concerned managers participated in the negotiating and in the final decision
making. Even when profit goals haven't been met; Japanese executives are
quick to emphasize their primary goal—establishing a harmonious, trusting business relationship. Moreover, because of the group decision making and participation, all the action provisions of the agreement are
quickly implemented.

It has been the experience of American firms that once the first deal has
been struck with a Japanese client or partner all successive negotiations proceed quickly. Therefore, it is generally not necessary to send a complete ne-

gotiation team when new issues are to be considered. Clearly, then, it is best to start with a small, relatively simple business proposal. Once the relationship has been established, substantial and complex negotiations will proceed more smoothly. This is the approach used by Japanese firms entering the United States, and it is a sensible strategy when American firms court Japanese business.

FOLLOW-UP COMMUNICATIONS

Just as personal considerations are more important during negotiations with Japanese clients, they are also important after the negotiations are concluded. Obviously, you will be in touch with your Japanese clients and partners regarding the business of the relationship. But it will be equally important to keep personal relationships warm.

A formal letter should be sent from your top executive to their top executive expressing happiness that the talks have been concluded successfully and confidence that the new relationship will be prosperous and long-lasting. But just as important as this formal correspondence will be short, more personal notes for each Japanese participant. It is a Japanese practice to include pictures of everyone to commemorate events and places associated with the negotiations—golf courses, factory visits, and so on. This provides the much-needed personal touch. The significance of these several follow-up notes is underscored by the recollection that all Japanese, top to bottom, were involved in the decision making.

Another standard Japanese practice will be frequent visits to your headquarters. Negotiators traveling to the United States for other purposes will take the time to stop off and visit. Even if their primary purpose for the trip is a new account in New York, they will come to see you in Omaha. Again, such visits serve to keep the relationship warm and are a form of nontask sounding. Where Americans are urged by AT&T to "keep in touch" via telephone, Japanese will not use such a medium for such a purpose. The telephone and e-mail in Japan tend to be used for business only. Therefore, personal comments should be reserved for face-to-face visits, letters, or occasional e-mails. For example, we often send personal notes to our Japanese business associates that include published accounts of political and economic issues in which they might be interested.

One final consideration is crucial when doing business with the Japanese. Do not switch executives managing your Japanese business relationships. In dealing with American clients this is not much of a problem. Here the economics of the business deal are more important than the personal relationships involved. Managers often shift positions within companies and between companies. But in Japan this is much less the case. Moreover, Japanese executives are given long-term (five to ten years) responsibility for managing intercompany relationships. After all, much was invested in building the personal relations that make business between the companies work smoothly. So when American companies switch key managers, Japanese clients get very nervous. Therefore, such shifts should be made with great care and should be accompanied by new efforts of nontask sounding and rapport building.

MODIFICATIONS TO AGREEMENTS

During the course of almost all business relationships changes occur in the environment and to either partner. For example, we know of a major Japanese trading company that agreed to purchase six million bushels of wheat at $1 per bushel. However, during the course of the contract the yen fell sharply in value relative to the dollar. The trading company had not budgeted for such a precipitous fluctuation in currency and was forced to renege. In such a situation in the United States, the conflicts arising from the changing circumstance would be settled through the use of direct and confrontational legal channels or, as is now more often the case, in arbitration.

In Japan, given the same set of changing circumstances, companies would ordinarily resolve the conflicts through conferral. Thus, Japanese contracts often include such wording as, "All items not found in this contract will be deliberated and decided upon in a spirit of honesty and trust." When differences can't be ironed out through simple conferral, then the next step is to express concerns through *shokai-sha* or *chukai-sha*, who hopefully can mediate a new understanding. Rarely will the confrontational and legal approaches be used in Japan, for they would destroy the harmony and trust required for continued business dealings. Even arbitration is viewed negatively in Japan. The Japanese Commercial Arbitration Association (JCAA) is designed both to educate executives on the option of arbitration and to conduct hearings in disputes. However, the process of arbitration is different in Japan. While in the United States the approach is usually one of confrontation, in Japan the overriding theme is compromise. The JCAA acts more like a *chukai-sha*, mediating and inducing settlements. Less than 1 percent of all cases brought to the JCAA end in binding arbitration.

Our recommendations are to include an international arbitration clause in your contract should conflicts arise. But even though such measures are included in the contract we suggest a Japanese approach to conflict resolution. That is, approach the dispute from a cooperative standpoint and talk with your Japanese client or partner. Given that you have maintained the *wa* and trust, and that you have an honest mutual interest in the deal, then such problems can usually be resolved through simple conferral. The next option is *chukai-sha* mediation. The last resort should be binding arbitration.

III

OTHER CRUCIAL TOPICS

10

Culture and Personality Issues

Some might suggest that the material we have presented in this book is the worst kind of stereotyping. Does everybody really act the same in Japan? Should we prejudge others based on their nationality or ethnic background? These are difficult but important questions, and we will attempt to answer them here.

THE DANGERS OF STEREOTYPING

There is danger in stereotyping American executives. The same caveat must be made about Japanese bargainers. Indeed, any Japanese businessperson would be quick to point out that personalities have a strong influence on bargaining styles. We certainly agree. In all dealings with Japanese clients you should consider the personalities of the bargainers involved.

Consider, for example, Akio Morita, founder of Sony Corporation—an unusual, albeit very successful, Japanese businessman. Before his death in 1999 he was described as outgoing, adventurous, and molded in the American entrepreneurial spirit. His top-down decision-making style was also well known. Such characteristics made him an outcast in Japanese industry initially, and his company concentrated on developing markets in the United States first. Soichiro Honda (founder and former chairman of Honda Motors), Isao Nakauchi (chairman of Daiei, once Japan's largest retailer) were also known for their "American" approach to management and negotiation. And perhaps most unusual is Masayoshi Son, the founder and CEO of SoftBank. (Please see his most non-stereotypical biography summarized in box 10.1.)

BOX 10.1. THE FASCINATING STORY
ABOUT AN ICON OF THE NEW JAPAN

Masayoshi Son is a second-generation Korean-Japanese who is the founder and current chief executive officer of Softbank Capital, and the chief executive officer of Softbank Mobile (the renamed Vodafone K.K.). According to *Forbes* magazine, his net worth is $5 billion and he is now the second richest person in Japan.

A third-generation son of a Korean family in Japan, Son was not considered a Japanese citizen until his family adopted the Japanese surname Yasumoto. He pursued his interests in business by securing a meeting with Japan McDonald's president Den Fujita. Taking his advice, Son began studying English and computer science.

At age 16, Son moved to California and finished high school while staying with friends and family in South San Francisco. He then enrolled at University of California, Berkeley, in which he majored in economics and took some computer science courses. Enamored by a microchip featured in a magazine, Son at age 19 became confident that computer technology would ignite the next commercial revolution.

Convinced that anything related to microchips could yield a fortune, Son decided to produce at least one entrepreneurial idea a day. He patented a translating device that he eventually sold to Sharp Electronics for $1 million. Applications of the patent include the Wizard series of Sharp PDAs.

Flush with cash, Son imported Space Invaders video arcade systems and dispersed them about the UC Berkeley campus. Soon after graduating from Berkeley with a BA in economics in 1980, Son started Unison in Oakland, California, which has since been bought by Kyocera.

In 1981, Son returned to Japan to start Softbank Capital in order to publish computer-related media and software. Despite discrimination and risk-averse bankers, Son secured a $1 million loan from Dai-Ichi Kangyo Bank. Unsuccessful at first, Son avoided failure when a computing goods retailer in Osaka accepted his offer to supply all the computer software and publications available—including his.

After a scandal-ridden Dai-Ichi Kangyo Bank was forced to cancel its loan, Son found new sources of capital from Industrial Bank of Japan. To compound problems, Son was hospitalized for hepatitis from 1984 to mid-1987. During this time, Son forged ties with Microsoft Japan and acquired a 25 percent stake in Novell Japan.

In the late 1980s, Son was still not a citizen of Japan. He had his Japanese fiancee change her last name to Son. After marrying her and legally assuming her new last name, Son became a Japanese citizen without having to adopt a Japanese surname, thus avoiding the intended naturalization laws for Korean-Japanese.

In 1994, Son lost to an investment bank in his attempt to buy Ziff-Davis. However, he won control of the Ziff-Davis tradeshows, which he purchased for $202 million. His luck changed in 1995, when he bought Ziff-Davis entirely for $2.1 billion (about $500 million more than he had offered the previous year).

By 1995, Son's Softbank had acquired 37 percent of Yahoo! and a controlling interest in E*Trade. By 1996, Softbank had purchased COMDEX for $900 million and Kingston Technology for $2.1 billion. In 1997, Softbank invested in a wide variety of Internet-related ventures.

A composite of Internet companies, Softbank became the Japanese powerhouse of the New Economy. At the peak of the "Dot-com bubble," Softbank was valued at about $200 billion—making Son's 38 percent stake worth almost $80 billion.

Softbank continued to absorb more companies despite their irrational valuations, which naturally Son considered cheap. Reducing his Yahoo! stake to 22.58 percent, Son was able to finance his myriad of acquisitions. One of the most prominent of these was Nippon Credit Bank, a once strong institution felled by bad loans.

Despite distractions such as Nippon Credit Bank (which subsequently changed its name to Aozora Bank), Son focused on becoming Japan's dominant broadband provider. By establishing Softbank Networks and BB Technologies, he set out to challenge Nippon Telegraph and Telephone, which had been slow to install broadband.

In 2006, Vodafone Group announced it had agreed to sell Vodafone K.K. to Softbank for approximately $12.5 billion. Since then the company has added subscribers but remains in third place behind NTT Docomo and KDDI. The acquisition has boosted revenues, but profits stumbled initially by two-thirds. The firm has most recently launched a Japanese version of MySpace with Rupert Murdoch's News Corp. Jack Ma, chief of China's Aliabab.com, has joined Softbank's board.

Sources: "Softbank: Receiving, Not Giving," *The Economist*, April 14, 2007; Kiyoe Minami and Justin Doebele, "Japan's 40 Richest," *Forbes Asia*, June 18, 2007, 37–40; Wikipedia contributors, "Masayoshi Son," *Wikipedia, The Free Encyclopedia*, http://en.wikipedia.org/w/index.php?title=Masayoshi_Son& oldid=137440141 (accessed March 14, 2007).

Further, we have witnessed unusual behavior from even the highest ranking Japanese officials. Kazuo Wakasugi, once director of MITI's trade policy bureau, has threatened to "trade with the communists" if Americans and Europeans refuse to trade. Wakasugi was immediately and roundly criticized for his remarks by other Japanese officials, including his boss at MITI.

Not only have we found personality differences to be important in our dealings with Japanese clients, we also have discovered apparent differences in negotiation style based on industry, expatriate experiences, and age.

NEGOTIATION STYLES DIFFER ACROSS INDUSTRIES IN JAPAN

We have found important differences in negotiation styles across industries in Japan. Perhaps the most dramatic comparison is that between the Japanese banking and retailing industries. Negotiations with Japanese bankers will almost always proceed in the more traditional way. However, major retailers in Japan seem to take a different approach to strategic decision making. We must point out that more routine or smaller transactions are usually handled in the more traditional ways even when large Japanese retailers are the clients.

One mistake the authors made a few years ago was to contact directly the president of one of Japan's largest banks about a relatively large American acquisition, a strategy we have found successful in the retailing industry. However, at the bank we were politely but firmly informed that this was not the proper way to conduct business with a Japanese financial institution. So we started over, contacting middle management first.

Generally, the major firms in established industries will negotiate in the traditional way. Smaller firms, particularly if they have been exposed previously to international transactions, and if they are in newer industries, may take a more flexible, less traditional approach to business negotiations. But the key word is "may." The *shokai-sha* will be the most important source of information as to whether your clients' negotiation styles fit the Japanese stereotype.

Japanese Negotiators with Expatriate Experiences

Japanese with experience living or working in the United States will usually adjust their bargaining style and appear to understand a Western approach. Indeed, we have noticed in our negotiation simulations that Japanese executives living only six months in the United States begin unconsciously to reflect the communication style (eye contact, conversational rhythm) of American bargainers.

But the degree to which these Japanese will understand and respond to the American style of negotiations can differ depending on the length and quality of their stay in America. The answers to simple questions such as, "How long did you spend in the United States?" and, "What were your responsibilities there?" will help gauge their understanding. Generally, higher level expatriate tours of duty (such as head of a subsidiary or middle manager) are shorter (three to five years) and involve primarily contact with headquarters personnel in Japan. Alternatively, staff or trainee assignments are for five to six years and entail much more contact with American suppliers and clients. The Japanese with lower-level staff experience in the United States can thus be expected to be more familiar with Western negotiation practices.

You should also be aware that most Japanese with such a bicultural competence are able to switch their American style on and off. We have seen such Japanese bargainers, fully capable of forthright responses to key questions, "clam up" and play the role of the typical indirect Japanese.

You are more likely to focus your attention on such executives because they speak English better, they appear to understand you better, and they appear to be smarter. This is a mistake. Often, the Japanese executive with long expatriate experience is the least influential in the group.

Age

All of Japanese youth tends to display more interest in foreign cultures, foreign languages, and international travel. The consequence is that each successive generation is more cosmopolitan in thinking and behavior. The older Japanese decry the lost culture; the younger generations celebrate the new freedom. Kazuma Uyeno[1] laments the lost art of *ishin-denshin*:

> *Ishin-denshin* is communication of thought without the medium of words. The expression means "what the mind thinks, the heart transmits." In other societies, particularly Western, communication generally has to be expressed in specific words to be thoroughly understood. To the Westerner, therefore, the Japanese sometimes seem to have telepathic powers because so often communication among Japanese is achieved without the use of words.
>
> This is because the many formalities, conventions and common standards developed in a society which gives priority to harmonious relations makes it easy to understand what goes on in the mind of the other person.
>
> The younger generation of Japanese who have become more individualistic are losing the *ishin-denshin* faculty.

And as is the case with any generation gap, both the older and the younger complain about one another.

HOMOGENEITY

Obviously we think there is value in describing both the typical American negotiation style and the typical Japanese negotiation style. Although the values and behaviors appear to be very different within each of the two cultures—the Yokohama negotiators are known to be the toughest in Japan, while the fast-talking New Yorker's communication style is very different from that common in Charleston, South Carolina—when viewed from outside there appears to be a great deal more homogeneity. This is particularly so when the two cultures are so different. We feel that by better understanding one another's cultures, values, and behaviors we can improve communication and anticipate one another's needs. Such understanding is critical to a mutually satisfying even creative exchange relationship. This is true for individuals, business enterprises, and countries.

RACIAL AND ETHNIC PREJUDICE

Very few countries in the world share America's ideals of racial and ethnic equality. We say "ideals" because sometimes Americans aren't very good at ignoring color and race—just hearken back to the 1980s and early 1990s, when Japan dominated the economic landscape, for example:

> Is the United States faced with a new "yellow peril"? There is abundant evidence that many Americans think so.
>
> Last year in Milwaukee, a Japanese flag was slashed and stomped on by an angry crowd of U.S. auto workers. In St. Louis, a shipment of Japanese made cars was mysteriously destroyed by bullets and knives. Labor unions have begun to pass out inflammatory literature, crying, "Remember Pearl Harbor." A national tabloid ran a story, reprinted as an advertisement by a major car manufacturer, charging that this country "whipped the Japanese in World War II but now they're getting even by shipping us millions of dangerous cars that kill tens of thousands of Americans every year."
>
> Inflammatory and questionable as such statistics are, more and more politicians are demanding protectionist legislation against Japanese imports. All of which makes the conclusion of syndicated columnist Mark Shields, published in these pages last week, seem an understatement "If Americans are looking for a political scapegoat this year, Japan may be it."[2]

And it's not just American autoworkers who have exhibited such racist tendencies. Kim Clark reports that American executives display their distaste for Japanese-style management during his seminars on corporate strategy at the Harvard Business School. "You can just see it. They roll their eyes and sort of turn off. The questions I do get are more strident and bitter. To my dismay, there are a lot of racist comments which I had never seen before."[3] Americans who demonstrate this kind of ethnic prejudice will not be successful in Japan. Your Japanese clients will easily read such feelings, and business discussion will simply not proceed.

The Japanese, too, harbor prejudices. In fact, some argue that racial prejudice is a particular problem in Japan because of the history of isolationism and the resulting ethnic homogeneity. And this ethnic homogeneity will certainly persist, given Japan's virtual ban on naturalization of aliens (see box 10.2 for more details). But our concern here is not social reform. Rather, we must consider how racial and ethnic prejudice influences the efficiency of business negotiations between American and Japanese companies.

Let us begin by saying that Japanese clients expect to deal with American executives who are Caucasian and male. This is their stereotype of "the American business executive." And although many Japanese have trouble handling foreigners in general, they at least know more about Caucasian males, who have earned their respect. After all, Commodore Matthew Perry and General Douglas MacArthur, the two individuals most responsible for westernizing Japan, were Caucasian males.

This expectation and stereotype has caused problems for both Japanese and American executives. Americans of African, Asian, or even Japanese heritage are often assumed by the Japanese to be second-class citizens. For example, we know of one second-generation Japanese-American municipal official traveling on business to Japan. He and his younger Caucasian male assistant were greeted at the airport by their Japanese hosts. The Japanese assumed the Japanese-American was second in command and treated him accordingly. When they learned otherwise, the Japanese hosts were mortified at their mistake. They had lost face, and much time had to be spent patching things up, including bringing in a new set of hosts. Such a circumstance may seem a bit comical, but the relationship suffered. And in a land where personal relationships are so important, this was a serious problem.

Americans who don't fit the Japanese executive's stereotype may make Japanese clients uncomfortable at first. African or Asian American executives traveling to Japan should realize this and anticipate having to work harder at establishing credibility. When minority executives are sent to negotiate with Japanese clients, the Japanese should be notified ahead of time who is coming and who is in charge.

In this respect, too, things are changing in Japan. Younger executives can be expected to have a broader, less prejudiced view of the world and international business. And generally, minority Americans are treated as foreigners first and minorities second. Once the initial surprise is overcome, most Japanese executives will get down to the business of personal relationships and the economics of the deal.

BOX 10.2. HONDA LEARNS LATE
ABOUT BIAS, BUT IT IS NOT ALONE

In settling discrimination charges last week, Honda of America had to acknowledge that it made a $6-million blunder in not hiring qualified blacks
and women for its U.S. operations between 1983 and 1986. In one sense
that's quite surprising. Honda is perhaps the best player in the world at a most
difficult game—international business. Selling products in other countries requires an intricate knowledge of not only foreign customers' tastes but also
the laws that regulate competition and operations in foreign lands. Honda's
history of product innovation and marketing competence is unequaled. Its
product quality is the envy of American and Japanese automakers. And its
bold and successful introduction of a new nameplate, the Acura, has stunned
auto makers in Nagoya, Stuttgart, and Detroit.

So, then, how could one of the world's best international companies bun-
gle its highly visible hiring practices in the United States? Part of the explanation has to do with its treatment of women and minorities at home, Japan is
perhaps the least ethnically diverse country in the world. In contrast to the
melting pot of America, Japan has always had stringent immigration policies.
People in the world's most crowded country (when arable land is considered)
just don't welcome foreign settlers.

Korean immigrants and their descendants make up a substantial minority in
Japan and are generally treated derisively. But blonds and blacks are novelties—
often sources of wonder in social settings. But something else happens in work
settings. The Japanese stereotype of an American manager is a white, Anglo-
Saxon Protestant male. This isn't so surprising when you consider the Japanese
historical appetite for John Wayne movies. And it isn't so surprising when you
consider the makeup of boardrooms in the United States today. Thus we heard
former Prime Minister Yasuhiro Nakasone two years ago publicly denigrate the
intelligence of American blacks and Latinos.

Furthermore, sex discrimination within Japan is absolute. Almost no
women hold management positions in major companies like Honda. Instead
women run the home, make all the domestic decisions—major investments
even—that the men don't have time to contemplate. They also tutor their children through the rigors of the Japanese school system.

Women working at the office are either receptionists or secretaries—never
managers.[a]

Because Japanese and American cultures are so different, all kinds of problems crop up in trans-Pacific business relationships. Many American managers will say, "Never send a woman to Japan." We've even seen that bad advice given among the opening comments of a training film about doing

---

[a]Circa 2008, Japanese women have more opportunities to enter management ranks. Culture does change, albeit slowly.

business with the Japanese. We have found that American women can get along fine with Japanese clients when they are properly supported by the other Americans on their own negotiating team and when the Japanese know ahead of time with whom they'll be bargaining. Surprises can be uncomfortable and embarrassing for the Japanese.

We are beginning to see things improve on both sides of the Pacific. Last year, for the first time ever, I had one of my graduate business-administration students from Japan ask about negotiations with American women. They can't ignore the crucial role of women in the American business systems when 40 percent of American MBA students are female. And firms like Honda, Nissan, and Toyota are changing their hiring practices in the United States. Indeed, the publicity surrounding the Honda case will provide an important role model for other Japanese firms establishing business operations in the United States.

The downside to all the press coverage given to Honda's hiring biases is the increased potential for Japan-bashing. And I don't mean to excuse its behavior or diminish the consequences of discriminatory Japanese hiring practices on the women and blacks involved. But what is truly surprising about the Honda case is that it hasn't come up before. Given the way Japanese culture and business systems work, why hasn't Honda been called to task sooner?

The answer has to do with the discriminatory hiring practices of comparable U.S. institutions. The Equal Employment Opportunity Commission has had to contend with such American giants as General Motors and State Farm Insurance in the past four years. And my own business is no better; at universities the real hiring decision comes with tenure. Women hold only 10 percent of tenured faculty positions in the entire UC systems, and only 14 percent at USC. Let him who has not sinned cast the first stone at the Japanese.

Source: John L. Graham, *Los Angeles Times*, March 31, 1988.

SEXISM

Time did a great disservice to women executives interested in international business. In an otherwise well-conceived article on business negotiations in Japan, the journalist reported, "Experts on Japanese business methods have compiled numerous guidelines for foreign negotiators. One of the first is that women should not be part of any formal talks. 'Women are simply not accepted as business equals in Japan,' notes a negotiator for a major U.S. electronics firm. Japanese women are all but barred from the management of big companies, and the important after-hours business socializing in Japan is exclusively stag."[4]

It is true that Japanese women are seldom managers (see box 10.3), but that does not necessarily mean that American women can't be successful. To

BOX 10.3. THE NEW WOMAN IN JAPAN, FREE AT LAST?

Japanese wives are famous for ruling the domestic roost. But there are signs that gently, with a padded elbow and a close-mouthed giggle (and, admittedly, the occasional lawsuit), Japanese women are also increasingly making their own rules outside the home. Consider the following:

A mere thirty-seven years after America ruled the low-dose contraceptive pill safe and effective, a Japanese government working group has at last agreed. Although two more government panels will have to approve its use, most expect it to be available within a year or so. This will give women the most reliable form of birth control (short of abortion) they have ever had.

In 1975, only one in eight Japanese women went to a four-year university, a prerequisite for the better jobs. By last year, the proportion was almost one in four. Women are also marrying later. Their average age at marriage is now approaching twenty-eight. Among college graduates more than half of those between twenty-five and twenty-nine are still single, compared with less than a third in 1970.

Although women tend to get laid off first in recessions, more women are working. In 1975, 32 percent of the workforce was composed of women; the figure now is about 40 percent. In big companies, women have one in twenty-five managerial positions, compared with one in forty in 1984.

Japan has not only created a word to deal with sexual harassment—*sekuhara*—but about two dozen such suits are pending. Recently, twelve female bank employees won ¥100m ($890,000) in compensation and were promoted by court order after they successfully sued the Shiba Credit Association. It was the first time a company had been held liable for sex discrimination in promotion.

The Tokyo Securities Exchange accepted its first woman floor trader in 1996. The first woman in more than a thousand years to perform the Knife Ceremony, a hallowed sushi ritual, did so last year. And, however improbably, women have started a sumo circuit as well.

It may sound as if Japanese women are treading the path marked out by Western feminists thirty years ago. Not so. Feminism with Japanese characteristics—a less combative tone and greater emphasis on protecting motherhood—is different.

For example, conventional wisdom in the West is that the birth-control pill was an essential step toward women's liberation. Japanese women are more ambivalent. A poll by *Mainichi Shimbun*, a newspaper, in 1992 found that only one in five women strongly favored legalization of the pill; 54 percent were unsure. Many worry that men will be less willing to use condoms.

Japanese women are also less determined to break down traditional sex roles. A 1996 survey, for example, found that 37 percent of Japanese women strongly believed that a home and children were what women really wanted; 7 percent of American women agreed. This outlook may have something to do with the unattractiveness of life as a *sarariman*. The stock image of the

Japanese man is of a henpecked, hard-pressed, bullied, and rather pathetic soul, more adept at interacting with his computer-generated girlfriend than with real people. There is little to envy in his lot.

The result of this ambivalence on the part of Japanese women, and of a 1986 law designed to encourage equal opportunity, has been that big companies have established two career tracks for women: one (which most choose) for those who do not want to be part of management, and one for those who do. In principle, this makes it possible for women to compete with men on an equal basis. In practice, men are not allowed to get on the non-career track and women find it difficult to stay on the management track. Given the frequent transfers, long hours, and lack of domestic help, moving up the corporate ladder all but requires a stay-at-home spouse. Corporate practice has done nothing to adapt to the woman who wants to reach the top and also to bring up a family. The *oyaji* girl—a twenty-something professional who works hard and plays hard—has been the clearest beneficiary of the new latitude for women. But not everyone wants to be like her, or at any rate to remain like her in an unmarried state. Many women, particularly mothers, are happy to stay out of the corporate rat race. Married women tend to prefer *onna tengoku*, women's heaven (a mix of part-time work, bringing up children, hobbies and community work), to the restricted life they would have as a *sarariwoman*.

Given a choice, men might opt for a less workbound existence as well. In a recent survey, "to be a woman" was the second most popular response among Japanese men when asked how they would like to be reincarnated ("a bird" was first). Their grandfathers would be appalled.

Source: Elizabeth Lazarowitz, "A Woman's Place Is in the Sumo Ring," *Los Angeles Times*, January 8, 1997, 1.

the *Time* article, Gerry Muir, in a letter to the editors, responded: "*Time's* report says women are not accepted as business equals in Japan. That is not always true. I was the Los Angeles creative director for a large Japanese advertising company and feared that my presence might jeopardize the presentation we were making in Japan. My Japanese boss assured me that his colleagues have nothing against women in business so long as the women are not Japanese."[5]

Indeed, we have found the performance of women executives in Japan to be mixed. Box 10.4 is one woman's report of how American women have handled advertising accounts for Japanese companies. Further, Nancy Adler, a professor of management at McGill University in Montreal, found that North American women executives are successfully managing relationships with Japanese clients. She echoes the idea that American women are first foreigners and second women, and they interact with Japanese managers as such.[6] It is true that they don't fit into the traditional routine

BOX 10.4. ADVERTISING WOMEN
AND THE JAPANESE PROBLEM

There are layers upon layers of gentle subtleties—"Sometimes when they nod and smile, you think that means 'yes'—you work based on the smile and the nod, only to find out that they really meant 'no.'" The Japanese are governed by an ironic politeness.

Sometimes the layers melt and the subtleties give way to a raw reality "Once, I was the one laying out a new campaign, and I was supposed to be in charge. Now you'd think, being the only woman there, they couldn't ignore me. But every question the Japanese had, every comment, was directed to someone else in the room. It was as if I didn't exist."

These experiences are rooted in a culture that rarely bends to embrace women: "In Japan, women don't participate in business decisions, so the rules for women simply haven't been defined. What it all boils down to is that the Japanese are not comfortable with women, and when they are not comfortable, they don't do business."

Indeed, many Japanese firms have training programs for U.S.-bound executives to help them adjust to the cultural differences they will face during the typical three- to five-year stint most spend in their U.S. subsidiaries—specifically, the ability to deal with a business world that sometimes delegates power to women.

It is the desire to adapt, in part, that is beginning to make it possible for women to survive the demands of the Japanese in this evolving advertising climate. When Bill Morelanci, then at Dailey & Associates, put Beri Leiberman on the Honda business three years ago as an account executive, one of the Japanese car company's executives pulled Moreland aside. "He laughed and said, 'You've got a lot of nerve putting a woman on this account.' But I told him to give her a chance, and in a month he was coming back saying she was the best hire on the account," says Moreland, now vp/management supervisor at BBDO/West.

In this evolutionary relationship, women working with Japanese clients find themselves trying to wade through a whole new set of workplace nuances—to know when to push and when to retreat, to understand that rank and position can ultimately mean more than being a man or a woman. "It took me two years to learn how to play their mental chess game. There is a tremendous sense of your position in the company, and if the other people in the agency make your position clear, it is my experience that the Japanese will respect it," says one female account executive working with a Japanese client.

A high-ranking American executive who has spent the last ten years in a Japanese-owned firm observes that "when the orientation is heavily skewed to Japanese hands-on management of the company, women are tolerated. The politeness is always there, but they probably wouldn't take a woman seriously. The same suggestions from a man would be given a lot more consideration. It's better than it was ten years ago, but many Japanese companies have made no internal transition to include women."

Source: Betsy Sharkoy, "Advertising Women and the Japanese Problem," *Adweek*, May 1983, 32–33.

of golf, drinking, and bath houses, but with time they are accepted because of their professional expertise.

Ford Motor Company has demonstrated progressive thinking when negotiating with Japanese clients and partners. Specifically, women executives have been given the responsibility to act as the lead business negotiator. While initially there was some resistance on the part of the Japanese, now women executives at Ford are accepted as competent representatives. Julie Willoughby, one of the first Ford women to sit across the negotiation table from Mazda and now a Ford Division marketing plans manager, told us about her initial experiences with the Japanese:

> My first trip to Japan was pretty much a disaster for several reasons. The meetings didn't run smoothly because every day at least twenty, if not more, people came walking in and out of the room just to look at me. It is one thing to see a woman at the negotiating table, but to see a woman in the lead position who happens to be blond, young, and very tall by Japanese standards (5'8" with no shoes) leading the discussions, was more than most of the Japanese men could handle.
>
> Even though I was the lead negotiator on the Ford side, the Japanese would go out of their way to avoid speaking directly to me. At the negotiation table I purposely sat in the center of my team, in the spokesperson's strategic position. Their key person would not sit across from me but rather two places down. Also no one would address questions and/or remarks to me—to everyone (all male) on our team—but none to me. They would never say my name or acknowledge my presence. And most disconcerting of all, they appeared to be laughing at me. We would be talking about a serious topic such as product liability, I would make a point or ask a question, and after a barrage of Japanese they would all start laughing.
>
> Finally, a senior Ford manager at the table broke into the conversation with, "I guess you are not interested in talking with us, because there is one person in this room that knows this program better than any of us. If you don't start addressing your questions to her, and answering her questions, we will conclude these meetings now and leave!"
>
> At that, the Japanese began to speak to me, but it took many more meetings before I truly felt accepted as a Ford spokesperson. Needless to say, that first trip was quite a frustrating experience—one I'll never forget."[7]

We asked Willoughby if she had done anything in particular to establish her credibility with the Japanese. She told us that the strong support of her male Ford team members, as exemplified above, was crucial. She also added that a key event in her relationship with her Mazda counterparts was a dinner party she had at her home. She tells the story best:

> My husband Mike Williams, also a Ford manager working with Japanese clients, and I decided to have a few of our Mazda associates over for an "All-American"

dinner during their next trip to Detroit. So, we started out inviting three people to our home. We thought this would be a nice intimate way to get to know one another and provide the Japanese with an honest-to-goodness homemade American meal. By the eve of the dinner, word had gotten out and we had thirteen for dinner. They sort of invited themselves, they changed their meetings around, and some even flew in from the Chicago Auto Show. We had a wonderful time and for the first time they saw me as a person—a mom and a wife as well as a business associate. We talked about families, some business, not particulars, but world economics and the auto industry in general. The dinner party was a key turning point in my relationship with Mazda."[8]

We talked with Muneo Kishimoto (then president of Mazda North America Inc.), and formerly one of Willoughby's counterparts at Mazda, to get the Japanese perspective on dealing with American women. He told us Julie was always professional in demeanor and dress. Interestingly, he emphasized the importance of the latter. He considered her very capable and noted her patience with his discomfort in speaking English. He didn't think of her as a woman but as an "American business executive."

But perhaps most important, Kishimoto independently confirmed the value of the dinner party at Willoughby's home. That's when he and his colleagues perceived her as a "person." And as we have emphasized throughout the book, personal relationships are crucial to successful dealings with the Japanese. American men can establish personal relationships in bath houses, golf club locker rooms, Ginza bars, and the like, if their livers can stand the strain. But American women have to be more creative. Many of the more traditional recreational activities are not appropriate for mixed company. But the personal touch is still necessary.

The aspects of the Ford/Mazda relationship managed by Willoughby and Kishimoto have proven worthwhile for both companies. Indeed, both executives were promoted to positions of greater responsibility. And they remain good friends even though their jobs have changed.

Nancy Adler, in her excellent article "Pacific Basin Managers: A Gaijin, Not a Woman," makes several key recommendations:

> Give a woman every opportunity to succeed. Send her in full status—not as a temporary or experimental expatriate—with the appropriate title to communicate the home company's commitment to her. Do not be surprised if foreign colleagues and clients direct their comments to the male managers rather than the new female expatriate in initial meetings, but do not accept such behavior. Redirect discussion, where appropriate, to the woman. Such behavior should not be interpreted as prejudice, but rather as the reaction to an ambiguous, nontraditional situation.[9]

The female expatriates had a number of suggestions for other women following in their footsteps. First, as they suggest, presume naiveté, not malice. Realize that sending women to Asia is new, perceived as risky, and still fairly poorly understood. In most cases, companies and foreigners are operating on untested assumptions, many of which are faulty, not out of a basis of prejudice.

Several women managers at Ford add that the attitudes and behaviors of their American colleagues are crucial to setting the right tone. An early reference or, better yet, deference to the expertise of the woman team members will help a great deal. The managerial implication here is the same as in the previous section on racial and ethnic prejudice. When women travel to Japan, they must anticipate the attitudes of their clients. With patience and an understanding of the Japanese, women can be effective. Indeed, President Bush's and President Clinton's appointments of three women as U.S. Trade Representatives well demonstrates this confidence that a woman can be successful with Japanese. Finally, Deborah Tannen argues that American women may be even more effective in Japan than American men:

> In general, women are more comfortable talking one-on-one. The situation of speaking up in a meeting is a lot closer to boys' experience of using language to establish their position in a large group than it is the girls' experience using language to maintain intimacy. That's something that can be exploited. Don't wait for the meeting; try to make your point in advance, one-to-one. This is what the Japanese do, and in many ways American women's style is a lot closer to the Japanese style than to American men's.[10]

CONCLUSION

Business negotiations across cultures are difficult undertakings, particularly in such a fast-changing world. Much can go wrong besides the economics of the deal. In this chapter we have tried to address the most delicate but very real problems of cultures meeting—personalities, prejudices, and sexism. We don't have all the answers because all the rules haven't yet been established. But we hope to have made you aware of these important, but hidden, pitfalls of business negotiations with the Japanese.

NOTES

1. Kazuma Uyeno, *Japanese Business Glossary* (Tokyo: Mitsubishi Corporation Toyo-Keizai-Shinposha, 1983), 68.

2. *Los Angeles Herald Examiner*, March 23, 1992, 1.

3. Nancy Yoshihara, "Japan's Strategies May Need Some Tuning to Work Here," *Los Angeles Times*, January 23, 1983, 42.

4. John Greenwald, "The Negotiation Waltz," *Time*, August 1, 1983, 42.

5. Letters to the Editor, *Time*, August 22, 1983, 2.

6. Personal interview with Nancy J. Adler.

7. Personal interview with Julie Willoughby.

8. Personal interview with Julie Willoughby.

9. Nancy J. Adler, "Pacific Basin Managers: A Gaijin, Not a Woman," *Human Resource Management* 26, no. 2 (1987): 169–191.

10. Deborah Tannen, author of *You Just Don't Understand: Men and Women in Conversation* (New York: William Morrow, 1990) in *Working Women*, July 1990.

11

Best Cases

Over the years many case studies have been written regarding negotiations between Japanese and Americans. We have selected the two best to include here in chapters 11 and 12. Both are written by leading experts in international business negotiations and diplomacy. Both case studies are only excerpted here in the interests of space (the citations of the complete works are listed in the references at the end of the book). Even so, both writers include rich details that exemplify and amplify many of the points we have made previously in the text.

The GM/Toyota joint venture plant in Fremont, California, after more than twenty years remains one of the most successful international alliances in corporate history. The NUMMI plant itself continues to win quality awards both for its cars produced, and most recently for energy savings—the U.S. Environmental Protection Agency granted its ENERGY STAR Sustained Excellence 2006 Award to the Fremont plant. It is also interesting to note that the Toyota Corolla is the best-selling passenger car in the history of the planet. Of the thirty-one Corolla models produced over the last four decades, 2.5 million were built at the NUMMI facility. The plant has some 5,700 employees and is represented by the United Auto Workers, Local 2244. Almost 70 percent of the workforce are minorities. General Motors has adopted many of Toyota's manufacturing processes in its plants all over the world. Toyota has expanded its international manufacturing operations from the 1982 NUMMI experiment to seven new countries including five additional plants in the United States.

Perhaps most interesting is Jeffrey Liker's *amae* laden explanation of Toyota's fundamental motivation for joining GM in NUMMI:

> But at least one consideration was that Toyota realized GM was the world's largest carmaker and was struggling in its manufacturing operations. By helping to raise the level of manufacturing at GM, they were helping American society and the community, as well as creating high-paying manufacturing jobs for Americans. The senior executives at Toyota speak of giving back something to the United States for the help they provided Japan to rebuild its industry after World War II. This is not mere lip service or pie-in-the-sky idealism. They really believe it.[1]

The two firms are now engaged in a five-year partnership to develop and possibly jointly produce advanced-technology vehicles, including those powered by fuel cells. Stephen Weiss, a professor of international business at York University in Canada and one of the most prolific writers on the subject of international business negotiations, well documents and analyzes the initial negotiations between the two auto giants.

STEPHEN WEISS TELLS THE STORY OF THE GENERAL MOTORS-TOYOTA JOINT VENTURE NEGOTIATIONS

During the last four years, the joint venture between General Motors and Toyota Motor Company to assemble subcompact cars has become a symbol of international cooperation within the auto industry and beyond.[2] Academics, managers, and government officials have all emphasized the parent companies' reputations and the joint venture's achievements in labor relations, production efficiencies, and product quality. Yet, as deserved as this attention to operations and performance may be, an important aspect of the venture has been neglected—its birth.

Creating an international joint venture is neither an easy nor certain process. Like other negotiations, joint venture negotiations may at worst fail completely. Undertaking negotiations in an international context, moreover, adds obstacles as well as opportunities. Before its talks with GM for example, Toyota negotiated with Ford (unsuccessfully as it turned out) for thirteen months. Even the GM-Toyota talks were in participants' words, "long," "hard," and "frustrating." So the agreement leading to the establishment of the joint venture now known as New United Motor Manufacturing, Inc. (NUMMI) represents an important accomplishment.

The story of the GM-Toyota negotiations is also significant as an illustration of the complexity common to international business negotiations. They entail complicated issues, parties that are large organizations, and multiple, dynamic, and differing environments—all of which are given little attention in existing management research on negotiation.

With respect to the actors involved, the analysis that follows treats GM and Toyota as the two primary organizations. In addition to their intercompany (primary) talks, they met in critical ancillary negotiations with the United Auto Workers (UAW) and with the Federal Trade Commission (FTC). Figure 11.1, which guides this discussion, places the foursome at the center of activity as the most deeply involved organizational actors (Ring 1a).

Other actors also influenced and were affected by the negotiations. Figure 11.1 identifies and classifies several organizations by their degree of involvement (Rings 1a–4a). The exhibit also recognizes three levels of analysis for behavior: (a) organizational wholes, (b) groups such as negotiating teams, and (c) individuals. The activities of each organization listed, which shaped conditions for the negotiations, could be analyzed at the two other levels. For clarity and brevity, only the groups and individuals representing the four major organizations appear in figure 11.1, and the most deeply involved actors are located in the very middle (b and c).

GM's decision to enter joint venture negotiations, like Toyota's, appears to follow naturally from the two companies' interests and complementary resources and skills. Through collaboration GM could learn production and management techniques from a company renowned for them, and Toyota could gain low-cost entry to the U.S. auto industry with the assistance of the industry leader. Other concerns and motivations are also worth noting.

On the skeptical side, one could speculate that each company could gain merely from the act of negotiating, regardless of the result. During the Toyota-Ford talks, after all, several American observers opined that Toyota was simply trying to demonstrate responsiveness to MITI and the U.S. government without intending to reach an agreement. The same motivation coupled with gathering information about GM is conceivable here. GM too could benefit from "side effects" such as learning more about its competitor and delaying Toyota's move to produce and to sell without restraints in the United States. The delays, expressed "worries," and actions that came up during the negotiations are consistent with these possibilities.

One GM participant who was interviewed mentioned that the possibility of Toyota's simply "buying time" did occur to the GM team and concerned them enough to ask Toyota about it. Toyota responded that they were negotiating in good faith and would go into the joint venture with an "open mind." GM itself had no desire to learn just from negotiating, according to another GM interviewee.

In the main, however, the participants interviewed by the author and reporters felt that the companies' motivation for pursuing a joint venture was a shared interest in exploring the feasibility of profitable subcompact

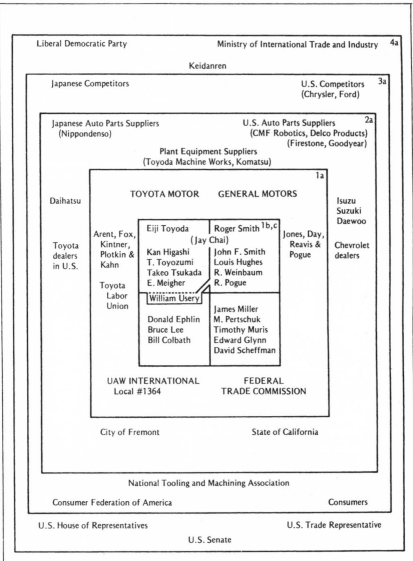

Notes: This structure was suggested by Ian Wise.
Larger rectangles (rings) represent diminishing degrees of involvement: 1—primary actors; 2—affiliates, network members, and supporting audiences; 3—industry and market actors (opponents); 4—environmental (political) actors. *Letters* designate levels of behavioral analysis: a—organizations; b—groups; c—individuals. With the exception of the FTC, Boxes 1b, c contain negotiating teams (excluding CEO's Toyoda and Smith) as well as primary individual players.

Figure 11.1. Actors and Audiences in the GM-Toyota Negotiations

Source: Stephen Weiss, "Creating the GM/Toyota Joint Venture: A Case in Complex Negotiation," *Columbia Journal of World Business* (Summer 1987), 23–25.

car production in the United States. GM stood to gain working experience with Japanese techniques that neither licensing alone nor companies other than Toyota might effectively provide. The prospective advantages included the demonstration to American labor that they could work in plants managed by Japanese techniques (a so-called "labor demonstration effect.") On the other hand, Toyota could respond to political forces, enter the United States at low risk, and move more quickly up "the learning curve." These and other interests listed above were all reasons for the companies to try and reach an agreement.

In November 1981, Jay Chai, an executive vice president of C. Itoh and Company (America) and the advisor to the chairman (of GM) on Japanese affairs, broached with Toyota executives in Tokyo the possibility of a joint venture with GM. Then on December 21, 1981, Seishi Kato, chairman of Toyota motor sales, met with Roger Smith in Detroit. Language barriers made the visit "bewildering" in Smith's words, but it got the ball rolling.

Phase One: Developing a Framework

The first formal intercompany negotiation concerning a joint venture occurred on March 1, 1982, in New York City, between Eiji Toyoda, president of Toyota Motor Company, and Roger Smith, chairman and CEO of GM. A GM source indicated that they discussed only the overall concept of a joint venture, not initial proposals. By the end of the month, he continued, the two company heads had agreed in principle to undertake a feasibility study for a joint venture. Interestingly, a Toyota interviewee read from an official company history of the talks that Smith had made a "very specific" proposal during March, namely a joint venture with equal capital contributions, use of an idle GM plant in California, production of a Corolla-class car beginning fall 1984, and an output of 200,000 to 400,000 cars.

Players

Responsibility for the day-to-day talks was given to John Smith, GM's director of worldwide product planning, and Kan Higashi, Toyota's general manager of overseas operations. The balance of both negotiating teams (figure 11.1) was made up of representatives from finance (Hughes, Toyozumi) and legal affairs (Weinbaum and staff, Tsukada). Flavio Cella, an assistant to Hughes responsible for special projects, also participated. Each team included outside counsel (Pogue, Meigher), and interpreters were present. Louis Hughes, an assistant treasurer with responsibility for GM's overseas group, and Toyota's Higashi would become chief spokesmen.

Jay Chai officially participated as a member of the GM team but took a facilitating, intermediary role once talks got underway. At several points, he acted as an interpreter. More critically, at impasses Chai would carry and explain to Toyota representatives proposals written by Roger Smith and others.

In addition to this core negotiating group, there were several auxiliary "working groups" that communicated with counterparts across company lines and fed information to their companies' main negotiators.

The Negotiation Process

In April 1982, talks at the operational level began (see table 11.1). The negotiating teams divided up the agenda and assigned pieces to working groups. The facility planning group, for example, comprised three to four engineers from Toyota and two from GM. Other groups were formed for costing, logistic planning, and labor. A schedule was charted; the target date for agreement was set for September 1982.

According to two reports, GM initially proposed a large venture involving two plants and production of some 400,000 subcompact cars. Toyota sought a limited venture based on one abandoned plant with a capacity of 200,000. GM also may have become concerned about the antitrust ramifications of the larger venture, for the limited plan prevailed.

GM sought the Corolla, Toyota's best-selling car worldwide, as the product for the joint venture. Toyota offered instead the Sprinter, a sporty subcompact that had been produced since 1968 solely for domestic sale in Japan. One GM participant stated that GM was "very happy" with this offer because it obviated the investment needed to differentiate a Corolla-based joint venture car from the common Corolla.

Formal and informal negotiation sessions took place over several months, moving from discussion of the joint venture concept to feasibility studies to costing studies (see table 11.1). By late summer 1982, news articles reported agreement on production volume, plant location, and sales channels as well as the type of product.

Sourcing of components had also been decided. Toyota would supply the engine and transmission, and all other parts would be procured through competitive bids. Most of the parts would be Japanese, and Toyota provided the list of bids from Japanese companies. They included affiliates (e.g., Nippondenso) and nonaffiliates (see figure 11.1). GM provided the bids from its affiliates (e.g., Delco Products) and other American companies who would primarily supply parts such as radiators, glass, seats, and tires. Since just-in-time *(kanban)* inventory was integral to its production system, Toyota sought explicit assurances from GM that supply decisions would be based on product quality and vendor reliability as well as cost.

The issues were more complicated and the discussion more arduous than either party had anticipated. Citing the number of parts to a car, one GM official reportedly stated, "Dozens of decisions have to be made with

Table 11.1. Timetable of GM-Toyota Negotiations

1981	Dec. 21	Kato visits R. Smith for the first time in Detroit.
1982	Mar. 1	R. Smith and E. Toyoda discuss the concept of a joint venture in New York City.
	Mar. (end)	Agreement in principle reached on undertaking a feasibility study for a joint venture.
	Apr. 5	GM board of directors informed of preliminary discussions with Toyota and their strategic implications.
	Apr. 14	First operational level negotiations begin in Tokyo.
	May 17–20	Second operational level negotiations held.
	June	Morita and other Toyota officials survey GM's U.S. plants.
	Summer (end)	Agreement reached on basic issues such as type of car, number to be produced, plant site, sales channels.
	Sept. 20	Another round of operational level negotiations begins in Tokyo.
	Nov. 30	R. Smith makes proposal to break impasse on valuation of Fremont property and capitalization of venture.
	Dec. 23	Yamamoto and Iwasaki meet with R. Smith in Detroit (E. Toyoda visited the U.S. in Nov.).
	Dec. 27	E. Toyoda accepts Smith's proposal, and they resolve to finalize a memorandum of understanding quickly.
1983	Jan. 20–26	Last operational level negotiations held in Japan.
	Feb. 7	GM board of directors approves final draft of agreement.
	Feb.	MITI announces extension of auto export restraints to a third year, April 1983–March 1984.
	Feb. 16	GM and Toyota's in-house and outside counsel inform Glynn at FTC of signing ceremony the following day.
	Feb. 17	R. Smith and E. Toyoda sign "Memorandum of Understanding."
	Feb. (end)	Hart-Scott-Rodino filing by GM and Toyota.
	Mar. 3	Usery retained to assist in negotiations with UAW.
	Mar. 21	T. Toyoda named president and CEO of the joint venture.
	Mar. (end)	FTC makes "Second Request" for information from companies and begins investigational hearings that last until July.
	Apr.	First negotiations between Toyota's counsel and FTC staff concerning release of requested information.
	May 18	Gieber succeeds Fraser as president of the UAW.
	May 25	Formal Toyota-UAW negotiations begin.
	June	Toyota provides FTC with a number of company documents.
	June 20	First deadline (120 days) for labor agreement stipulated in Memorandum of Understanding; extension granted.
	Aug.	Toyota's council informs FTC that firm cannot release cost and profit data; Miller publicly demands the data.
	Sept. 2	UAW Local #1364 (former GM Fremont workers) sue GM and UAW International for negotiating without them.
	Sept. 22	UAW International reaches agreement in principle with GM and Toyota ["Letter of Intent"].

(continued)

Table 11.1.   Timetable of GM-Toyota Negotiations (*continued*)

	Nov. 16	New FTC Commissioner Calvani begins term.
	Nov. 24–27	FTC staff has access to depository of Toyota documents at offices of outside counsel, breaking two-month impasse.
	Dec. 22	GM and Toyota sign consent accord with FTC.
1984	Feb. 21	Joint venture shareholders agreement executed, by-laws accepted, company established in California as New United Motor Manufacturing, Inc.
	Apr. 11	FTC grants final approval to joint venture in 3–2 vote.
	May	NUMMI begins hiring workers.
	Dec. 10	Dedication of first NUMMI Nova (CL Sedan) off the line.

practically every part. . . . If any project ever required patience, this is it." Participants interviewed by the author echoed that assessment for additional reasons.

Communication was difficult due to culturally based factors. For example, Japanese negotiators for Toyota addressed issues in ways that appeared "oblique" to the GM team. Some silences and affirmations at the negotiating table were mistaken for agreement. Translation also slowed the negotiation process considerably.

Negotiating and decision-making styles also contrasted. According to the participants interviewed, the Japanese tended to start talks with statements of general principles and usually did not respond to proposals before checking with their headquarters. The Americans preferred specific proposals and responses at the table. In fact, the GM team received so few proposals from Toyota initially that they wondered where they stood. Further, Toyota was struck by GM negotiators' ability to source information quickly from particular individuals within their organization; GM saw the Toyota team's ability as less clear-cut. In the end, the September 1982 target date for agreement passed, and the date was moved to December.

During the fall of 1982, unresolved issues included the licensing fee to Toyota for its car design, management of operations, prices of the cars (destined for GM) and exchange rate fluctuations.

A major impasse developed on capitalization of the venture and the evaluation of the idle GM plant in Fremont, California, that the companies had selected. GM had reportedly renovated the plant at a cost of $280 million in the months before its closing in March 1982. Toyota, according to its written history of the talks, considered the equipment too old to be effective in increasing production. Toyota also must have figured that GM could at least write off much of that amount. On November 30, 1982, Roger Smith personally wrote to Eiji Toyoda softening GM's stand. Toyoda accepted Smith's proposal on December 27.

A final set of negotiations was held in January 1983 in Tokyo. Early in the month, Shoichiro Toyoda, president of Toyota said, "It is too early to predict the possibility of reaching a final agreement between our companies by the end of January." Among other issues, the pricing of the joint-venture car, which had been repeatedly set aside, remained unsettled. Even at the end of the month as the *Wall Street Journal* reported the plan, a Toyota spokesman denied that the companies had an agreement. By February 7, GM's board of directors had already twice authorized Roger Smith to sign an agreement. GM awaited Toyota.

The Outcome

On February 14, 1983, only days after MITI notified the U.S. government that it would extend auto export restraints to a third year, GM and Toyota formally announced their agreement on a joint venture. Signed on February 17, the fifteen-page "Memorandum of Understanding" stipulated:

1. Limited production of a car derived from Toyota's "new front wheel drive Sprinter" for sale directly to GM
2. Equal shares of capital from the parent companies—as it turned out, $100 million cash from Toyota; from GM, $11 million cash and the Fremont plant ($89 million); and another $250 million was later raised
3. Equal ownership by the parents
4. Design of the Fremont manufacturing layout by Toyota, construction of a stamping plant
5. A "reasonable royalty" to Toyota for the license to manufacture the car
6. Technical assistance from GM and Toyota on a cost-plus basis
7. Nominal annual production capacity of 200,000 cars
8. Pricing joint venture cars on a market-basket standard
9. Startup for the 1985 Model Year

Some American observers complained in the American press that Toyota out-negotiated GM. Toyota did gain operational control of the venture, although that could have been seen by GM as necessary for creating an accurate and didactic model of Toyota's system. Most of the components were to be Japanese. Toyota also had a built-in client and royalties and other fees that considerably lowered its risk. Toyota clearly gained a great deal. But the achievement of each company's primary goal, learning from the other, depended on yet to be designed mechanisms and on experiences of the joint venture well after startup.

Phase Two: Completing the Details

From the February 1983 signing of the Memorandum to the May 15 target for a contract, and even up to the February 1984 incorporation of the joint venture, a number of additional issues required negotiation. Many concerned the United Auto Workers and the Federal Trade Commission. There also remained detailed items for intercompany negotiations.

For this phase Eiji Toyoda and Roger Smith assumed very limited roles. Some of the working groups (e.g., costing) had also largely completed their tasks. The core group of negotiators (figure 11.1) stayed in place to work out the fine points.

STRATEGIC IMPLICATIONS

1. *Preparation and Monitoring.* In light of the information and activity required in complex negotiations, careful planning seems especially important. Interests and options should be identified and evaluated for one's own company as well as the prospective partner(s). Assessment must continue through the negotiations. Moreover, the activities of a counterpart beyond the negotiating table and other forces in the dynamic multifaceted environment may call for reevaluations of anticipated benefits and costs.

   The timing of a venture and the expected duration of negotiations also deserve consideration. Restraints on Japanese auto exports are still in place today six years after the Kato-Smith meeting, but now products from even lower-cost sources (Korea, Taiwan, Brazil, Mexico) have entered the U.S. market. Moreover, in July 1985, Toyota announced plans for its own assembly plants in the United States and in Canada, and in September 1986, began producing cars at NUMMI under its own nameplate. In late 1984, GM arranged to source from Korea's Daewoo, and in August 1986, set up a joint venture with Suzuki in Canada. Such factors must be monitored and anticipated without injuring the budding joint-venture relationship.

2. *Top-Level Support.* The GM-Toyota negotiations also illustrate the impact of top-level support on one's own organization and negotiators and on the counterpart. Both sides look for signals of commitment. At the same time, if too active, CEOs run the risk of diminishing the perceived authority of their more involved negotiators. Executive intervention may be most effective if used sparingly, for example, at major impasses.

   Leadership among the more involved negotiators also seems important given the diffusion of activity—the multiple negotiating arenas, internal and external negotiations—and dependence of resolution of issues in one arena on resolutions in other arenas. It was because of the "highly motivated" core group of negotiators, according to one participant, that the GM-Toyota talks succeeded.

3. *Intermediaries and Other Outside Experts.* For negotiations involving a number of disparate issues and parties having different negotiating styles, outside experts may be especially helpful. The GM-Toyota talks entailed labor and antitrust as well as auto parts issues. Further, the two companies' predominantly domestic outlooks, ethnic differences and unknowns, and corporate cultures and attitudes based on being "Number One" complicated the talks. GM employed Chai for strategic and cultural affairs, Toyota hired Usery for labor concerns, and both companies hired outside counsel for the antitrust issues. Intermediaries and other outside experts have facilitated other international auto negotiations as well (e.g., AMC and Beijing Automotive Works).

4. *"Fractioning" the Agenda and the Format.* One way to handle very large agendas is to break them into manageable issue clusters. GM and Toyota, for example, formed working groups such as logistic planning to "feed" the main negotiating teams. Moreover, formal, full team-on-team formats should probably not be the only venue for talks. Individuals can also accomplish a great deal in formal and informal one-on-one meetings.

5. *Referring to the "Big Picture."* For several reasons (the complexity and detail of the agenda, the various arenas of activity, the months of effort involved, and strong partisan positions), key players should refer regularly to the basic relationship being sought and to the potential benefits of the companies' cooperation. Internally, Toyota seems to have done so by concentrating on a single, draft memorandum of understanding. In joint sessions, the negotiators can also reframe in order to stimulate and sustain momentum as needed. (This also counterbalances some of the drawbacks of (4) above.) This tack is effective as long as the companies see more benefits than costs in the joint venture relationship.

NOTES

1. Jeffrey K. Liker, *The Toyota Way* (New York: McGraw-Hill, 2004), 75.

2. Stephen E. Weiss, "Creating the GM-Toyota Joint Venture: A Case in Complex Negotiation," *Columbia Journal of World Business* (Summer 1987): 23–37.

12

Food Fights

While the remarkable successes of the GM/Toyota cooperative effort in the NUMMI plant in Fremont continue to demonstrate the maturity of the bilateral relationship between the companies and the countries, the ongoing story of disputes about food exports suggests another reality—one John Belushi (aka "Bluto" Blutarsky in the 1979 hit movie *Animal House*) would have enjoyed.

This second case study regards the opening of the Japanese rice market to foreign producers. Given the cultural salience of rice to the Japanese as described in chapter 4, this represents a historic breakthrough in U.S.-Japan relations. Michael Blaker, author of the seminal book *Japanese International Negotiation Style*, provides a most insightful discussion of the intricate negotiation processes involved in this surprising and important accomplishment of American diplomacy. As dessert to follow Blaker's rice entree, we add our own discussion about the most recent major trade dispute between Japan and the United States. It too regards a food item, this time beef and the mad cow disease scare.

JAPAN NEGOTIATES WITH THE UNITED STATES ON RICE: JAPAN CAN SAY "NO, A THOUSAND TIMES, NO!" BY MICHAEL BLAKER

Negotiating skills are one key facet of the multifaceted art of diplomacy.[1] Scholarly studies of Japanese and other national negotiating "styles" rest on three basic arguments: first, that a particular country's diplomatic representatives' style of negotiating is identifiable; second, that these identifiable negotiating styles differ; and, third, that these identifiable, country-specific styles significantly affect negotiating outcomes.

While particular bargaining moves are not unique to any country, the mix of moves provides a distinctive composite portrait for any country's diplomatic behavior. Japan is no exception. Enough has been written by Japanese and other analysts to permit one to offer a portrait of the Japanese style of negotiation. The behavior—what may be labeled "coping"—is consistently evident both at the loftier plateau of diplomacy and down in the trenches at the level of direct negotiations.

"Coping" captures the go-with-the-flow essence of the Japanese bargaining approach: cautiously appraising the external situation; methodically weighing and sorting each and every option; deferring action on contentious issues; crafting a domestic consensus on the situation faced; making minimal adjustments or concessions in order to block, circumvent, or dissolve criticism; and adapting to a situation with minimum risk. This negotiating style mirrors the vaunted low-key, low-profile, risk-minimizing, defensive, damage-limiting patterns in Japan's overall foreign-relations conduct.

Drawing from the extensive literature on the topic, we can identify the "top ten" characteristics of Japanese bargaining behavior:

1. Use of vague, ambiguous, noncommittal language in framing negotiating proposals
2. Heavy stress on process-related elements of negotiation (such as person-to-person communication and back-channel contacts)
3. Few initiatives, especially on political, security, and controversial economic topics
4. Avoidance of front-line, assertive, visible, leadership positions and roles
5. Slowness in reaching negotiating positions, after lengthy deliberations among domestic interests affected by subject(s) to be discussed
6. Preference for adaptive, short-range, ad-hoc, case-by-case approaches over comprehensive, integrated plans
7. Preference for bridging, mediating, go-between role when faced with highly adversarial situations
8. Concessions presented slowly, in small increments
9. Significant compromises offered only when conditions have become highly politicized and a "crisis" stage has been reached
10. Relatively great weight given to instruments bolstering commitment to Japanese positions as against arguments and techniques to persuade or convince others to change their views or positions

Based on the sheer consistency of these and other traits over time, Japanese negotiating style has lent itself to a variety of characterizations. "Probe, push, panic, and postpone" is one. "Silence, smiling, and sleeping" is another. "Deny, delay, defer, deadlock, and discontinue" could be yet another. While Japanese analysts are uncomfortable with the rather mocking tone of such descriptions, few have disputed their general accuracy in portraying the behavior of Japanese negotiators.

In assessing Japanese negotiating behavior and performance, this study seeks to define Japanese objectives. After all, should not Japanese negotiators be judged on the basis of Japanese goals? While this may seem an obvious point, it is not, because Japanese goals are typically opaque and therefore must be inferred from behavior. Moreover, as mentioned above, Japan is typically on the defensive side in negotiations, and the Japanese side deals with an imported agenda. Also, even though Japanese negotiators often draw criticism for failing to take initiatives, to articulate Japanese positions clearly, to assume political risks, or to respond quickly to changes in the bargaining situation, one may well ask whether or not the Japanese were interested in such matters at all. Identifying Japan's "medium of exchange" is therefore critical to grasping correctly the Japanese style.

THE RICE NEGOTIATIONS

The Subject of Rice

For Japan, rice is a near-sacred product, deeply embedded in history, culture, economics, politics, and symbolism. For the Japanese, rice is "our Christmas tree," and rice-producing land is reverently called "our holy land." In Japanese eyes, rice—far more than beef, citrus fruit, or textiles—represents the ultimate non-negotiable market-access topic. "Not a single grain of foreign rice shall ever enter Japan," was the solemn vow of Japanese politicians of all stripes, backed by public opinion, the press, the business community, academics, and the bureaucracy. Opposition to imported rice reflected a national consensus.

Small wonder that American demands in 1986 for opening the Japanese rice market were seen as a frontal assault on Japanese culture itself. There is some irony in the Americans' criticizing Japan's inefficient rice-farming system. After all, it was the American-led Occupation that had broken up existing large land holdings into the small tracts that would become the bastions of rice farmers whose votes politicians rewarded with generous subsidies perpetuating these economically inefficient plots.

PRELIMINARY PHASE

U.S. pressure on Japan to open its rice market to foreign rice began with the U.S. complaint in 1986 that Japanese restrictions on imports of twelve agricultural products, including rice, were in violation of GATT rules. The U.S. complaint stemmed from prodding from a well-organized American lobbying group, the Rice Millers' Association (RMA).

Over seven years would pass, and six prime ministers would hold office, before a negotiated settlement was reached in December 1993.

The Japanese goal on the issue of rice imports was simple: keep foreign rice from Japanese mouths. On an opposition-to-liberalization scale of one to ten, with oranges rating "3" and beef about a "5," rice would have registered a perfect "10." Along with the heavy value Japanese attached to the subject was the virtually universal Japanese perception of the domestic rice market as sacrosanct. Permitting foreign rice to enter Japan was tantamount to letting foreign firms build condos inside the walls of the Imperial Palace. The Japanese response to American demands for opening the domestic market was akin to "How dare you!"

During the pre-negotiating period on rice, Japan's basic objective was negative, to block entirely the subject from being placed on the bargaining agenda, at either the bilateral or the multilateral GATT level. Once the RMA's petition was filed, and U.S. Trade Representative (USTR) Clayton Yeutter had to decide how to deal with the petition, Tokyo unleashed a defensive counterattack with every weapon at its disposal.

Both houses of the Diet voted unanimously in favor of a resolution binding Japan to self-sufficiency in rice production. Politicians, the press, big business, academic experts, and of course farm lobby groups voiced a single message: no, on rice imports. In order to communicate this resolve to the Americans—to make Washington "understand" the Japanese situation and to prevent it from pressing rice liberalization upon Japan—letters were sent, envoys were dispatched, meetings were arranged, and demonstrations were organized.

"The List"—Japanese Arguments against Rice Imports

Among the long list of reasons cited in support of the Japanese position in the various pre-bargaining communications to the American side were the following:

Rice is historically significant in Japan.
Rice is culturally significant in Japan.
Other countries also award preferential treatment to certain economic
  sectors.
Japan is the world's top importer of foreign agricultural products.
Japan's National Food Control Law establishes rice as a "basic food," and
  self-sufficiency in rice as essential to national-security interests.
The Japanese Diet will never accept rice liberalization.

The Japanese public will not accept rice liberalization.

Japan's situation on rice is "unique," "special," and "different."

If Japan is forced to import rice, Japanese-American relations will suffer.

Rice is a domestic issue of no concern to other countries.

Japan needs more time to consider the subject, so other governments should be "patient."

Rice liberalization is not a bilateral but a multilateral subject.

Arguably, presentation of two of the above reasons proved to be a mistake for the Japanese in their preliminary jousting on the issue. When negotiations on the subject subsequently switched to the multilateral level, Tokyo rejected the idea of liberalization because, for Japan, rice (unlike steak and oranges, staples of the Japanese daily diet) was a basic food. Japan's multilateral-level approach was to seek an exception for Japan's rice-producing sector.

In 1988, with a second Rice Millers' petition under consideration at USTR, Ambassador Matsunaga met Yeutter. In that conversation, after urging Yeutter to reject the petition, Matsunaga communicated Japan's willingness to include rice on the Uruguay Round negotiating agenda. Based on the ambassador's assurance, Yeutter turned down the RMA request on the condition that Japan deliver on its stated commitment by addressing the issue multilaterally.

As Yeutter was putting the Japanese commitment on the public record, multilateral pressures were beginning to build on Japan. In October 1988, the "Cairns Group" at the Uruguay Round asked for "minimum access" for imported rice into Japan. In December, Japan assembled a mammoth delegation to the Uruguay Round negotiations in Montreal, including a bloated *oendan* ("support group") of party politicians, as is typical for Japanese multilateral delegations, to gain information, score political points by having been at the scene, demonstrate commitment to the Japanese cause in the negotiations, and, perhaps, keep a watchful eye on Japanese bureaucrats in the event they might be inclined to compromise excessively.

By the Montreal meetings, Japan had crossed the line: Tokyo was on record as supporting the liberalization of agricultural products and was irreversibly enmeshed in the negotiating process. There would be no turning back.

Communication—Static and Shifting Goal Posts

During the course of the 1988 U.S.-Japan negotiations over renewal of the beef and citrus fruit agreement, Yeutter had told the Japanese minister of agriculture Takashi Sato that the United States would not press Japan bilaterally to liberalize its rice market. Rice, to Japanese the dreaded "r" word, was taken by Tokyo officials as off limits at the bilateral level, according to this mutual understanding.

Also important, in Japanese eyes, was Agriculture Secretary Richard E. Lyng's statement later that year that the United States would be willing to accept a percentage-based "partial access" (*bubun kaiho*) arrangement for Japanese rice imports.

Through the summer of 1990, in fact, the heated Japanese domestic political debate over the rice question was based upon this understanding, namely, that the Americans would allow the issue to be addressed at the GATT on the basis of "partial access"—a gradual opening of Japan's rice market—without tariffication.

Not surprisingly, in light of this belief, Japanese officials were jolted in mid-1990 when Deputy Secretary of State Lawrence R. Eagleburger informed the Japanese that "partial access" would not satisfy Washington but, instead, tariffication of rice imports would be required. Overnight, the rug had been yanked from under Japanese assumptions as to what type of Japanese compromise on rice would be necessary to meet American desires.

THE MIDDLE PHASE: TO THE BRINK
OF COMPROMISE AND BACK

Kiichi Miyazawa became prime minister of Japan in November 1991. He quickly assigned top priority to working toward the successful conclusion of the Uruguay Round. His personal commitment to that process, however, did not imply that he supported rice imports based on a tariffication formula. The most likely explanation was that his Liberal Democratic Party had lost its majority in the upper house of the Japanese Diet in mid-year elections. Tariffication of rice imports would mean revising the Food Control Law. Upper house approval would be required for revising the law. Thus, as the prime minister told Secretary of State James Baker in Tokyo that month, "It's impossible to accept tariffication-based rice imports, because that would require revising the Food Control Law."

The Agriculture Ministry Softens Its Stance

Ministry of Agriculture intransigence softened in July 1992, with the appointment of Akio Kyotani as administrative vice-minister. Four years before, Kyotani, as livestock production bureau chief, had participated in the beef and citrus negotiations with the United States. He favored liberalization. A highly influential official, Kyotani was revered by his bureaucratic brethren in the ministry. Why? Kyotani had a particular gift, a personal quality much prized in Japanese officialdom, of "being able to respond to the situation correctly" (*jokyo ni tekikaku ni taio dekiru*).

In the fall of 1992, Kyotani warned a group of Liberal Democratic Party agriculture group members that negotiations with the United States would "go nowhere" unless Japan was prepared to "set forth specific numbers." According to a later newspaper account of the meeting, Kyotani asked the politicians to "give me the responsibility to handle this."

Reading between the lines, the Japanese side, and even Agriculture Ministry officials, were now willing to use the "t" word (tariffication) as well as the dreaded "r" word in policy planning for the negotiations. From the Ministry of Agriculture's perspective the shift was extraordinary. After all, until just a few years before, no official interested in long-term employment at the ministry would have dared utter the "r" word, much less discuss the idea of tariffication. Thus, Japan's one-dimensional "we won't accept tariffication" approach had now changed.

In December 1992, at a press conference after his cabinet was reshuffled, Miyazawa hinted at the softening of Japan's negotiating stance: "We don't want to ruin the [Uruguay Round] negotiations and yet we don't want to ruin rice farming in Japan. How can we satisfy both goals?"

Miyazawa's impromptu remarks (not included in the press conference briefing materials aides had prepared) were taken to mean the Japanese side was on the brink of compromise on rice. According to insiders' accounts published in the press, Miyazawa had reached the conclusion that tariffication was "unavoidable" (*yamu o ezu*).

Behind Miyazawa's significant statement was the fact that Japan had found itself in an untenable position in the multilateral negotiations. As long as the EC and the United States remained at loggerheads on agricultural imports, Japanese leaders seemed quite content merely to watch from the sidelines, to let others take the head for continued deadlock and the blame if the Uruguay Round talks collapsed. But the United States and the EC had announced an agreement on November 24. Miyazawa evidently was amazed that the French, who "disliked" the Americans, could have buckled to Washington's pressure on the agricultural issue.

As it happened, however, and fortunately for the Japanese side, the EC-U.S. confrontation had not ended but continued to persist, giving Tokyo a respite, at least until the new Clinton administration took office in January. Miyazawa's earlier readiness to compromise on rice imports, albeit at the final hour, as well as his subsequent readiness to postpone taking action on the issue, underline the extent to which the Japanese side's position varied according to fluctuations in U.S. policy and circumstances at Geneva.

By 1992, the once impregnable dike against imported rice was about to give way. Only the party politicians from rural districts and Agriculture

Ministry bureaucrats still had fingers in the dike. As happened during the earlier orange negotiations, the bureaucrats at Agriculture proved themselves ahead of the politicians in accepting the need for compromise. Ministry officials thus turned willing, even eager, to have the ministry negotiate the best deal possible under the circumstances. Once the ministerial fingers were pulled from the dike, the vote-conscious politicians surrendered, permitting Agriculture bureaucrats negotiating authority. By this point, the rice-import issue no longer was "whether or not" but "when" and "how much."

The Final Phase of the Negotiations

The Bush years ended with a standoff on the subject of rice imports, with Washington standing firmly behind its "no exceptions" position and Tokyo doggedly continuing to seek preferential treatment on rice. The new Clinton administration trade team, working against the backdrop of the looming deadline for wrapping up the Uruguay Round multilateral negotiations, moved aggressively—in both style and substance—to resolve the issue. When he met Clinton at a bilateral summit session on April 16, Miyazawa recited the standard Japanese script, that tariffication of rice would require changing the Food Control Law, which would be impossible. Instead of responding with the American "no exceptions" argument, as Bush had done repeatedly, Clinton chose to avoid a harsh response.

The multilateral negotiations revived in May when a quadrilateral (United States, Canada, Japan, EC) trade ministers' meeting agreed to open comprehensive negotiations in the fall, a decision that intensified pressure on Japan to face and force resolution of the rice problem.

THE O'MARA-SHIWAKU CONNECTION

An American initiative provided the catalyst for advancing the rice negotiations to the final stage. In June 1993, Charles J. O'Mara, chief agricultural negotiator in the Department of Agriculture, arranged a meeting with his counterpart in Japan's Ministry of Agriculture, Jiro Shiwaku.

Shiwaku and others in the Agriculture Ministry believed that with tariffication and free competition in the domestic Japanese rice market, U.S.-grown rice would be at a serious disadvantage to rice grown in Thailand, where labor costs were significantly lower. Shiwaku thought, as had proved to be the case with wheat, nation-based set amounts of imports would be more advantageous to the United States than an open-market approach. Agriculture Ministry officials also thought that the Clinton administration, being more interested in results-oriented, managed trade than devotion to free-trade ideology, would be receptive to applying the wheat precedent to resolve the rice issue on a non-tariffication basis. Shiwaku ran this argument by the U.S. side, which listened. After all, thanks to a decade of preferential import treatment, compliments of the Ministry of Agriculture, half the wheat sold in Japan was American grown.

The U.S. side did more than listen. In June 1993, O'Mara submitted a compromise draft proposal to Shiwaku that suggested deferring tariffication on rice for six years, during which period rice would be imported into Japan according to a "minimum access" formula. In a personal interview, O'Mara confirmed the accuracy of reports published in the Japanese press regarding his private meetings with Shiwaku, including the fact that the offer was an American initiative. According to the formula that O'Mara submitted, tariffication of rice would only begin in the year 2000, after the six-year "minimum access" period.

Joe O'Mara's plan, which allowed Japan to avoid immediate tariffication of rice, was a welcome surprise to the Japanese team. "It was more than we expected," was the reaction of one delighted Japanese negotiator.

In July, Agriculture Ministry officials assembled to review the O'Mara draft. The bureaucratic lineup and relatively receptive thinking of officials in the ministry continued even through the domestic political chaos of mid-1993, the end of the thirty-eight-year reign of the Liberal Democrats, and the beginning of a series of multipart coalition governments. Despite the tumble of domestic political events in Japan, these were the officials whose views mattered most in determining the Japanese side's negotiating position. These officials promptly decided to accept the American draft.

On the other hand, the Liberal Democratic Party politicians ready to accept rice liberalization a year before, when their party was in power, had become members of the "opposition." Now they were unfettered by concerns about shouldering the burden, and the blame, associated with making a decision to open the rice market.

In August, as Japan commenced emergency imports of foreign rice, Ministry of Agriculture officials secretly approached the Rice Millers' Association. That meeting brought yet another surprise to the Japanese side, as RMA officers expressed their willingness to go along with the deferred-tariffication approach. In fact, following their discussion with the ministry representatives, the RMA sought Department of Agriculture guarantees on rice imports to Japan.

The Shiwaku-O'Mara meetings focused on several specific issues, including coming up with an acceptable translation for the key word *yuyo* (which means "postponement" or "delay"): Shiwaku balked at this English translation, favoring more ambiguous language. In the end the problem was averted through a circumlocution. The two officials also dealt with details on handling the period after the "minimum access" framework terminated following six years, and the exact percentage amounts of imported rice to be set for the six-year "minimum access" period. The Dunkel draft had set forth a staggered percentage increase of 3 percent (year one) to 5 percent (year six). Japan pushed for the Dunkel figures; the United States countered with percentages twice as high (6–10 percent over six years). In the end, the sides landed squarely in the middle, agreeing on a 4–8 percentage formulation.

The negotiated deal had several pluses: it met the minimum acceptable to the central player (the United States); it seemed to meet the expectations of Japan at the Uruguay Round; it would, for a time, postpone resolution of the still politically iffy matter of rice tariffication; it committed Japan to a rice import structure that other rice importing countries would follow; it entailed a politically and economically manageable process of step-by-step increases in imports; and it only required Japan to import comparatively modest amounts of rice.

MULTILATERAL PRESSURE

In mid-October, GATT director general Peter Sutherland trekked to Tokyo where he spent two exhausting days trying to convey to Japan's leaders the urgency of the imminent deadline for finishing up the Uruguay Round. During his stay he conferred with bureaucrats, Liberal Democrats, and Socialist party leaders who, to a surprised and exasperated Sutherland, seemed determined just to state Japan's unrelenting commitment against rice imports and to recite from "The List" (including "Japan's cultural heritage" and "Japan's food security imperatives"). Perhaps because he was less used to Japanese-style arguments on the issue than were Americans, Sutherland reacted with surprise, and even astonishment, that the Japanese leaders he met seemed indifferent to the fact that agriculture was but one of fifteen other major negotiating group topics at the Uruguay Round, including subjects of trade-in-services and intellectual property rights that he expected would have been of concern to his Japanese hosts. Aside from leaders of Keidanren, who were "the only people I could talk to," he noted in a sarcasm-laced statement to the press, "the only thing anyone seems interested in talking about is rice." "They seem to think rice imports mean the end of the world," he went on, "but they are not."

Only after seven years of haggling had Tokyo relented, grudgingly, incrementally, minimally, to a strings-attached settlement. Japan's behavior during the rice negotiations was consistently self-centered, narrow-minded, and parochial. In light of that dismal bargaining record, it seems ironic indeed that when announcing their decision to accept the final agreement, Japanese leaders explained the decision as motivated by Japanese devotion to free-trade principles, dedication to the GATT process, and commitment to fulfilling their nation's responsibilities as a global economic power.

SUMMARY ANALYSIS

What does the rice case suggest about the "Japanese style" of conducting international negotiations?

Negotiating Structure and Process

Centrality of the Bilateral Process.

The heart of the negotiating process in both cases was bilateral. Bargaining over rice imports (quota-based and tariff-based) began at the bilateral U.S.-Japan level. Subsequently, even while farm product issues were addressed multilaterally at the Uruguay Round trade negotiations, the process axis on rice continued to be the U.S-Japan connection. Final resolution of the rice issue was achieved via negotiations between the two governments within the structural umbrella of the Uruguay Round.

Japanese diplomacy buffs refer to such bilateral-in-a-multilateral-framework interactions as *maruchi-bi*. In the rice example, the critical process level was clearly *bi*, with not much *maruchi*-type impact until an impending global trade accord provided isolation-conscious Japanese leaders with a final-hour incentive to accept the previously arranged U.S.-Japan compromise formula.

The United States Plays "Offense"

The American side played the "offensive" role: Washington established the bargaining agenda, issued direct and indirect threats, undertook the significant initiatives, set the deadlines, and, at the multilateral level, acted to mobilize other governments to buttress its negotiating stance vis-à-vis Japan.

Japan Plays "Defense"

In sharp contrast, the Japanese played a "defensive" role: Japanese negotiators did not frame the initial bargaining agenda, but reacted within the framework of a U.S.-dominated bargaining agenda and process. Its proposals were counterproposals. Its conditions were attached as strings to accepting American demands. Its bargaining game plan was executed upon an American playing field—with an American rule book, American referees, an American scorekeeper, and an American crew adjusting the height of the goal posts. No matter at which level negotiations took place—bilateral, multilateral, or bilateral within multilateral—the policies, approach, and behavior of Japanese negotiators were conditioned by Japan's defensive position.

This is not to say the Japanese were passive, for they were actively engaged in the bargaining process. Their active involvement in the process, however, took place in an externally defined context. Their initiatives were not designed to replace or fundamentally alter the existing, made-in-America negotiating agenda. Throughout negotiations on rice, the Japanese negotiating team was in the position of reacting and adapting to other governments'—notably the American government's—initiatives, proposals, statements, demands, pressures, and expectations.

Strategies and Tactics

In interviews with the author, several Gaimusho officials have described Japanese bargaining strategy as "a strategy of no strategy." While few in number, perhaps, compared to other countries, there were Japanese bargaining strategies and tactics—shaped in form and nuance by the Japanese defensive orientation described above.

For analytical purposes, the strategies and tactics that were adopted and pursued by the Japanese side during the rice negotiations can be arranged into two general types: "issue avoidance" and "issue minimization."

"Issue-Avoidance" Behavior

The Japanese government's fundamental goal in the rice case was not to enter into negotiations on the issues in the first place. Accordingly, a variety of "issue-avoidance" techniques were used, to block or defer consideration of what to the Japanese side were off-limits subjects from the bilateral and/or multilateral agendas. A sampling of the behavior drawn from the rice example:

gaining prior understandings or promises (through personal meetings with American officials) that topics will be off limits or that Japan will receive exceptional, special, or preferential treatment;

seeking to "multilateralize" negotiations, thus side-stepping the United States and averting action;

adopting a watch-and-wait posture at the multilateral level;

blocking and/or delaying multilateral-level action in GATT panels based on unanimity rule;

using available tools to demonstrate the Japanese side's commitment to its basic stance (as against stressing techniques to persuade others to change their positions); and

repeatedly maintaining subject(s) as "off limits" (tariff-based imports).

"Issue-Minimization" Behavior

Once "avoidance" efforts had failed, the Japanese side turned to ways to reduce the scope and content of compromises required to resolve the issues involved. These are a few illustrations from the rice negotiations:

conceding less significant items (wheat and dairy products, tomato paste, and the like) to minimize concessions on more important items;

offering minor concessions and postponing further compromise until American response was received and assessed;

avoiding explicit pledges; and

expressing Japanese proposals in ambiguous language (notably during the preliminary and early phases).

Domestic Institutions and Politics

Decision making in Japan's political culture requires the expenditure of enormous energy and time in consensus-building tasks. Only by a politically correct process—extensive discussions, behind-the-scenes consultations, formal and informal conferences—can a viable decision be arranged. According to Japanese norms of politics, all relevant opinions must be heard and be taken into consideration when reaching policy decisions. Japan's fractious, fragmented political processes extend to international negotiations and shape Japanese bargaining style in direct ways.

Nongovernmental Actors

The extensive involvement of unofficial actors on both sides reflects the diversity, complexity, and intensely interrelated quality of relationships between the two societies. In the rice case the Japanese negotiators' consensus-building (*nemawashi*) efforts included a visit to RMA offices to test the waters on the final compromise plan.

Similarly, dispatching missions, delegations, and personal envoys to the United States was a *nemawashi*-type tactic employed for domestic political reasons. These visits facilitated the softening of the Japanese stance and thus were a critical part of the process of reaching final agreements.

Manipulating "Outside Pressure"

In the rice case, various Japanese official and nonofficial actors used external pressure—real, imagined, expected, and typically American—to provide added support for policies they personally espoused but might not have been able to accomplish without a dash of *gaiatsu* (foreign pressure).

Time-Consuming Policy Making

In the rice case, the Japanese side typically took two to three months to prepare and present its positions at the negotiating table. The lengthy response time did not stem from intentional delaying or stalling tactics by the Japanese side but from the snail-like pace of consensus-building toward lowest-common-denominator decisions among all parties having a stake in the issues being considered.

Japanese Compromise Behavior

Beyond a rock-hard commitment to its minimum position, what was acceptable to the Japanese side depended on what was acceptable to the Americans. Japanese concessions were seen as giving up less of what the Americans were asking, rather than winning more from the Americans.

What prompted Japanese concessions in these two cases? Significant Japanese compromises (in the final stage) were offered only when circumstances surrounding negotiations had become heavily politicized, a "crisis" stage had been reached, and the Japanese side had come to see itself to be in a "no-choice" position.

A significant, final-stage source of pressure to concede was multilateral, if unanimous agreement there, and the possibility of being isolated, criticized, and blamed for the collapse of the Uruguay Round. Japanese fears of American retaliation for noncompliance with its proposals (and consequent threat to other, relatively more significant sectors of the Japanese economy) constituted another major, final-stage reason for Japanese compromise.

The apparent Japanese sense of relief when Washington dropped its more ambitious demands (for example, its demand for immediate tariffication of rice imports in mid-1993) seemed to make the Japanese side more willing to accept earlier American proposals it had initially rejected. In what must be a uniquely Japanese way of rationalizing compromise, Japanese final concessions in both bases were justified because they permitted a final agreement with better terms than those Washington had been demanding earlier!

American Bargaining Style as a Factor

Japanese Complaints

At various times during the years of negotiating agreements on rice, Japanese negotiators and officials complained about Washington's negotiating conduct. Among these alleged American shortcomings were the following:

1. Unannounced shifts in position
2. Unexplained, sudden escalation of demands
3. Discrepancies between American positions expressed at multilateral and bilateral meetings
4. Violation of previous Japanese-U.S. "understandings" or "promises"
5. Excessive use of pressure and threats
6. Repeated submission of demands known to the American side as "off limits," clearly beyond Japan's maximum concession range

Impact on the Negotiations

The escalation of American demands in both cases clearly imposed added hardships on the consensus-driven Japanese domestic decision-making process, making the process even more time consuming. American shifts in position during negotiations had similar effects.

Such American behavior had a particularly striking impact on the Japanese side's conduct of the negotiations, precisely because Japan's bargaining "menu" was provided by the United States. When the American side changed or added items to that agenda, the existing Japanese internal consensus disintegrated. Tokyo then had to arrange a fresh consensus, more or less from scratch, on the basis of the latest U.S. plan.

While Japan was not able to exploit effectively these conflicting messages from the American side to its advantage, the frequently different and occasionally contradictory messages added static to the communication process.

Whether the U.S. demands were artificially inflated ("phony") or not, their later withdrawal affected the bargaining process (by hastening settlement between the sides) and the final outcome (by improving final terms in favor of the U.S. side). However loudly and often Japanese officials cried foul over this violation of bargaining norms by the Americans, from the U.S. perspective the tactic (if it was, in fact, intentional) of submitting and then retracting especially harsh conditions was an effective tool. Why the American "ploy" worked so well is explained, again, by Japan's place in a fundamentally defensive bargaining structure and by the Japanese side's view of its position within that framework, as weak, vulnerable, and necessarily reactive.

Japanese bargaining style in the rice case is "classic." The style mirrored the "coping" or "go-with-the-flow" approach described earlier. Japanese negotiators sought, to the greatest extent possible, to avoid losses, to limit damage, and to avoid mistakes. Their bargaining behavior in these instances fits one American observer's apt likening of Japan's diplomatic style to that of "an interested bridge partner, waiting to follow the first good bid from the American side."

COWBOYS VERSUS CONSUMERS, OR THE BEEF ABOUT BEEF

In chapter 3 we elaborated on the cowboy role model and metaphor for the American negotiation style. Here we find ourselves reporting on the odd circumstance of cowboys (literally) negotiating with Japanese consumers over the ban of importation of American beef products. The beef story carries eerie parallels to the rice story Dr. Blaker related just above. But, this story, at least at this writing, continues without resolution.

In June of 1988, U.S. Trade Representative Clayton Yeutter was pleased to report the breakthrough he and his team had achieved in opening up the Japanese market for beef and oranges. The context of the larger GATT negotiations over agricultural products helped him move the negotiations along in Tokyo. Congressional clamoring and new trade laws had also helped break the deadlock, and in some senses had paved the way for the eventual movement on rice.

By 2003, Japan became America's most important export market for beef at more than $1 billion per year. That was consistently more than ten times the exports of rice over the last decade. By comparison, rice was small potatoes. Then mad cow disease hit North America. In May 2003, the 1980s scourge of European beef, bovine spongiform encephalopathy (BSE) was discovered in Canada. BSE is believed to cause brain deterioration in humans as well as cattle and can be transmitted by ingestion of contaminated beef. Imports to the U.S. of Japanese Kobe beef had been banned in 2001 shortly after the discovery of BSE in cattle there; but that commerce was a quarter-million-dollar trickle compared to the billion-dollar beef exports going in the other direction. Since the American meat companies export beef raised in Canada, but slaughtered in the States, Japan in 2003 demanded more stringent inspection of U.S. exports. The U.S. Department of Agriculture (USDA) balked at the stiffer regulations, but quickly compromised. Dan Murphy, a spokesman for the American Meat Institute explained, "At some point . . . the debate ultimately becomes, do we give our customers what they want? Certainly we'll negotiate, we'll strategize, we'll debate and discuss something that is mutually acceptable as possible, but at the end of the day this does really come down to a marketplace decision. Our members will comply because that's the business they're in—satisfying the customer."[2] Mr. Murphy's words reflect the key issue in this ongoing case of commercial machinations between the United States and Japan. USDA officials predicted exports to Japan would not be hurt by the Canadian case.

Then just three months later, in December 2003, all beef exports to Japan came to a halt because of the first American case of BSE, discovered in a cow in Washington State. The billion-dollar trade evaporated instantly. That March a desperate ranking member of the U.S. Senate Finance Committee,

Max Baucus, a Democrat representing the beef-producing state of Montana, declared interest in a free-trade agreement with Japan that would reduce the 37–50 percent tariffs on beef to zero. But, the Republican appointed U.S. Trade Representative, Robert Zoellick, quickly denounced the innovative olive branch as "not an option."

After months of sparring over the bans on cattle trade between the two countries, in September 2004 the Japanese negotiators reported that their American counterparts had informally agreed to importing cattle untested for BSE as long as they were twenty months or younger. Japanese scientists had found no BSE symptoms in younger cattle and had allowed Japanese producers to sell domestic beef using that safety criterion. The American side originally argued for a twenty-four-month cutoff, but relented as the Japanese stood pat. One week later, on September 20, 2004, while attending a United Nations General Assembly meeting in New York, Japanese Prime Minister Koisumi and President Bush affirmed the intention to resume the beef ban negotiations "at an early date." However, the two-day October meeting in Colorado yielded a useful information exchange, but no agreement.

In late October, U.S. Agriculture Under Secretary J. B. Penn traveled to Tokyo to continue the discussions and after three days of negotiations announced an agreement had been reached to resume beef exports to Japan under the Japanese conditions of twenty months or younger. Penn boasted, "We're talking here about a matter of weeks" before Japan begins importing U.S. beef. American officials also expressed the notion that the "breakthrough" was important in other markets, as only Mexico had resumed imports from the United States since the BSE discovery in the States; and South Korea and Taiwan would be watching the U.S.-Japan discussions closely. Also carefully listening to the discussions were Canadian exporters hoping to resume exports to the U.S. Only agreement on testing procedures and compliance mechanisms stood in the way of American beef making it to Japanese mouths once again. "Only!"

By January 2005 no agreement had been reached on how to determine the age of cattle. The technical discussions were continuing over the telephone and e-mail, and the Japanese said they would soon be convening a meeting of their food safety experts on the matter. An involved American official predicted "just another week" and an agreement would be reached. But four days later, Japanese officials reported the first Japanese human death caused by the human variant of BSE. The man had spent a month in Britain in years past, and most human cases have been reported there. But, Japanese consumers stopped consuming beef in 2001 after the first domestic case of BSE, and consumer anxiety there has been mollified only with strict testing of all cattle of all ages. Ouch!

Excerpts from a *New York Times*[3] article concisely summarize the festering beef imbroglio circa April 2005:

TOKYO, April 20—Where's the American beef? That's a question more and more American officials and many Japanese consumers are asking here.

Six months after American negotiators thought they had a deal to resume beef exports to Japan, historically the largest foreign market for American ranchers, this $1.2-billion-a-year market remains closed, as a result of a single case of mad cow disease detected in Washington State in December 2003.

But Japan's barriers to American beef are now drawing heavy fire in Congress, conjuring up a 1980's-style battle over American export access to Japan. Partly because of earlier battles, Japan bought about one-third of American beef exports in 2003, the last year of imports.

Members of Congress "don't want this issue to boil over into the larger relationship," J. Thomas Schieffer, the new American ambassador here, warned Monday in his first news conference. Calling on Japanese to "divorce the emotion from the science," he noted: "After all, 300 million Americans are eating that beef every day, and there are no health concerns in the United States."

Next week, a delegation of American specialists is to arrive here from Washington to testify about measures taken in the last 15 months to prevent new cases of the fatal brain-wasting disease, bovine spongiform encephalopathy, as mad cow disease is formally known. But late summer looks like the earliest that Japan's food safety bureaucracy might reopen doors to American beef.

In Japan, polls show that a majority are in no rush to open to American imports. "I hope Japan will import American beef only when it is confirmed safe enough," Kayo Mochizuki, a housewife, said Wednesday.

The centerpiece of the American effort is a federal agriculture program that has increased mad cow testing from 20,000 animals a year in 2003 to a forecast for 500,000 this year. No infected cows have been detected since the lone case, a 6-year-old Canadian-born cow, was found 16 months ago. In contrast, 17 infected cows have been detected in Japan since August 2001, the latest two weeks ago.

But Japan tests all cows that are slaughtered. The United States plans to test about 14 percent of cows slaughtered this year, focusing on the oldest animals, which are most at risk. Last October, American officials say, Japan agreed to resume imports of beef from cows under 21 months, an age group not deemed to be at risk from the disease.

"It is spilling over from an agricultural issue to a trade issue, which is unfortunate," Howard H. Baker Jr., who stepped down as ambassador here in February, said in a news conference. Referring to the beef ban, he said, "I tried very hard to bring that thing to closure, and three times, at least, maybe more, I thought we had."

Pressure on Japan started in February when 20 senators, largely from Republican-dominated Western states, threatened "retaliatory actions against Japan" in a letter to Japan's ambassador in Washington, Ryozo Kato. The letter noted that Japan's tire exports to the United States were roughly the same value as American 2003 beef exports to Japan.

Talking to Japanese reporters after meeting April 6 with 22 members of the House of Representatives, Ambassador Kato said: "I felt their growing frustration firsthand. I also felt that anything could happen if the current situation persists."

In Congress, support is growing for resolutions warning Japan to reopen its market to American beef. If not, the Senate text says, "the United States trade representative should immediately impose retaliatory economic measures against Japan." The House text warns that Japan is "putting a long and profound bilateral trading history at risk."

Japan's ban on American beef imports dominated Mr. Schieffer's confirmation hearing in Washington in early March. Senators approved Mr. Schieffer, evidently seeing a reliable ally in this former state legislator from Texas, the nation's largest beef-producing state.

"All these are red states, and that's why President Bush is so concerned," John E. Carbaugh Jr., a political consultant, said here Monday, running his finger down a list of Republican majority states.

Fearing political damage, President Bush made a telephone call to Prime Minister Junichiro Koizumi of Japan in early March. The two leaders, allies in Iraq, talked about American beef, aides later told reporters. Later in March, the secretary of state, Condoleezza Rice, visited here and devoted more of her comments to American beef than to North Korean bombs.

Speaking privately, American diplomats here charged that Japan failed to live up to a deal reached last October to open up to American beef. According to the Americans, Japan promised to loosen its testing rule and allow imports of beef from untested cows under 21 months. A Japanese official working on the beef issue elaborated Monday in an interview: "The Japanese government also thinks that early resumption of the beef trade is important. But it is directly related to the food safety issue, and, in Japan, people are very sensitive on the food safety issue."

But judging by crowds of Japanese diners last month at the Outback Steakhouse in Guam, there is a minority who want to eat American beef. Some diners say American beef is cheaper and tastier than Australian beef, often the alternative.

Indeed, nearly 1.2 million Japanese consumers signed a petition last month calling for the resumption of beef imports from the United States. In February, when the Yoshiro D & C Company, the nation's largest "beef bowl" chain, drew on its stocks of frozen American beef for a one-day offering of its *gyudon* shredded beef on rice, the restaurant chain sold 1.5 million meals in six hours.

The second case of BSE discovered in the United States in June 2005 didn't help matters, nor did the expected third case in August. J. Patrick Boyle, president of the American Meat Institute offered at the time, "Our government and Japan should apply international guidelines adopted under the World Animal Health Organization to determine whether it is safe and appropriate to trade in beef products between countries that may have BSE." In October, House representatives during an "ill-tempered hearing" threatened to file a WTO complaint about Japan's sloth on the beef issue. Meanwhile, Japanese consumers continued to express misgivings about even their own government's ability to provide safe beef, particularly from the States. Indeed, in 1996 British officials had prematurely proclaimed their beef to be safe. And all the while, beef exporters from New Zealand and Australia had been making huge gains in markets denied U.S. cattlemen. Lee Meyer, a cattle specialist at the University of Kentucky, predicted that Japanese markets would re-open in early 2006.

On November 16, 2005, Prime Minister Koizumi and President Bush met in Kyoto, and promises were made about beef against the backdrop of discussions about continuing Japanese troop deployment in Iraq, U.S. military bases in Japan, relations with China, Japan's permanent seat on the UN Security Council, North Korean past abductions of Japanese citizens, and the larger trade liberalization negotiations under the WTO Doha Round. Indeed, beef was the first item on the president's agenda. Koizumi assured Bush that Tokyo was poised to make a decision "in a few weeks" on the beef ban and asked for Bush to lift the U.S. ban on Kobe beef. Consequently, on December 13 the Japanese agreed to import American beef that met the twenty-month age limit. But, by then, Japanese consumption of beef had fallen by 18 percent as high prices and BSE anxiety had pushed many to pork and such. Polls of Japanese consumers at the time showed more than half willing to eat American beef.

So, in December 2005, finally the meat began to flow again across the Pacific. The first shipment was from Denver by air. American cowboys celebrated. But only for a couple of weeks. On January 20, 2006, the Japanese announced a reinstitution of the ban because a Brooklyn, New York, company had shipped bones along with its veal, and vertebrate bones (near nervous system tissue) were not permitted as part of the hard-won U.S.-Japan agreement. Sunday, following the Friday announcement by the Japanese, then Deputy Secretary of State Robert Zoellick met with Japanese Agriculture Minister Shoichi Nakagawa. To Zoellick's credit he profusely apologized, calling the shipment of prohibited materials an unacceptable mistake and expressed "sincere regret." Nakagawa scolded that the United States must "ensure that such an incident never occurs again." The ban persisted.

In April, the USDA announced that it would be scaling back its own inspections for BSE in beef for domestic consumption. In May, beef state senators began complaining. Missouri Cattlemen's Association representative Brent Bryant put it in true cowboy form, "These two countries [Japan and South Korea] were some of our best customers prior to this unwarranted ban." During the June negotiations in Washington, DC, the American side demanded a guarantee that Japan would not shut down trade again over problems with individual shipments. Japan countered with a demand for their own inspection of American facilities before the ban would be lifted, and snap inspections thereafter. Meanwhile, senators continued to threaten new trade sanctions. In the House, a Montana representative introduced a sanctions bill on July 1.

By August, the Capitol Hill pressure seemed to have worked; again the Japanese lifted their ban after their inspections of U.S. facilities. Five tons were flown to Japanese supermarket shelves. But whether the meat would make it to Japanese dinner tables was another matter—polls of consumers were still quite negative. By December, because of the more stringent regulations imposed by the Japanese, exports to Japan were still a trickle at only $20 million during the five months since lifting the ban. Japanese restaurateurs were beginning to complain about the short supply. Susan Schwab, the newly appointed U.S. Trade Representative, urged in January 2007 an easing of Japanese restrictions, including raising the twenty-month age limit to thirty months. Indeed, the thirty-month standard had by then been accepted by the World Organization for Animal Health (OEI). The Japanese Minister of Agriculture Toshikatsu Matsuoka responded with a classic, we are "not able to immediately begin consultations at this stage."

At this writing the whole issue is turning a bit silly. Montana senators complained in February that the Senate Dining Room included an entree of Kobe Beef! The very next day Japanese officials suspended imports from a Tyson meatpacking plant in Nebraska for violations of labeling regulations. Most ironically, another illegal shipment, this time from a California meatpacker, was discovered by Japanese inspectors at the Port of Kobe! And the Japanese still refuse to allow American beef older than twenty months to be imported. Still American cowboys are unable to sell their products to Japanese consumers.

LESSONS LEARNED

Both the rice and beef cases clearly represent the Japanese delays as a tactic that exasperates their American counterparts. Also, we see in both cases the Japanese side making concessions after presidential demands and/or, as Michael Blaker puts it, after "crisis" situations have developed. Moreover, Blaker's list of "Japanese complaints" fits well the behaviors of American negotiators in the beef case as well.

Based on our own reading of the cases, we find the continual predictions of breakthroughs by American negotiators to be particularly annoying and unproductive. Perhaps the American negotiators are using the inevitable disappointments associated with temporally specific predictions of success to stimulate the anger of their own constituents? In any case, we do not recommend having, let alone raising, expectations of success when negotiating with the Japanese. The Japanese take notice and use the information to their own benefit. And, of course, this specific set of problems is surely related to the Americans' inabilities to measure progress when negotiating with Japanese.

Finally, in this ongoing beef over beef we see another common American mistake. Perhaps threats from Capitol Hill move foreign politicians, but they don't move foreign people. By raising the volume of their threats about punitive trade sanctions, American politicians are literally screaming out loud that they do not care about the welfare of Japanese consumers. It's not clear that the American politicians are winning the battle with their Japanese counterparts, but it is clear that they are losing the war with Japanese consumers. The bottom line is that everything coming out of the mouths of American cattlemen should be directed at the Japanese consumer. Japanese politicians and bureaucrats aren't the customer. Not even Japanese restaurateurs or supermarket chain operators are customers. In order for Japanese to eat American beef, they have to trust it. They have to like it. Cattlemen should realize that their complaints about quality controls say a great deal about the quality of the product they're offering. They should be spending money educating the Japanese public about international (OEI) standards for beef safety, not on lobbying Washington, DC, politicians. This is Marketing 101.

NOTES

1. Blaker, Michael, "Negotiating on Rice: 'No, No, a Thousand Times No,'" in *International Negotiation: Actors, Structure/Process, Values*, ed. Peter Berton, Hiroshi Kimura, and I. William Zartman (New York: St. Martins Press, 1999). The author provides copious citations from his own interviews and the Japanese news media in his original article.

2. Bill Thomson, "ODJ USDA Sees No Loss of Beef Exports to Japan—US Official," *Dow Jones Newswire*, August 11, 2003.

3. James Brooke, "Japan Still Bans U.S. Beef, Chafing American Officials," *New York Times*, April 21, 2005, 4.

13

Booms, Burst Bubbles, Recovery, and Perhaps Resurgence

THE BOOM YEARS

Back in 1977 the American love affair with Japanese imports was just getting underway. In that one year the volume of Japanese television sets exported to this country soared by 256 percent. Nothing like it had ever happened in global economic history. A flood of stereos, cameras, watches, and more soon followed, crowding their American counterparts off our merchandise shelves. Then, in the late seventies, as the price of OPEC-controlled petrol zoomed alarmingly, our freeways and byways became dotted with curious little high-mileage cars bearing strange names like Toyota, Honda, and Datsun—cars that had superbly timed their arrival here to become replacements for Detroit's gas guzzlers. This sudden avalanche of imports astounded us. For the second time in this century, Americans were forced to awaken to the existence of "distant little Japan." Fortunately, this time our interest was whetted by a "miracle" economic recovery rather than by military aggression.

Startled by the Japanese whirlwind economic surge, the question was: "How did they do it?" A lazy, and not altogether inaccurate, answer to that question would have been that a number of factors were involved. And, indeed, a number of factors were. But, as is usually the case, some factors were vastly more influential than others.

Early Explanations

Let us first examine what we believe to be some of the less compelling factors, many of which were initially given undue attention by Americans.

185

During the late seventies, a period that now seems almost like ancient history, many an American observer thought he saw the answer in Japan's low labor costs. But through the years, as American wages stagnated while Japanese wages zoomed, it soon became clear the Japanese competitive edge in the marketplace was due to something well beyond the cost of labor. Today the labor cost picture in some ways actually favors the Americans. It is well to remember, however, that Japan's earlier low labor costs did indeed provide them with an opening wedge when they needed it most. But today, not so. We must now look elsewhere for answers.

In the early eighties some economic scholars seized on a pair of differences between practices prevailing in our two economies to explain Japan's superior economic progress. First, they pointed to the Japanese emphasis on expanding market share, as contrasted with American industry's emphasis on assuring profitability. Scholars who normally sniffed at profits were particularly fond of this idea. We now know that what looked like an emphasis on market share had much more to do with maintaining stable sales during cyclical busts. During the booms, some Japanese firms gave up market share for the sake of stability.

Second, some observers were impressed by the longer-term economic view favored by the Japanese as compared with the American shorter-term business horizon. Those of us who have labored under American quarter-by-quarter demands from the investment marketplace were at first inclined to give some credence to this hypothesis. But we probably over-emphasized it. Many Japanese banks or corporations were building hugely profitable enterprises, and they were not doing it by eternally postponing profits. Later on, many a Japanese corporation found its longer-term view plunging it into extremely hot economic water. Too many of their investments, both in the United States and at home, had been faultily based on a belief in ever-escalating property and stock market values. Today, the Japanese probably wish their earlier wild investment flings had been disciplined by a shorter-term horizon. To say the very least, tradeoffs exist on this subject. In terms of Japanese advantage, it explains very little.

Now let us examine still another purported reason once given for Japan's startling economic surge. In the early eighties researchers discovered Japanese industry could produce an auto in half the man-hours spent by Detroit. "How come?" they asked. Many a technical expert then surfaced to assure us the answer lay in the extensive use of automation in Japanese factories. Well, we had been in those factories, and while we had seen a few "show off" automated assembly lines, they were rare exceptions. Gradually we came to realize that superior work organization and worker application, not automation, tipped the scales in Japan's direction. So another explanation of Japanese success fell by the wayside.

Over the years, among the many reasons given for Japan's resurgent economy, one seemed to stand out. Remember how in the late seventies a veritable parade of American corporate executives jetted off to Tokyo, seeking to discover the holy grail of Japan's industrial success? Back they came wide-eyed with wonder, carrying with them glory tales of such things as: quality circles, just-in-time parts supply, worker participation in decisions, bottom-up communication, and a dozen other "doing" practices. Before long American business journals overflowed with stories of American corporations attempting to copy these practices by installing them. We no longer read such accounts, do we? Gradually it became apparent that because of cultural differences these practices, like fine wine, didn't travel all that well. Attempts to apply them here in their Japanese form have met, at best, with modest success. Besides, and most importantly, they were not the fundamental ingredient underpinning Japanese industrial success in the first place. So now comes the question, "What was?"

National Consensus

To us, the standout—the towering—reason for Japan's 1950 to 1990 incredible industrial success was this—superb national economic management! Please underscore the word *national* here. During those years no nation matched Japan in, as we say, "putting it all together."

From early on after the Pacific War, all the institutions of Japanese society worked together to pursue a strategy that could rapidly repair their shattered land. Uniformly, across-the-board, they all agreed to one thing—a single-minded pursuit of economic advancement. Business, government, finance, labor, science, education, *all* united in a concerted, tireless effort toward reaching that single objective. In unity they found strength. Japan used that strength uncommonly well.

Now does this mean we believe something often derogatorily called "Japan Inc." actually exists? Well yes, if by that term you mean government and business there work more or less in harness toward a common goal. In that sense Japan Inc. certainly does exist. If, however, you mean, as some critics have insisted, that this unified effort constituted some sort of illicit cabal designed to subvert the interests of the United States of America, we say the interpretation is poppycock. Rather, Japan is fundamentally a consensus (some say "negotiated") society. The harmonious relationships we have seen prevailing among the institutions in that country are nothing more than the consensus concept writ large at the highest levels. We doubt their society could operate in any other way. Their consensus system was designed to assure internal harmony, not to subvert outsiders, no matter how much at times it might appear to have that effect. When the Japanese complain to outsiders, as they often do, "We are misunderstood," this distinction surely reflects part of that misunderstanding.

Confucian Work Ethic

Many observers once pointed to the superior productivity of the Japanese industrial worker. Fortunately for Japan, the edifice of superior morale and productivity could be built on a sturdy cultural foundation—built on something now often called the Confucian work ethic. Where did it come from? Of what does it consist? These are questions observers still ask.

We are told that, circa 500 BC, Confucius wrote a letter to his prince. In it he advised, "Conscientiousness and reciprocity are the two elements basic to all moral law. Man should be guided to duties that flow from the existence of a universal obligation toward men." Twenty-five centuries later, it is apparent that the venerable sage's writing has not been forgotten, at least not in Japan. Japanese work behavior is shot through with those three Confucian qualities: conscientiousness, reciprocity, and obligation. Above all, obligation. The obligation to one's fellow workers to do one's share of the work and to do it well—reciprocity in action.

What, then, has been the underlying force at work here? No, it is not the reward of a cherished pot at the end of some envisioned economic rainbow. It centers, rather, on a passionate need by each worker to be seen as doing one's part, whatever that part may be, doing it well and in harmony with others. Not to be so perceived in Japan brings about personal shame. And, of course, shame brings about that most odious of Asiatic tragedies, loss of face.

This Confucian ethic has been a driving force providing Japan with an ideal springboard for progress in the multinational corporate age. No need to encourage cooperation; it's automatic. No need to create incentives to stimulate effort; the incentive is already there. No worry about adversarial labor relations; unions become part of a unified effort.

Life teaches us that for every gain there exists at least some loss. The Japanese work ethic sacrifices the American go-getting, hell-bent-for-leather individual initiative, and the creativity it inspires. Assertive individualism, American-style, is too disharmonious to be comfortable in a Japanese workplace. In a cross-Pacific contest of work ethics, the Asian emphasis on harmonious effort has been pitted against the unabashed individual creativity that holds sway in the American workplace. In Japan's rise to economic glory, the moral element in the Confucian version once seemed to give it a bit of an edge. But, the jury is still out.

THE BUBBLE BURSTS

Come the early 1990s, Japan's economy came up with a stunning surprise. Almost abruptly it slowed, sputtered, and stalled. Stagnation set in and tenaciously persisted. Four explanatory themes have emerged; each has a basis in observable fact: (1) Japan's faulty economic policies, (2) their inept political apparatus, (3) their disadvantages from global circumstances, and (4) their cultural inhibitions.

Each of these four has its proponents, each its own rationale. So let's examine each separately.

1. Faulty Economic Policies

A wealth of facts reflects Japan's economic pain during the 1990s. None more so than its stock market collapse. In the early nineties, its Nikkei index level plummeted from over 35,000 to under 13,000. Its woefully inflated real estate values similarly hit the skids. The once huge (and to some Americans alarming) flow of investment into this country simply dried up. The end result found Japan with an economy once accustomed to nearly double-digit annual growth rates now struggling—at first to stay barely above no-growth levels, and then crashing to a 2.8 percent "minus growth" in 1998.

Economic recessions are not, of course, unknown. But the peculiar feature of Japan's 1990s' version was its decade-long persistence. Unsurprisingly, most economists sought to convince us that faulty economic policies both triggered the onset and the persistence of Japan's troubles. They explained with commendable brevity: "The bubble burst." But why the bubble, and why did it burst? The most common answer went somewhat as follows.

Decades of galloping economic recovery success had bred a prideful national overconfidence. Growing willingness to take exaggerated risks followed. Heavy borrowing soon drove up levels of marginal investment. Eventually, lending agencies began to edge away from confidence toward caution. With the caution flag up, almost suddenly the whole inflated structure collapsed. Caution also filtered down to consumer levels. Spending habits were curtailed. With a fall in product demand, industry was forced to cut back both output and hiring. Unemployment soared to unheard of levels for that nation. The main casualty, however, was the widespread deterioration of national confidence.

No sector was hit harder than Japan's lending institutions, especially their huge world-class banks. Came the crash and the banks looked at loan portfolios splashed with red ink. Lending had to be restricted, a practice that dried up sources of capital needed for financing economic recovery. And so it went, one discouraging development following another, until a verifiable national crisis existed.

Seeing all this, American authorities and economists could not resist a temptation to offer remedies.

"Draconian measures are needed," they chanted from across the Pacific. Understandable advice from on high, no doubt, but reflecting ignorance of the Japanese society's cultural prejudice against any action that might call for bold or rapid change. Please always remember, Japan values stability above all else. Part of the problem here is that most economists focus on overall economic performance and the dramatic slowdown in Japan's growth, tax revenues, and the potential disaster of deflation. And, therefore most economists have missed the real miracle of Japan's economic prowess (please see figures 13.1 through 13.4).

First, please notice that when you control for purchase price parity (PPP) in the per capita GDP calculations Japanese growth simply wavered during the 1990s. That is, the PPP calculation takes into account deflation and most simply illustrates the average wellbeing of the Japanese people. In figures 13.1 and 13.2 you can see the United States and Japan divergence, but Japanese consumers were still becoming better off even in the late 1990s. Also, you can see that Japan pretty much avoided the Asian financial crisis that resulted in a precipitous economic decline in neighboring South Korea. Figure 13.2 perhaps best illustrates the connectedness of U.S., German, and Japanese economic performance. Indeed, using this metric the stability of the Japanese economy is miraculous, particularly given the troubles their close neighbors experienced in 1997 (see figures 13.3 and 13.4) and particularly the dimensions of both their stock and property market declines in the early 1990s. Indeed, it is hard to imagine how the United States' economic performance would respond to simultaneous 60 percent declines in both the NYSE and housing markets.

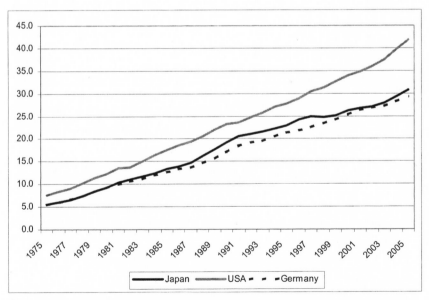

Figure 13.1. GDP per capita: Japan, America, and Germany (current international $)

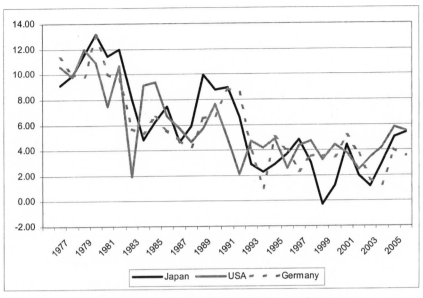

Figure 13.2. GDP per capita, % Change: Japan, America, and Germany

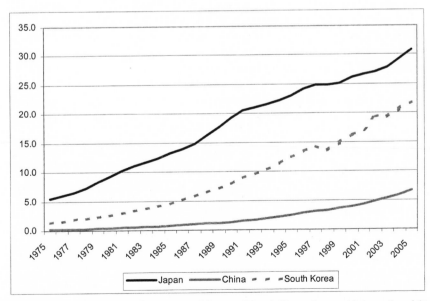

Figure 13.3. GDP per capita: Japan, China, and South Korea (current international $)

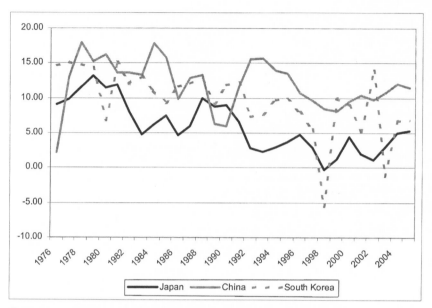

Figure 13.4.   GDP per capita, % Change: Japan, China, and South Korea

2. The Political Explanation

Views of economists on Japan's crisis were not the only ones heard. Political pundits soon rose to the challenge. They found two major villains: Villain #1—The Country's Long Entrenched Liberal Democratic Political Party; Villain #2—The Hidebound Japanese Bureaucracy.

Back in the 1970s, an authority on just about everything Japanese, one Frank Gibney, had written a seminal book on the nation. He called it *Japan: The Fragile Superpower.* His insight into the possible future of their then surging economy was confirmed when the 1990s brought on crisis conditions. "Fragile" proved to be an apt tag.

In a new appraisal, Gibney now wrote that Japan had become the victim of "one party sickness," an ailment brought on by a forty-year hardening of political arteries. Meanwhile, many observers thought politicians had to share blame with Japan's powerful bureaucracy. In fact, many both inside and outside Japan had long since come to believe that the bureaucracy actually controlled their elected politicians. Of course, in a consensus-type society it is not easy, particularly for outsiders, to tell where one institution's power leaves off and another's begins. In any event, to those who championed a political explanation of Japan's woes, these two national institutions were viewed as joint culprits. Meanwhile, other observers, particularly many within Japan, were dissatisfied with either the economic or political explanations they were hearing. They felt compelled to look for deeper roots.

3. Global Circumstances Have Hurt

The third explanation for Japan's end-of-the-century economic problems has more to do with three circumstances beyond their control.

First, the Japanese population, like the western European, is shrinking faster than the American. While American baby boomers circa 2005 were at their peak of productivity, both the Japanese and Europeans are about ten years ahead of us in adjusting economic, political, and cultural systems and institutions to population decline and graying hair. And this adjustment is costly—just wait until 2015 in the U.S. to see how costly.

Second, Japan has a serious disadvantage in the information age—its complex language. Not only do three alphabet systems hinder software innovations appropriate for world markets, but the fundamental indirectness of the Japanese linguistic system hinders electronic information flows generally. So Japan hasn't participated in the information technology explosion which has driven the American economy to precarious heights in the late 1990s. (Please see figure 13.5 to see the quantitative expression of this disadvantage.) We would be the first to argue that Japan is now catching up,

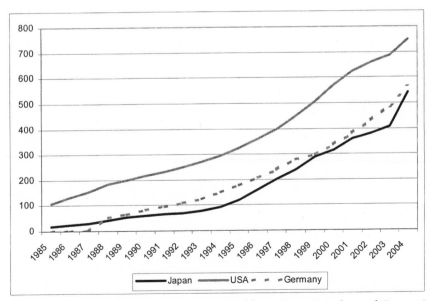

Figure 13.5. Personal Computers per 1,000 Residents: Japan, America, and Germany

particularly as software advances have made the structure of the Japanese language less a hindrance in the digital age. Also, as mentioned in previous chapters, a 9/11 caused slowdown in international travel has pushed Japanese businesspeople to become more adept with e-mail and other electronic communication media.

Finally, with American baby-boomer households operating at peak consumption levels and oil at historically low real prices, sports utility vehicles (SUVs) were the rage in the U.S. during the last decade. Japanese auto firms, which drove the 1980s boom in Japan, came quite late to the American SUV market. Honda was the last and very late entrant. Certainly, in the short run, this was a huge national economic disadvantage for Japan. But, now the reluctance to bet so much on big-car designs has proven to be much to the advantage of Japanese carmakers. A good argument can now be made that they are leading Japan toward a new resurgence.

4. The Cultural Explanation

In the mid-nineties, we became aware of what might be called "The Cultural Causation" theory of it all. This theory went somewhat as follows: Immediately after World War II a shattered Japanese nation arrived at a consensus goal for national recovery. That consensual goal provided the incentive for their spectacular progress decade after decade. Then, during the late 1980s, the Japanese people stepped back and looked around at their manifest achievement. It was easy to conclude they had indeed reached their coveted goal. So the question for them now became, "All right, what's next?"

Perhaps more than any other society, the Japanese have an affinity for united effort. They seem inspired by common striving toward a common goal. Lack of one can present a problem.

Others who champion a cultural explanation of Japan's 1990s woes don't limit their reasoning to an absence of a national goal. They point out that, during most of our twentieth-century, building of a strong enterprise structure provided the key to continuing success. Then, with the advent of globalized competition, their inflexible structure became a hindrance. Agility, not structure, became the prime need. As has been pointed out, American corporate enterprise has met this need by wholesale restructuring and a blizzard of mergers, acquisitions, and consolidations. Standard Japanese practices such as lifetime employment, job promotion based not on merit but on length of service, reciprocal contractor/subcontractor loyalties, and a dozen others have inhibited adaptive corporate measures. To put it simply, the American enterprise scene handled its adjustment to our new economic era better than the Japanese had done.

CONCLUSION

For American business interests, a vital question remains: "Have the Japanese now put their era of long economic stagnation behind them?" We believe a majority of knowledgeable observers would now answer with a cautious "Yes." In this instance, any caution reflected would be more a matter of prudence than a reflection of unease.

For business practitioners, this outlook should be seen as heartening. For foreign capital, the risk/reward pendulum in Japan has edged into positive territory.

14

The Future of U.S.-Japan Relations

A bad compromise is better than a good battle.

—Russian proverb

Good foreign relationships flow overwhelmingly from a singe source—common interests. The Unites States and Japan have more in common—really basic stuff—than almost any other two major industrial powers. We share an exceptionally impressive list of commonalties: established free institutions, regard for human rights, belief in the rule of law, creative free enterprise, free flow of international trade, and open societies. We also seem to share the same distastes: Marxist ideologies and totalitarian rule.

We find yet another quaint item in common: among the world's leading democracies, the income tax bite we put on the citizens of our two countries is comparatively low, only a little over half the crunch inflicted on most northern Europeans.

Since we share so many of these fundamentals, why is it we don't wrap our arms around each other in warm embrace? Sadly, we don't. True, neither country is suing for divorce, but as yet anything resembling marital bliss has escaped us. The last quarter century has regularly erupted with fractious bickering.

During these decades a sharp change transformed the nature of our two-nation ties, a change largely unnoticed. To illustrate, let us quote a few paragraphs from something Jim Hodgson wrote about the then existing state of our relationship in the late seventies:

Japan's long-time feeling of dependency on the United States is suffused with emotion. Many Americans are unaware of a powerful psychological characteristic

197

of the Japanese people involved here. In return for accepting its dependency status Japan expects, even demands, a quid pro quo from America. It feels it has every right to exact a price for assuming such a role. A concept of mutual obligation the Japanese call *"amae"* exists. As applied here *amae* means Japan not only expects but has a right to insist on preferred and benign treatment from the United States. To Americans this may seem shocking. To the Japanese it seems entirely natural. When the United States shows "indifference" to this obligation, great consternation ensues in Japan. The resulting imbroglio comes as a shock to the United States. This circumstance suggests two things. Japan must try to understand that while *amae* may be a useful concept at home, it cannot be readily applied abroad. It also suggests that the United States must show greater sensitivity not only to this, but to their unique Japanese cultural singularities.

The above cited "dependency" element in our relationship has now faded from the screen. In Japan, now little if any of the *amae* feeling toward the U.S. still exists. With the Japanese bursting with pride over their spectacular economic climb in the 1970s and 1980s, and having reached the reluctant conclusion that an indifferent America will never acknowledge the concept, so *amae* lies dead and buried, at least at the national level.

America has sought to replace the now defunct dependency relationship with a partnership concept. "Pacific partners" has become inserted in our political rhetoric for several years. The Japanese are wary of this idea for a couple of reasons. First, partnership between a militarily weak and politically insular Japan and a military and geopolitical giant like the United States strikes them as being long on rhetoric but short on realism. Second, although we share this wide range of common interests, we come at our mutual problems from wildly contrasting cultures. So today, among the things we "share," we find a trade gap sustained by the culture gap.

The Japanese have viewed our trade issue almost wholly in economic terms, contending America's trade deficit with them springs from our own ill-chosen business and economic policies. In other words, it is all *our* fault. We counter that the issue must be viewed, not so much in economic as in political, even moral, terms. We Americans have a special fondness for creating moral imperatives out of political desires. This found us endlessly taunting the Japanese with slogans about fairness. "Level playing field" and trade as "a two-way street" rank high in our moralizing.

But, not surprisingly given our contrasting cultures, the Japanese have seen fairness on trade far differently than we do. They stress fairness of opportunity—equal opportunity for competitors to access and penetrate the market. We counter with fairness of result, finding supposed virtue in equal levels of imports and exports. So what happens? In our trade negotiations, fault clashes always with fairness. We talked right by each other, seldom getting on the same wave length.

Over the years, diplomats of both countries gradually became so frustrated and locked into corners by their respective rigidities, they do little but flail about, each seeking to protect the narrowest of their own narrow economic and political interests. For each country the yardstick of a "good" settlement has become how well it could play politically back home, not what it has done to reduce the trade imbalance.

The two of us have not yet been quite able to lift ourselves out of this well-worn rut. But with so much turbulence elsewhere in the world, as an issue, a trade imbalance has drifted to benign neglect among Asian nations. China, with its spectacular economic upward surge, now captures priority attention, not all of it favorable. Hardly a month passes without word of some new spat arising between that country and the United States.

As our long-time reliable ally, the Japanese would no doubt resent being displaced by China as America's prime Asian focus. Yet without doubt they are pleased to get our recurrent protests on trade off their back.

RESPECT AMID THE GRUMBLES

In such a relationship as ours things are rarely simple. Push our differences on trade to one side and what remains? What remains are bonds of mutual respect and common interests. Americans admire the way postwar Japan worked hard to build a strong economic recovery. We buy their quality consumer products by the carload. We appreciate the nation's support on practically every international issue of the day. The United States, in its role of international leadership, needs good followers. Japan has filled that role uncommonly well.

Beyond all this Americans have become aware of and impressed by the quality of Japanese society. Low crime, high literacy, superior standards, unfailing courtesy—the list of their social virtues runs on.

The Japanese in turn look to us not only for international leadership but for a committed defense of their teeming islands. They also are impressed by the dynamism, sweep, and creativity Americans bring to all we do. And they have not wholly forgotten our benign postwar occupation and the help we gave them when they needed it most.

With all this going for us, by now Japan and the United States could well have firmly in place the most positive bilateral ties in the world. But sadly enough we don't. Perhaps that is too much to expect of two proud countries of contrasting cultures and well-honed competitive instincts.

What then is needed? In his masterly work, *Diplomacy*,[1] Dr. Henry Kissinger counsels greater patience by Americans, and then goes on to suggest that Japan must "come to grips with meaningful long range policies on which the future cooperation between our two nations will ultimately depend." In others words, the Japanese must change and the United States must give them time to do it.

American patience has certainly been tested. Even back in the mid-eighties all participants of the Reagan/Nakasone U.S.-Japan Economic Advisory Committee jointly declared, "The large, persisting and growing trade imbalance between Japan and the U.S. has become intolerable." Yet despite subsequent years of diplomatic skirmishing, what was judged "intolerable" years ago has actually worsened in size if not importance.

One reason for Japan's seeming indifference to American exasperation on the trade imbalance may be that she recently has gained an alternative to the lush U.S. market for her products. While the economies of East Asia are thriving, Japan is now exporting more to those economies than to the United States.

Meanwhile, until the United States and Japan can reach a better understanding on the pesky trade issue, we will coast along in a bond seriously aggravated by competing economic forces but sustained by common geopolitical interests. That may not reflect a picture of the best relationship in the world but neither is it the worst.

JAPAN 2020

Three decades ago the Japanese were saying they had reached a turning point in their national history. Today they still say the same thing. One is tempted to observe that they are certainly taking their time about turning that corner. Yet for Japan, delay is understandable. Their postwar recovery phase has been such a spectacular success, they are reluctant to change any part of the formula that brought them so far so fast. This hesitancy also finds them puzzled about just which direction they should next turn. The Japanese can be uncomfortable with speculation about their country's future. Mostly they consider it a silly waste of time.

Two of their rich lode of proverbs confirm this sentiment. "Talk of next year and the devil laughs." That derisive assessment is then topped by this one: "One inch ahead all is darkness." Clearly the Japanese have but little confidence in forecasts of what the future may hold in store. In one way we find this sentiment downright curious. We know no nation on earth works harder to achieve a better tomorrow. The Japanese must have satisfied themselves that if they work hard the future will pretty much take care of itself.

Those of us outside Japan sense a paradox here. What are we to think of a people who work exceptionally hard yet disdain attempts to envision what it is they are working for? This, of course, is but a single example of the many paradoxes that outside observers profess to see in today's picture of Japan. Let's look at some of these paradoxes.

THE PRICE OF DIFFERENCE

A bit of history here. The Japanese are well aware of their variation from the international norm. Ever since they started going out into the world 150 years ago they have repeatedly asked, even begged, to be understood. "We are different," became their century-long theme song. Little did they realize where this plea would lead. Gradually, as the world became aware of the unique features of their culture, of the distinctive pattern of their thinking, and of the mercantilist nature of their economic policies, the world started to agree.

That the Japanese were indeed different from other industrial nations became a widely accepted view. Then, sometime in the 1980s, this view led to what seemed to be a logical conclusion.

"If the Japanese are as different as they say," many decided, "then Japan should be treated differently than other nations." Thus it was that several countries began anew to push for quotas, tariffs, or other restrictions on Japanese imports, actions intended to reflect the purported difference.

The Japanese hastily scrambled to reverse course and jettison their "different" label.

Perhaps this "different but not really different" episode illustrates as well as any single circumstance, the quicksand the Japanese often encountered when they set foot on alien soil. To the Western world it became clear that Japan realized it was different. Yet the Japanese resented having that recognition result in their nation being treated differently. In terms of Western logic and idiom, Japan's position on this matter is seen as "wanting to have it both ways." This duality obviously doesn't trouble Asian logic, but it appears incongruous to most Western minds.

One reason offered to explain this Japanese problem with outsiders goes like this. While they are totally sincere in asking the outside world for a sympathetic understanding of their distinctive national features, they, in turn, have as yet shown very limited talent for understanding others.

Perhaps many in Japan would object to a conclusion that they possess an inadequate understanding of others. They can point to the intense effort they have made during the last one hundred years to study what goes on in the world beyond their islands. We are certain, for instance, they know ten times as much about the United States of America as we know about their country. If so, what could be the problem?

Simply this. Ungrammatically—knowledge *about* is not understanding *of*. Knowledge may lead to understanding, but it is insufficient by itself. Hence the lag.

THE ROAD AHEAD

Some amateur observers of Japan's many external and internal paradoxes seem to delight in predicting that disaster looms for the country in the years ahead. We disagree. We suggest these problems merely reflect the "bad news" side of a two-sided national equation.

As we see it, a "good news" future exists for Japan. A review of their past reveals that no people have greater talent for living with paradox and ambiguity than do the Japanese. For one thing they are not prisoners of the either/or pattern of thought that infests Western minds. They have demonstrated an almost unique ability to thrive by doing things their own distinctive way. And their way certainly is distinctive. No other people on earth ever consciously cut themselves off from the rest of the world for two and a half centuries, an act that clearly reflects their penchant for unique behavior. The rest of us must recognize that doing things their way is a proven Japanese specialty. To us this may often look like doing it the hard way, but the Japanese thrive on it.

To sum up then, we suggest that despite Japan's paradoxes we are not about to see the nation come unglued. Sure, like other nations, the Japanese will show adaptive strains from time to time. But they have made a habit of recovery from these strains. We believe they will continue to do so for the foreseeable future, doing it their own way and at their own pace.

Meanwhile the outside world will continue to watch them with a mixture of fascination, frustration, and envy. It will often strongly take issue with Japanese positions that appear to outsiders to be overly protective and selfish. But we must agree that the Japanese have a powerful set of attributes going for them—exceptional intelligence, a flinty pragmatism, and above all, a communal unity that has served them well in bad as well as good times. The prognosis for a strong and healthy Japanese future is excellent.

NOTE

1. Henry Kissinger, *Diplomacy* (New York: Simon and Schuster, 1994).

Appendix

Research Reports

The Japanese Negotiation Style: Characteristics of a Distinct Approach

During the last fifteen years, a group of colleagues and I [John Graham] in the behavioral science laboratory have systematically studied the negotiation styles of business people in fifteen countries (seventeen cultures)—Japan, Korea, Taiwan, China (northern and southern), Hong Kong, the Philippines, Russia, the Czech Republic, Germany, France, the United Kingdom, Brazil, Mexico, Canada (anglophones and francophones), and the United States. More than 1,000 business people have participated in our research. What we have discovered so far in these studies confirms that the Japanese negotiation style is quite distinct.

Methods of Study

The methods of our studies included a combination of interviews, field observations, and behavioral science laboratory simulations, the last using videotaping. The integration of these approaches allows a "triangulation" of our findings—that is, we can compare results across research methods. Indeed, we have found mostly consistency across methods, but we have also discovered discrepancies. For example, when we interviewed Americans who had negotiated with Japanese, their comments were consistent with those of Van Zandt:[1] "Negotiations take much longer." And, when we match American negotiators with Japanese in the behavioral science laboratory, the negotiations take longer (an average of about twenty-five minutes for Americans with Americans, thirty-five minutes for Americans with Japanese). So, in this respect, our findings are consistent for both interviews and laboratory observations. When we talk with Americans who have negotiated with

Japanese, universally they describe them as being "poker-faced," or as displaying no facial expressions. However, in the laboratory simulations, we focused a video camera on each person's face and recorded all facial expressions. We then counted them, finding no difference in the number of facial expressions (smiles and frowns) between Americans and Japanese. Apparently, Americans are unable to "read" Japanese expressions, and they wrongly describe Japanese as expressionless. Thus, discrepancies demonstrate the value of balancing and comparing research methods and results.

Preliminary Fieldwork

The preliminary fieldwork consisted of two parts—interviews with experienced executives and observation of actual business negotiations. An open-ended questionnaire was used to interview eight American business people with extensive experience in cross-cultural business negotiations. Less structured discussions were held with eight native Japanese executives working in the United States for a variety of Japanese manufacturing and trading companies. In all cases, extensive research notes were taken during and after the interviews. The second step in the fieldwork was observation of business meetings in both the United States and Japan. The meetings observed involved sales personnel from an American capital equipment manufacturer and a variety of clients. I observed eight such transactions with American clients in Southern California and eight with Japanese clients in Tokyo. Again, extensive notes were taken in each case and participants were interviewed afterward. I completed similar interviews and observations in eight of the other countries.

Behavioral Science Laboratory Simulation

The participants in the study included business people from Japan, the United States, and fifteen other cultures. The specific numbers of each group are reported in table A.1. All have been members of executive education programs or graduate business classes, and all have at least two years' business experience in their respective countries. The average age of the 1,014 participants was 35.6 years, and the average work experience was 11.5 years.

We asked participants to play the role of either a buyer or a seller in a negotiation simulation. In the case of the Japanese and Americans, three kinds of interactions were staged: Japanese/Japanese, American/American, and American/Japanese. In the other countries, only intracultural negotiations (that is, Koreans with Koreans, Brazilians with Brazilians, etc.) were conducted. The negotiation game involved bargaining over the prices of three commodities. The game was simple enough to be learned quickly but complex enough to provide usually one half hour of face-to-face interaction.

Following the simulation, results were recorded and each participant was asked to fill out a questionnaire that included questions about each player's performance and strategies and his or her opponent's strategies. The profits attained by individuals in the negotiation exercise constituted the principal performance measure. We used a variety of statistical techniques to compose the results of the several kinds of interactions.

Finally, we videotaped some of the exercises for further analysis. Several trained observers then documented the persuasive tactics negotiators used, as well as a number of nonverbal behaviors (facial expressions, gaze direction, silent periods, etc.). Each of the Japanese and American participants was also asked to observe his or her own interaction and to interpret events and outcomes from his or her own point of view. Each participant's comments were tape-recorded and transcribed to form retrospective protocols of the interaction. Here, also, we employed a variety of statistical techniques in the analysis, as well as a more inductive, interpretive approach.

Phase One

As can be seen in table A.1, Japan is the most unusual among the seventeen groups. The Japanese buyers achieved the highest individual profits (that is, 51.6, out of a possible 80, see column 1). The Japanese pairs (buyers and sellers) also achieved the highest joint profits (95.9 out of a possible 104—see column 3). The difference between buyers' profits and sellers' profits was among the greatest. However, Japanese buyers apparently "took care of" their respective sellers, because only the sellers in northern China, Hong Kong, and Brazil achieved higher profits (see column 2). Finally, the statistics in column 5 provide strong evidence that status/rank plays a crucial role in negotiations between Japanese. Twenty-three percent of the variation in negotiations' profits is explained by the role (buyer or seller) of the negotiator.

These findings dramatically confirm the adage that in Japan the buyer is "kinger"—indeed, "kingest." These results not only are interesting but illustrate an important lesson also. Look at how things work in the United States. Buyers do a little better than sellers here, but not much. Americans have little understanding of the Japanese practice of giving complete deference to the needs and wishes of buyers. That's not the way things work in America. American sellers tend to treat American buyers more as equals. And the egalitarian values of American society support this behavior. Moreover, most Americans will, by nature, treat Japanese buyers more frequently as equals. Likewise, American buyers will generally not "take care of" American sellers or Japanese sellers.

Finally, table A.1 gives some indication of how negotiations work in the other countries. Rank and the associated deference given to buyers is also

Table A.1   Outcomes of Simulated Negotiations

Country (Culture)	1 Buyers' Profits	2 Sellers' Profits	3 Joint Profits (Buyers' + Sellers')	4 Profit Difference (Buyers' − Sellers')	5 % Variance Explained by Role (ANOVA R²)
Japan (n = 44)	51.6	44.3	95.9	7.3*	23.2
South Korea (n = 48)	46.8	38.6	85.4	8.2*	14.0
Taiwan (n = 54)	44.3	40.1	84.4	4.2	3.9
China					
Northern (Tianjin) (n = 40)	45.6	46.7	92.3	−1.1	0.4
Southern (Guangzhou) (n = 44)	45.7	40.0	85.7	5.7	7.4
Hong Kong (n = 80)	49.2	44.7	93.9	4.5*	5.1
Philippines (n = 76)	44.5	39.5	84.0	5.0	4.8
Russia (n = 56)	45.4	40.5	85.9	4.9	4.8
Czech Republic (n = 40)	42.6	41.8	84.4	0.8	0.3
Germany (Western) (n = 44)	42.8	39.0	81.8	3.8	2.3
France (n = 48)	49.0	42.2	91.2	6.8	8.0
United Kingdom (n = 44)	50.0	44.3	94.3	5.7*	11.5
Brazil (n = 78)	47.3	45.5	92.8	1.8	1.0
Mexico (n = 68)	48.6	37.7	86.3	10.9*	17.5
Canada					
Anglophones (n = 74)	47.9	42.5	90.4	5.4*	7.4
Francophones (n = 74)	42.3	44.1	86.4	−1.8	1.0
United States (n = 98)	46.8	43.5	90.3	3.3	2.4
All Groups	46.5	42.1	88.6	4.4	

*Difference is statistically significant (p less than 0.05).

important (albeit not as important) in South Korea, Hong Kong, the United Kingdom, English-speaking Canada, and Mexico.

Phase Two

We studied the verbal behaviors of negotiators in ten of the cultures (six negotiators in each of the ten groups were videotaped). Again, Japanese negotiators proved to be unusual (see table A.2). The numbers in the body of table A.2 are the percentages of statements that were classified into each category. That is, 7 percent of the statements made by Japanese negotiators were promises, 4 percent were threats, 20 percent were questions, and so on. The verbal bargaining behaviors used by the negotiators during the simulations proved to be surprisingly similar across cultures. Negotiations in all ten cultures studied were comprised primarily of information-exchange tactics—questions and self-disclosures. However, it should be noted that once again the Japanese appear on the end of the continuum of self-disclosures. Their 34 percent was the lowest across all ten groups, suggesting that they are the most reticent about giving information.

Reported in table A.3 are the analyses of some linguistic structural aspects and nonverbal behaviors for the ten videotaped groups. While our efforts here merely scratch the surface of these kinds of behavioral analyses, they still provide indications of substantial cultural differences. And again the Japanese are at or next to the end of almost every dimension of behavior listed in table A.3. Their facial gazing and touching are the least among the ten groups. Only the northern Chinese used the word "no" less frequently and only the Russians used more silent periods than did the Japanese.

A broader examination of the data in tables 2 and 3 reveals a more meaningful conclusion. That is, the variation across cultures is greater when comparing structural aspects of language and nonverbal behaviors than when the verbal content of negotiations is considered. For example, notice the great differences between Japanese and Brazilians in table A.3 vis-à-vis table A.2.

Summary Descriptions

Following are further descriptions of the distinctive aspects of each of the ten cultural groups we have videotaped. Certainly, we cannot draw conclusions about the individual cultures from an analysis of only six business people in each, but the suggested cultural differences are worthwhile to consider briefly.

Japan

Consistent with most descriptions of Japanese negotiation behavior in the literature, the results of this analysis suggest their style of interaction to be the least aggressive (or most polite). Threats, commands, and warnings appear to be de-emphasized in favor of the more positive promises, recommendations, and commitments. Particularly indicative of their polite conversational style is their infrequent use of "no" and "you" and facial gazing, as well as more frequent silent periods.

Korea

Perhaps one of the more interesting aspects of this study is the contrast of the Asian styles of negotiations. Non-Asians often generalize about the

Table A.2   Verbal Negotiation Tactics: The "What" of Communications

Bargaining Behaviors and Definitions	Cultures (in each group, n = 6)									
	JPN	KOR	TWN	CHN[a]	RUSS	GRM	FRN	UK	BRZ	USA
Promise. A statement in which the source indicated his intention to provide the target with a reinforcing consequence which source anticipates target will evaluate as pleasant, positive, or rewarding.	7*	4	9	6	5	7	5	11	3	8
Threat. Same as promise, except that the reinforcing consequences are thought to be noxious, unpleasant, or punishing.	4	2	2	1	3	3	5	3	2	4
Recommendation. A statement in which the source predicts that a pleasant environmental consequence will occur to the target. Its occurrence is not under source's control.	7	1	5	2	4	5	3	6	5	4
Warning. Same as recommendation, except that the consequences are thought to be unpleasant.	2	0	3	1	0	1	3	1	1	1
Reward. A statement by the source that is thought to create pleasant consequences for the target.	1	3	2	1	3	4	3	5	2	2

Punishment. Same as reward, except that the consequences are thought to be unpleasant.	1	5	1	0	1	0	3	0	3	3
Positive normative appeal. A statement in which the source indicates that the target's past, present, or future behavior was or will be in conformity with social norms.	1	1	0	1	0	0	0	0	0	1
Negative normative appeal. Same as positive normative appeal except that the target's behavior is in violation of social norms.	3	2	1	0	0	1	0	1	1	1
Commitment. A statement by the source to the effect that its future bids will not go below or above a certain level.	15	13	9	10	11	9	10	13	8	13
Self-disclosure. A statement in which the source reveals information about itself.	34	36	42	36	40	47	42	39	39	36
Question. A statement in which the source asks the target to reveal information about itself.	20	21	14	34	27	11	18	15	22	20
Command. A statement in which the source suggests that the target perform a certain behavior.	8	13	11	7	7	12	9	9	14	6

*Read "7% of the statements made by Japanese negotiators were promises."
[a]Northern China (Tianjin and environs).

Table A.3 Structural Aspects of Language and Nonverbal Behaviors: "How" Things Are Said

Bargaining Behaviors (per 30 minutes)	Cultures (in each group, n = 6)									
	JPN	KOR	TWN	CHN[a]	RUSS	GRM	FRN	UK	BRZ	USA
Structural Aspects										
"No's." The number of times the word "no" was used by each negotiator.	1.9	7.4	5.9	1.5	2.3	6.7	11.3	5.4	41.9	4.5
"You's." The number of times the word "you" was used by each negotiator.	31.5	34.2	36.6	26.8	23.6	39.7	70.2	54.8	90.4	54.1
Nonverbal Behaviors										
Silent Periods. The number of conversational gaps of 10 seconds or longer.	2.5	0	0	2.3	3.7	0	1.0	2.5	0	1.7
Conversational Overlaps. Number of interruptions.	6.2	22.0	12.3	17.1	13.3	20.8	26.2	5.3	14.3	5.1
Facial Gazing. Number of minutes negotiators spent looking at opponent's face.	3.9	9.9	19.7	11.1	8.7	10.2	6.0	9.0	15.6	10.0
Touching. Incidents of bargainers touching one another (not including handshaking).	0	0	0	0	0	0	0.1	0	4.7	0

[a]Northern China (Tianjin and environs).

Orient. Our findings demonstrate that this is a mistake. Korean negotiators used considerably more punishments and commands than did the Japanese. Koreans used the word "no" and interrupted more than three times as frequently as the Japanese. Moreover, no silent periods occurred between Korean negotiators.

China (northern)

The behaviors of the negotiators from northern China (i.e., in and around Tianjin) are most remarkable in the emphasis on asking questions, at 34 percent. Indeed, 70 percent of the statements made by the Chinese negotiators were classified as information-exchange tactics. Other aspects of their behavior were quite similar to the Japanese—the limited use of "no" and "you" and silent periods.

Taiwan

The behavior of the business people in Taiwan was quite different from that in China and Japan, but it was similar to that in Korea. The Chinese on Taiwan were exceptional in terms of time spent on facial gazing—on the average, almost twenty out of thirty minutes. They asked fewer questions and provided more information (self-disclosures) than did any of the other Asian groups.

Russia

The Russians' style was quite different from that of any other European group, and, indeed, was quite similar in many respects to the style of the Japanese. They used "no" and "you" infrequently and used the most silent periods of any group. Only the Japanese did less facial gazing, and only the Chinese asked a greater percentage of questions.

Germany

The behaviors of the western Germans are difficult to characterize because they fell toward the center of almost all the continua. However, the Germans were exceptional in the high percentage of self-disclosures at 47 percent and the low percentage of questions at 11 percent.

France

The style of the French negotiators is perhaps the most aggressive of all the groups. In particular, they used the highest percentage of threats and warnings (together, 8 percent). They also used interruptions, facial gazing, and "no" and "you" very frequently compared to the other groups, and one of the French negotiators touched his partner during the simulation.

United Kingdom

The behaviors of the British negotiators are remarkably similar to those of the Americans in all respects.

Brazil

The Brazilian business people, like the French, were quite aggressive. They used the highest percentage of commands of all the groups. On average, the Brazilians said the word "no" forty-two times, "you" ninety times, and touched one another on the arm about five times during thirty minutes of negotiation. Facial gazing was also high.

United States

Like the Germans and the British, the Americans fell in the middle of most continua. They did interrupt one another less frequently than all the others, but that was their sole distinction.

Phase Three

The results of the final phase of our studies are perhaps the most enlightening. Here, we consider only Japanese and American negotiators, but in much greater detail.

The data for this analysis include the videotapes (three Japanese/Japanese, three American/American, and six Japanese/American dyads), each participant's account of the negotiations, descriptions of three uninvolved observers, and all data previously analyzed and reported. The method is presented below in five stages:

1. The first step was to view the videotaped interactions to gain a gestalt or a context-informed understanding of the content. Then, to locate "focal points," notes were made while each tape was being viewed a second time. Focal points were identified by obvious misunderstandings, breakdowns in conversational rhythm, and changes in thematic progression. The principal researcher and two assistants (one of them Japanese) independently identified focal points.
2. Next, in a session with individual participants, the tapes were again reviewed, with the participants stopping the tape periodically (at

their discretion) to report their "thoughts and feelings at the time of the negotiation." Comments solicited by the researcher were limited to a minimum during these interviews. All participants' comments were tape-recorded, thus providing retrospective protocols for future analysis.

3. Informed by the first two stages, specific focal points were selected for in-depth analysis. The criteria of selection included the intrinsic interest of the focal point, its completeness, its theoretical salience or practical salience for participants, and the quality of picture and sound on the tape. These focal points of interaction, as well as two or three minutes of interaction before and after the focal point, were edited onto another tape.

4. In the fourth step, the focal points were reviewed repeatedly. Additionally, all relevant data previously collected, including questionnaires, verbal and nonverbal measures, and participant protocols were reviewed. The goal of this inductive form of analysis was to identify the antecedents and consequences of these focal points.

5. The final stage of the analysis involved demonstration of the generality of the models determined from the single cases developed in stage four. Here, all twelve tapes from the entire series of interactions were searched for analogous instances of these single cases. In viewing this series of analogous cases, attention was given to those communication forms and functions that had demonstrated structural salience in stage four. When discrepant evidence appeared during this stage, the original case was reexamined and possibly redesigned.

The analyses of the ten focal points selected follow. Included are excerpts from eight of the twelve interactions (no focal points were chosen from four).

Focal Point 1

The first focal point consisted of a gap in the rhythm of conversation between two Japanese participants. This gap was noted by the principal researcher and specifically commented on by one of the participants. The Japanese seller reported "puzzlement" because the buyer took control of the interaction and described his situation (e.g., company background, product quality, etc.) first, rather than allowing the seller to do so.

This "abnormal" beginning to the Japanese negotiation was the antecedent to the breakdown in conversational rhythm. A search of the rest of the available information indicated some plausible explanations for this circumstance. The Japanese buyer reported that he wanted to talk about one product first, so he took control. It should also be noted that the buyer held a relatively powerful position—the two were well acquainted, the buyer was older, more experienced, and more extroverted (these last three characteristics were measured using questionnaires completed after the negotiation sessions).

The consequences of this abnormal start were: (1) the seller reported discomfort with the buyer's aggressive behavior; (2) the seller reported adjusting his strategy to deal with the buyer's attack, taking control, agreeing with the buyer's assessment, and then describing his own situation; and (3) an outcome to this negotiation that consisted of one of the largest gaps between buyer and seller profit levels, with the buyer doing much better.

A search of the other interactions reveals additional instances where negotiations did not begin with Japanese sellers describing background factors and product quality. However, in every case, Japanese participants made unsolicited comments regarding the normal order of topics in a Japanese negotiation. In circumstances similar to those in the negotiation simulation, Japanese appear to have expected that sellers would describe their situation before price discussions began. Alternatively, Americans frequently began the negotiation game with price quotes or price-quote requests.

Typical of cross-cultural interactions is the following excerpt from one of the negotiations:

American buyer: "All right, so you want to start out to make the first offer?" Japanese seller: "First offer? Oh yeah, first, I like to explain these goods to you. . . ."

Focal Point 2

The second focal point examined consisted of a series of long silent periods or gaps in the conversation between two Japanese participants. Both participants stopped the tape at this point and made unsolicited comments during the reviews. Additionally, both the principal researcher and the Japanese assistant noted this period in the interaction.

The immediate antecedent to these silent periods was an unacceptable offer made by the seller. The silence was used as a negative response by the buyer. Additionally, a large gap existed between initial offers, and neither participant made concessions on second offers. The buyer rated both himself and his partner as highly exploitive. So, these silent periods apparently resulted from two individualistically oriented bargainers coming to an impasse. Particularly insightful are the comments made by each participant in their respective protocols.

Japanese buyer's protocol: "That price satisfied me, so I just say okay . . . but I try to get more high profit. I was thinking, silence rather than shaking hands."

Japanese seller's protocol: "This is his style of negotiation; he doesn't say a word sometimes, he's just thinking about something. I felt a little bit uncomfortable."

The consequence of these silent periods was discomfort for the seller and eventually, capitulation to the buyer's "negotiation style." Indeed, the buyer made only one counteroffer throughout the game. The buyer achieved significantly higher profits than the seller.

Proof of the generality of this "style of negotiation" is that thirteen such silent periods ensued in this interaction—one for as long as forty seconds. As already noted, such silent periods occurred more frequently in Japanese negotiations than in either American or cross-cultural negotiations. Moreover, no silent periods of twenty-five seconds or more in length were found in American or cross-cultural interactions. Although other researchers have reported periods of silence to be a frequent occurrence in everyday Japanese interactions, here, silence was used consciously as a bargaining tactic.

Focal Point 3

The third focal point was an obvious gap in conversational rhythm in a negotiation between two Americans. The principal researcher and the American assistant independently noted the incident. Further, both participants commented on it during the participant reviews.

The break in the conversation immediately followed the buyer's disclosure of information about his utilities for the different products in the game. The buyer, who was much more aggressive in his bargaining strategies (i.e., strong topical control, more facial gazing, more frowns, more extroverted), reported intentionally misinforming the seller about his utilities for the three products. The seller reported confusion and taking time to think rather than responding immediately.

The consequences of this break in conversational rhythm were wholly negative for the seller. The seller eventually capitulated on the issue. The buyer expressed no feeling of being pressured. The buyer attained very high profits in the game. The seller indicated the buyer had more influence in the negotiation. The buyer rated the seller as relatively unattractive.

Regarding the generality of this type of focal point, it can be noted that the same type of thing occurred three more times during the interaction. However, as mentioned previously, silent periods happened less frequently in negotiations involving Americans.

A brief contrast of focal points 2 and 3 is worthwhile. In the case of the Japanese, silence was consciously used, typically from a strong position, as an aggressive, persuasive tactic. For Americans, silence seems to have had a negative impact for "the silent one," perhaps because not having a quick and cunning response can be sign of weakness. For Japanese, silences apparently mean, "Take some time to think it over and offer me a better deal," while for Americans it means, "Give me some time to think it over."

Focal Point 4

Obvious discomfort on the part of both participants in a cross-cultural interaction marked the fourth focal point. The principal researcher noted the Japanese seller "laughing out of place" and being unusually unresponsive. Both Japanese and American assistants reported a period of mutual discomfort. Neither negotiator commented on the incident.

The antecedent conditions were relatively complex. The Japanese seller reported discomfort at playing the role of the seller. Further, he indicated that his "poor English" dictated a strategy of listening rather than manipulating. The American buyer's strategy was an aggressive one—"to put the other guy on the defensive." Indeed, the American rated himself as more self-interested and engaged in aggressive, persuasive appeals throughout the interaction.

As a consequence of this combination of strategies, the American did most of the talking. Both players agreed that the American had more influence in the game, and, for the most part, that the American controlled the topic of conversation. However, the difference in outcomes was minimal. Evidently, the American's arguments had little impact. Indeed, the Japanese seller seemed most interested in prices—quantitative information rather than qualitative.

This "turning out" of qualitative arguments appears to be one way of dealing with language difficulties and was common to at least two other cross-cultural interactions.

Focal Point 5

The fifth focal point consisted of a series of interruptions or conversational overlaps during a cross-cultural negotiation. The principal researcher noted these incidents, as did both the Japanese and American assistants. The American buyer apologized for his interruptions during the negotiation and specifically commented on them in the protocol.

The antecedents of these turn-taking problems appear to have been mostly cultural differences in signaling when conversational contributions had been concluded. Both the Japanese research assistant and the Japanese participant alluded to language problems. Additionally, the American buyer reported a strategy of letting the Japanese seller "carry the interaction" and "listening to refute." The Japanese seller reported being "puzzled" by some of the American's arguments.

Although the American apologized for interrupting, the turn-taking difficulties became worse as the negotiation progressed. Additionally, the Japanese began to register discomfort in response to the American's interruptions. Even though the American reported letting the Japanese "carry the interaction," he mostly controlled the topic of conversation. A final consequence was a very large difference in outcomes; the American did very well.

Regarding the generality of this type of communication problem, it was noted that interruptions occurred throughout this interaction. Moreover, such serious problems in turn-taking were typical in two of the five other cross-cultural interactions.

Focal Point 6

This focal point involved the same participants as the previous one, an American and a Japanese. It is characterized as a definite change in atmosphere in the interaction. The principal researcher and the American assistant noted the change, and both participants commented on it during the reviews.

Previous to the change in atmosphere, the interacting was going smoothly, despite the numerous interruptions. The American buyer reported in the protocol that he was encouraged by the Japanese seller's continual head nodding, registering agreement and understanding, and that he felt comfortable. However, when the American asked for price quotes, the Japanese responded by offering very high prices, which further annoyed the American. The comments of both, listed in protocol 1 (see table A.4), are particularly insightful.

As a consequence, the American took control and began his persuasive strategies, never returning to the "give-and-take" characteristic of the first half of the negotiation.

In one other cross-cultural negotiation, a Japanese seller began with the highest prices. He, too, was greeted with a strong negative response from the American buyer. A review of all the tapes revealed that Japanese made first offers in four of the six cross-cultural negotiations. And, on average, they asked for significantly more (higher profit prices) than did the American in their first offers.

Focal Point 7

The seventh focal point is characterized by an obvious misunderstanding between a Japanese seller and an American buyer. All three researchers noted the particular incident.

The principal antecedent was a language problem. The Japanese bargainer said at the beginning of the conversation that he considered himself

Table A.4.   Transcript and Retrospective Protocol Data from a Crosscultural Interaction (Focal Point 6)

10:10:25 (1)		Transcript
10:05:40	American Buyer:	Well, I might ask you then, are there any particular prices that you are interested in charging us?
10:06:03	Japanese Seller:	Well, uh, I'm thinking of, uh, the price of the trucks (2), maybe Price I (3).
	American Buyer:	Um hum, for which product?
10:06:30	Japanese Seller:	For trucks. And airplanes, Price I. And for dolls, Price I.
10:06:55	American Buyer:	Okay, well, to be real honest, that wouldn't be advantageous for us at all. . . .
10:07:40	Japanese Seller:	So maybe we can, taking into considerations the factors you're mentioning, and also into consideration that this is the first step to establish a very good business communication with each other. I've also had an instruction from head office to give you, to offer more discount.

Japanese Seller's Retrospective Comment	American Seller's Retrospective Comment
I set the highest price for every merchandise because I thought, I felt the necessity of compromising finally, but I thought it was the usual step to set the highest price, the reasonably highest price we have to start the negotiation. I was not sure it hurt the buyer's impression of me or not. Then the buyer can give me an offer from his side.	I thought, "you greedy [expletive]." I wasn't too keen on the remark after trying to take me to the cleaners; then he said, "Well, since that didn't work, I suppose I can admit I can come up with a better deal."

(1) Place where participants stopped videotape to make comments.
(2) The products involved in this simulation were toy trucks, dolls, and airplanes.
(3) Price I is the highest possible price.

to be a poor listener of English. The American reported in his protocol that he had set his minimum goals before the start and his strategy was "just sit back" and listen until price negotiations began. Then, he would accept nothing lower than his minimum.

The consequences were an apparent lack of communication throughout the negotiation. A smooth conversational rhythm was never established, although the Japanese reported improving his listening toward the end. The outcome of the interaction was the highest mutual solution and also met the American's goal. The American was rated as very accommodating by the Japanese seller.

The American's response to communication problems was to focus only on the quantitative information. Thus, by limiting the information exchanged, he achieved the lowest profit level of any American buyer in a cross-cultural interaction. This kind of response to communication problems—ignoring them and the associated information—was common to at least three of the other cross-cultural interactions. (Indeed, a similar situation was described in focal point 4.)

Focal Point 8

Here, the Japanese buyer was noticeably uncomfortable at the beginning of the negotiation. Both the principal researcher and the American assistant noted the discomfort. The Japanese participant commented on it in the protocol. The antecedents of this problem were rather obvious. The American seller began with aggressive, persuasive appeals immediately. The Japanese buyer asked the seller to describe his situation first. (See protocol 2 in table A.5 for details of the interaction.) This aggressive behavior was not anticipated by the Japanese buyer.

The consequences were also rather obvious. The American ignored the Japanese request and continued his attack. Both participants later reported experiencing continuing discomfort during in the interaction and using individualistic bargaining strategies. Each participant rated the other as very exploitive but did not rate himself so. The outcome of the game was not particularly advantageous for either party as the joint-profit level was below average.

Comments made regarding generality in another "abnormal" negotiation sequence as described in focal point 1 hold true here.

Focal Point 9

This focal point occurred later in the same interaction as focal point 8 and consisted of an uncomfortable moment identified by the principal investigator, the American assistant, and the Japanese participant. It directly followed the American seller's response to a price reduction request from the Japanese. The American's comment was, "No, absolutely not . . ." The Japanese responded with an obvious negative affect. Moreover, he commented during the review of the videotapes, "His response was very strong to me." As mentioned, the American's "strong" response resulted from the request by the Japanese for a lower price.

Table A.5   Transcript and Retrospective Protocol Data from a Crosscultural Interaction (Focal Point 8)

13:31:45 (1)		*Transcript*
13:30:45	*American Seller:*	Well, I know that Japan doesn't grow much in the way of fruits (2), like grapefruit, lemons, and oranges. I know you have a very difficult time in getting them into Japan, and I think it would benefit your company greatly if you were to purchase from my company. Since we're here on the West Coast, the shipping costs would be less than if you purchase from a company in Florida or the Midwest, for example, and our . . .
13:31:09	*Japanese Buyer:*	I would try to understand your situation first.
13:31:15	*American Seller:*	Well, also I know it's difficult. The quality of fruits from other parts of Asia, Southwest Asia, is not very high, and so I think our product is quite good, which is, I'm sure, why you're talking to us, rather than a company down in Australia or Malaysia or Singapore, or something like that. . . .
		Japanese Buyer's Retrospective Comment
		In America, which first to talk about business, buyer or seller?

(1) Place where the Japanese buyer stopped videotape to make comments.
(2) The products involved in this simulation were citrus fruits.

The Japanese buyer admits in the protocol that this particular request was meant to confuse the seller's understanding of the buyer's subjective expected utilities by placing false emphasis on that product.

As a consequence of this incident, the individualistic attitudes referred to in focal point 8 seemed to be reinforced.

It was mentioned in a previous section that no difference was found between the number of negative influence behaviors (e.g., threats, warnings, etc.) used by Japanese and Americans. A closer examination of the data reveals an interesting finding. The Japanese bargainers used a higher percentage of negative influence behaviors in intracultural negotiations than did Americans. But, they apparently toned down their use of these behaviors in cross-cultural negotiations. Additionally, three Japanese bargainers (including the one referred to here) made unsolicited comments about American frankness and its discomforting effects on them.

Focal Point 10

The final focal point to be considered is really an entire cross-cultural interaction. The interaction is a special one because it is the only videotaped negotiation in which no agreement was reached within the one-hour time limit. It is also special because it includes many instances of the various problems already described in other focal points. An obvious language problem existed, which was typified by numerous interruptions, a low percentage of shared smiles, and numerous responses unrelated to questions. The American often used aggressive, persuasive tactics leading to discomfort and annoyance for the Japanese. The American expressed his frustration regarding the lack of responsiveness of the Japanese.

Additionally, another unique problem seems to have compounded all the interactional problems already mentioned. In the discussion regarding focal point 6, it was pointed out that Japanese made first offers in four of the six cross-cultural interactions and, obviously, in all three intracultural interactions, and that these offers were considerably higher than the Americans' first offers. In the present negotiation, the Japanese seller offered the lowest price of the seven Japanese first offers. He explained his offer in the protocol, "I extend at the first stage the lowest price, so I cannot step back to a lower price." At the same time, the American buyer held some specific expectations about Japanese bargaining behavior. These expectations are manifest in his protocol: "Asians never quote final prices the first time. . . . Often they lose respect for you, a great deal, if you go after the initial price." With most other Japanese negotiators, this bit of folklore might not have negatively affected his performance, but, given the Japanese seller's comments, both parties were headed for a frustrating experience.

The Japanese had previously expressed feeling self-conscious in the role of a seller to an American client. Additionally, he rated himself as being relatively accommodating. These factors are the only ones available that might explain his unusually low first offer.

Both participants were asked to explain why the negotiation had failed. However, as might be anticipated, the two explanations were very different. The Japanese seller explained it as a difference in approaches to solving the mutual problem. He wrote, "Price negotiation is not same orientation: (1) partner may be based on the price of each product, (2) I try to figure out the total profit." The American stated, "We were both out for ourselves too much and neither of us wanted to give in to the other; I sensed that both he and I would've felt a personal sense of defeat if we didn't get exactly what we wanted." Additionally, he mentioned in the protocol, "I was having trouble deciding whether it was he the person or he the Japanese [i.e., personality or culture] that was causing the delay. He seemed perhaps to be delaying a little more than most Asians I would have expected, so even for a Japanese person he seemed a little more reticent at discussing hard figures." So, the Japanese described the problem as differences in the decision-making process, while the American attributed it to individual motives and personalities.

CONCLUSIONS

In some senses the Japanese negotiation style was similar to the American style in our findings. Herein lies the opportunity for cooperation across the cultures. However, the primary finding of our studies is that substantial differences also exist. In many ways, the Japanese approach to business negotiations is the most unusual of the seventeen cultures we have studied so far. The American approach seems to be less distinct and more of a compromise between other styles.

Cultural differences in negotiation styles are apt to cause misunderstandings between well-meaning business partners. The first step toward improving the effectiveness and efficiency of cross-cultural commercial transactions is to become aware that such differences lie not only in "what" is said (content) but in "how" it is said (linguistic structure and nonverbal behaviors) and in the "social context" of the discussions. The initial goal should be to avoid misinterpreting or over-interpreting the overt and subtle signals sent by our negotiating counterparts from other countries.

Training and preparation regarding the culturally determined nuances of individual negotiation partners should be the second step toward improving cross-cultural negotiations. Certainly, individual personalities influence behaviors at the negotiation table, but so does national culture, and the latter does so in quite predictable ways. Our studies of the Japanese negotiation style have proven to be the basis of useful training programs for Americans working with Japanese. Perhaps the best example is a three-day program in which some 700 managers at Ford Motor Company have participated. The videotapes have been an invaluable medium for communicating cultural differences in these programs. While we do not claim to have all the answers regarding the Japanese negotiation style, our research and the extant literature do provide enough information to allow for the development of successful training programs regarding the Japanese.

But Japan, albeit a crucial one, is just one of our foreign trading partners. More systematic studies of negotiating styles in other countries must be undertaken in the future. Our findings in Phases One and Two just hint at the kinds of problems which systematic study may reveal and document. Participant observations, case studies, field surveys, and simulations with videotaping can all provide useful pieces of the pictures of the negotiating styles of our foreign partners and clients.

NOTES

1. Howard Van Zandt, "How to Negotiate in Japan," *Harvard Business Review* (November–December 1970): 45–56.

Bibliography

Note: Asterisks indicate references that have been particularly useful in our work.

Adler, Nancy J. "Pacific Basin Managers: A *Gaijin,* Not a Woman." *Human Resource Management* 26, no. 2 (Summer 1987): 169–191.

Anglemar, R., and L. W. Stern. "Development of a Content Analytic System for Analysis of Bargaining Communication in Marketing." *Journal of Marketing Research* (February 1978): 93–102.

Anterasian, Cathy, John L. Graham, and R. Bruce Money. "Are U.S. Managers Superstitious about Market Share?" *Sloan Management Review* (Summer 1996): 67–77.

Blaker, Michael. "Negotiating on Rice: 'No, No, A Thousand Times No.'" In Peter Berton, Hiroshi Kimura, and I. William Zartman, eds., *International Negotiation Actors, Structure/Process, Values.* New York: St. Martin's Press, 1999.

DeMente, Boye. *The Japanese Way of Doing Business: The Psychology of Management in Japan.* Englewood Cliffs, N.J.: Prentice-Hall, 1981.

Diamond, Jared. *Guns, Germs, and Steel: The Fates of Human Societies.* New York: Norton, 1999.

Doi, Takeo. "Some Psychological Themes in Japanese Human Relationships." In J. C. Condon and M. Saito, eds., *Intercultural Encounters in Japan,* pp. 17–26. Tokyo: Simul Press, 1974.

Evans, Franklin B. "Selling as a Dyadic Relationship." *American Behavioral Scientist* 6 (May 1963): 76–79.

Fisher, Roger, and William Ury. *Getting to Yes.* New York: Penguin Books, 1981.

Gibney, Frank. *Japan, the Fragile Superpower.* Tokyo: Tuttle, 1979.

Graham, J. L. "A Hidden Cause of America's Trade Deficit with Japan." *Columbia Journal of World Business* (Fall 1981): 5–15.

———. "Business Negotiations in Japan, Brazil, and the United States." *Journal of International Business Studies* (Spring/Summer 1983): 47–62.

———. "The Influence of Culture on the Process of Business Negotiations: An Exploratory Study." *Journal of International Business Studies* (Spring 1985): 79–94.

——. "Learn Foreign Languages and Catch Innovations at the Source." *Los Angeles Times*, October 8, 1985.

——. "Today the Summit—Tomorrow, Business." *New York Times*, May 5, 1986.

Graham, J. L., and D. Andrews. "A Holistic Analysis of Cross-Cultural Business Negotiations." *Journal of Business Communications* (1987): 63–77.

Graham, John L., and Yoshihiro Sano. *American Negotiation Techniques: Differences Between Japanese and American Styles*. Tokyo: Toyo Keizai Simpo Sha, 1987.

*Hall, Edward T., and Mildred Reed Hall. *Hidden Differences: Doing Business with the Japanese*. Garden City, N.Y.: Anchor Press/Doubleday, 1987.

*Hall, Edward T., and M. R. Hall. *Understanding Cultural Differences: Germans, French, and Americans*. Yarmouth, Maine: Intercultural Press, Inc., 1990.

Hinkelman, Edward G., ed. *Japan Business: The Portable Encyclopedia for Doing Business with Japan*. San Rafael, Calif.: World Trade Press, 1994.

Ishihara, Shintaro. *The Japan That Can Say No*. Trans. Frank Baldwin. New York: Simon and Schuster, 1991.

Karrass, Chester L. *The Negotiating Game*. New York: Crowell, 1970.

Kissinger, Henry. *Diplomacy*. New York: Simon and Schuster, 1994.

Kotha, Suresh, Roger L. M. Dunbar, and Allan Bird. "Strategic Action Generation: A Comparison of Emphasis Placed on Generic Competitive Methods by U.S. and Japanese Managers." *Strategic Management Journal* 16 (1995): 195–220.

Liker, Jeffrey K. *The Toyota Way*. New York: McGraw-Hill, 2004.

"Long Workdays." *Time*, January 12, 1981, 56.

March, Robert M. "Business Negotiation as Cross-Cultural Communication: The Japanese-Western Case." *Cross Currents* 9, no. 1 (Spring 1982): 55–65.

* ——. *The Honourable Customer: Marketing and Selling to the Japanese in the 1990s*. London: Longacre, 1990.

*——. *The Japanese Negotiator*. New York: Harper and Row, 1988.

*Nakane, Chie. *Japanese Society*. Berkeley, Calif.: University of California Press,1970.

Nakarmi, Laxmi, Dori Jones Yang, Peter Galuszka, and William J. Holstein. "South Korea Is Warming Up to China and Russia." *Business Week* (April 8, 1988): 42–44.

Nisbett, Richard E. *The Geography of Thought: How Asians and Westerners Think Differently . . . And Why*. New York: Free Press, 2003.

*Ouchi, William S. *Theory Z*. Reading, Mass.: Addison-Wesley, 1981.

*Pascale, Richard T., and Anthony G. Athos. *The Art of Japanese Management*. New York: Simon and Schuster, 1981.

Penetrating the Japanese Market. Pamphlet by the Manufactured Imports Promotion Organization.

Richman, Louis S. "The Japanese Buying Binge." *Fortune* (December 7, 1987): 77–94.

Rowland, Diana. *Japanese Business Etiquette: A Practical Guide to Success with the Japanese*, 2nd ed. New York: Time Warner, 1993.

Schmidt, Klaus D. *Doing Business in Japan*. Palo Alto, Calif.: Stanford Research Institute International, 1978.

Tannen, Deborah. *You Just Don't Understand: Men and Women in Conversation*. New York: William Morrow, 1990.

Thurow, Lester C. *Building Wealth: The New Rules for Individuals, Companies and Nations in a Knowledge-Based Economy*. New York: HarperCollins Publishers, 1999.

Tung, Rosalie L. *Business Negotiations with the Japanese.* Lexington, Mass.: Lexington-Books, 1984.

Uyeno, Kazuma. *Japanese Business Glossary.* Tokyo: Mitsubishi Corporation Toyo-Keizai-Shinposha, 1983.

Van Zandt, Howard F. "How to Negotiate in Japan." *Harvard Business Review* (November–December 1970): 45–56.

Weiss, Stephen. "Creating the GM: Toyota Joint Venture: A Case in Complex Negotiation." *Columbia Journal of World Business* (Summer 1987): 23–35.

Yoshihara, Nancy. "Japan's Strategies May Need Some Tuning to Work Here." *Los Angeles Times*, January 23, 1983, p. 42.

Yoshimura, Noborui, and Philip Anderson. *Inside the Kaisha: Demystifying Japanese Business Behavior.* Boston: Harvard Business School Press, 1997.

Zimmerman, Mark. *How to Do Business with the Japanese.* New York: Random House, 1985.

Index

About the Authors

James Day Hodgson was U.S. Ambassador to Japan from 1974 to 1977 and U.S. Secretary of Labor from 1970 to 1973. Previous to his government service he was an executive with Lockheed Aircraft Corporation (1941–1968) and held positions with the firm as vice president, industrial relations, and senior vice president, corporate relations. He has served as a corporate director of twelve companies, including Hewlett-Packard and Mitsui Bank, and consultant to nine others, including Toyota, Manufacturers' Bank, and Hill & Knowlton's Japan Unit. He has taught or served on the advisory board of more than twenty major universities, including UCLA, Berkeley, Harvard, Stanford, and Penn State. His civic activities have included the National Red Cross Board of Governors, director of the Los Angeles Chamber of Commerce, and the Eisenhower Exchange Fellowships. He was named to the Order of the Rising Sun, First Class, by the Japanese government in Toyko in 1982.

Yoshihiro Sano is the founder and president of Pacific Alliance Group, an international investment banking and consulting firm. Prior to that, he was a principal at Ernst & Young's western regional office, where he formed the Japanese Business Group. As an expert in Japanese business practices, he has assisted numerous American and other international firms on acquisitions, divestitures, and joint ventures with Japanese strategic partners. Sano was the founding associate director of the International Business Education and Research (IBEAR) Program at the University of Southern California. His books include *Introduction to Category Management*. He is also a frequent contributor to Japanese food and retail professional journals.

John L. Graham is professor of marketing and international business at the Merage School of Business, University of California, Irvine. He is also director of the UCI Center for Citizen Peacebuilding. Graham's primary professional interests focus on international business negotiations, and he has completed studies on negotiation styles in eighteen countries. His publications include *China Now: Doing Business in the World's Most Dynamic Market, International Marketing, Global Negotiation: The New Rules*, and numerous articles in leading international business and marketing journals. Graham has advised several major corporations, including Ford, Toyota, Intel, AT&T, and Prudential Insurance, and the U.S. State Department, the United States Trade Representative, the United States Institute of Peace, the International Research Center for Japanese Studies (Kyoto, Japan), the School for Advanced International Studies at Johns Hopkins, and the Harvard University Program on Negotiations.